TOEFL® MAP

ACTUAL TEST

New TOEFL® Edition

Writing 1

DARAKWON

TOEFL MAP ACTUAL TEST New TOEFL® Edition

Writing **1**

Publisher Chung Kyudo
Editors Zong Ziin, Cho Sangik
Authors Susan Kim, Michael A. Putlack
Designers Kim Nakyung, Park Narae, Lee Seunghyun

First published in April 2022
By Darakwon, Inc.
Darakwon Bldg., 211, Munbal-ro, Paju-si, Gyeonggi-do 10881
Republic of Korea
Tel: 82-2-736-2031 (Ext. 250)
Fax: 82-2-732-2037

Price ₩18,000
ISBN 978-89-277-8014-4
       978-89-277-8007-6 (set)

www.darakwon.co.kr

Photo Credits
Shutterstock.com

Components Main Book / Script and Translation Book
7 6 5 4 3 2 1   22 23 24 25 26

TOEFL® MAP

ACTUAL TEST

New TOEFL® Edition

Writing **1**

머리말

미국에 처음 왔을 때, 저녁 모임에서 교수님 한 분께서 제가 한국 학생들에게 토플을 가르쳐 왔다는 말을 듣고, 질문을 하셨습니다. 한국 유학생들은 토플이나 GRE 점수가 만점에 가까운데 왜 토론 수업에 참여를 거의 안 하느냐는 질문이었습니다. 당장 점수를 올려서 좋은 학교를 보내야겠다는 목표만 가지고 학생들을 가르쳤던 저로서는 어떤 대답을 해야 할지 당황스러웠지요.

그 이후, 토플 점수를 내는 것만이 성공적인 유학의 삶을 보장하는 것이 아니라는 사실을 깨닫고, 학생들이 다른 나라로 유학을 가서도 언어로 인해 너무 힘들지 않고 본인들의 전공에 집중할 수 있도록 도와야겠다는 결심을 했습니다. 그리고, 단지 점수를 높이기 위해 토플에서 원하는 형식의 답만 쓰는 것이 아닌 기본적인 문장 구조를 알아가고, 분석을 하고, 그 내용을 다시 스스로 쓸 수 있는 방법을 찾으려 노력해 왔습니다.

이 책에서 저는 기출 지문의 토픽은 물론이고, 현재 일어나고 있는 환경, 기술, 교육 등의 다양한 주제를 다루는데 심혈을 기울였습니다. 그래서 영어권 사람들과 대화를 할 때, 언어뿐 아니라 중요한 이슈에 관련된 단어들과 표현에 익숙해지는 것에도 목적을 두었습니다. 따라서, 제 아이들과 아이들의 친구들에게도 라이팅 실력 향상을 돕기 위해 자신있게 선물할 수 있는 교재를 만들었습니다.

실제로 토플 시험을 볼 때, 화면에 주어진 시간이 1초씩 없어지는 걸 보고 있으면 잘 알고 있는 것들도 머릿속에서 뒤죽박죽 섞이거나 아예 생각이 안 날 수도 있습니다. 제가 가르쳐 온 학생들의 고민과 의견을 토대로 실제 시험을 볼 때 도움이 되는 포인트들을 TIPS for SUCCESS에 담았습니다. 그리고 어떤 주제가 나와도 상대방을 설득시킬 수 있는 능력을 발달시킬 목적으로 독립형 문제에서는 찬반 혹은 선택의 모든 옵션을 샘플 에세이에 실어서 동일한 주제 및 동일한 서론 하에 자신의 주장을 개진해 볼 수 있도록 하였습니다.

본 교재를 통해 토플 시험을 준비하는 여러분들이 반드시 좋은 결과를 얻어 여러분들의 꿈을 향해 조금 더 다가설 수 있게 되기를 진심으로 기원합니다. 학생들에게 조금이나마 도움을 주고자 하는 제 바람을 펼칠 수 있도록 책이 출판되기까지 도움을 주신 다락원 편집부에 감사의 말씀을 전합니다. 마지막으로, 언제나 사랑과 응원으로 제 하루하루를 행복하고 가치 있게 만들어 주는 가족들께 깊이 감사드립니다.

저자 김수진

목차

이 책의 특징

최신 경향의 최다 문제 수록

- 각권 18회분 총 36회분의 문제 수록
- 최신 기출 문제를 분석하여 빈출 주제 및 단어로 문를 재구성

모든 문제에 대한 샘플 에세이 제공

- 수험생에게 실질적인 도움이 될 수 있는 모범 답안 제공
- 독립형 문제의 경우 찬/반에 대한 각각의 샘플 에세이 수록

고득점으로 이어지는 필수 팁 제공

- 고득점을 얻기 위해 에세이 작성시 반드시 알아야 할 팁 제시
- 각 독립형 문제에 관련된 연관 토픽 제시

모든 지문과 스크립트, 그리고 샘플 에세이에 대한 해석 수록

- 리딩 지문과 리스닝 스크립트, 그리고 각 샘플 에세이에 대한 해석 포함

리스닝 MP3 파일

이 책의 구성

TASK

주제들이 한 쪽으로 치우치지 않도록 빈출 주제들을 균형감 있게 재배치하였다.

NOTE-TAKING

통합형의 경우 리딩 및 리스닝에 대한 노트테이킹 요령을 제시하고 있으며, 독립형의 경우에는 노트테이킹 요령뿐만 아니라 브레인스토밍을 원활히 할 수 있는 가이드라인 또한 제시하였다.

WORD REMINDER

해당 주제와 관련되고 실제 토플 시험에서 자주 사용되는 단어들을 일목요연하게 정리해 두어, 수험생들이 빠른 시간 내에 단어 학습에 대한 효과를 볼 수 있게 했다.

SAMPLE ESSAY & TIPS for SUCCESS

수험생들이 실제 쓸 수 있는 레벨을 감안하여 눈높이에 맞춘 샘플 에세이들을 제공하였다. 특히 독립형의 경우, 찬/반에 대한 각각의 샘플 에세이를 제공해 줌으로써, 자신의 의견에 맞는 모범 답안을 분석해 볼 수 있다. 또한 작문에 유용한 문법 사항 등을 TIPS for SUCCESS에 정리하였다.

RELATED TOPICS

독립형의 경우 해당 주제와 관련되어 출제될 수 있는 다양한 문제들을 추가적으로 제시하고, 아울러 간단한 노트테이킹 작성 요령들도 함께 수록하였다.

TOEFL® iBT에 대한 소개

1. 구성

시험 영역	지문 형식과 문제 수	시간	점수

Reading	• 시험당 3~4개의 지문
	  – 지문 하나는 약 700개의 단어로 구성됨
	  – 각 지문마다 10개의 문제가 출제됨
		54–72분	30점

Listening	• 시험당 2~3개의 대화
	  – 약 3분 동안 12~25차례의 대화가 오고 감
	  – 각 대화마다 5개의 문제가 출제됨
	
	• 시험당 3~4개의 강의
	  – 강의는 3~5분 동안 500~800개의 단어로 구성됨
	  – 각 강의마다 6개의 문제가 출제됨
		41–57분	30점

Break 10 minutes			

Speaking	• 독립형 문제 1개
	  – 15초의 준비 시간과 45초의 응답 시간
	  – 선호 및 의견에 근거한 말하기 문제 1개가 출제됨
	
	• 읽고 듣고 말하기의 통합형 문제 2개
	  – 30초의 준비 시간과 60초의 응답 시간
	  – 대학 생활과 관련된 문제 1개와 특정 학문과 관련된 문제 1개가 출제됨
	
	• 듣고 말하기의 통합형 문제 1개
	  – 20초의 준비 시간과 60초의 응답 시간
	  – 특정 학문과 관련된 문제 1개가 출제됨
		17분	30점

Writing	• 읽고 듣고 쓰기의 통합형 문제 1개
	  – 20분간 읽기 및 듣기 내용을 150~225개의 단어로 요약하는 문제가 출제됨
	
	• 독립형 문제 1개
	  – 30분간 제시된 주제에 따라 최소 300개의 단어로 에세이를 작성하는 문제가
	    출제됨
		50분	30점

2. 특징

전 세계의 지정된 시험장에서 인터넷을 통해 실시

TOEFL® iBT에서 iBT란 인터넷 기반 시험을 뜻하는 Internet-based Test의 약자이다. 시험은 인터넷 시설이 갖추어진 지정된 시험장에서만 실시되며, 시차에 따른 문제 유출의 소지를 없애기 위해 전 세계에서 동시에 하루 만에 시행된다. 총 시험 시간은 3시간에서 3시간 30분 사이이고, 읽기와 듣기 영역 시험이 끝난 후 10분간의 휴식 시간이 주어진다.

읽기, 듣기, 말하기, 쓰기 영역을 통합적으로 평가

TOEFL® iBT는 네 가지 언어 영역을 평가하는 시험으로, 일부 영역의 시험만 선택할 수는 없다. 특히 말하기와 쓰기 영역에서는 읽고 듣고 말하기, 듣고 말하기, 읽고 듣고 쓰기 등과 같은 통합적인 언어 구사 능력을 평가한다. 문법은 별도의 평가 항목 없이 위의 네 영역에 나오는 문제와 과제를 통해 간접적으로 평가된다.

노트 필기 허용

TOEFL® iBT는 핵심 사항을 필기할 수 있도록 시험장에 입장할 때 연필과 종이를 나누어 준다. 따라서, 읽기, 듣기, 말하기, 쓰기 영역에서 지문을 읽거나 들으면서 중요한 내용을 메모해 두었다가 문제를 풀 때 참고할 수 있다. 노트 필기한 종이와 연필은 시험장에서 퇴실할 때 반납해야 한다.

미국식 이외의 발음 추가

TOEFL® iBT의 듣기 영역에서는 강의 가운데 한 개가 미국식 발음 이외의 영국, 캐나다 등 다양한 국적의 발음으로 나올 수도 있다. 하지만 실제 시험에서 대체적으로 미국식 발음이 가장 많이 들리기 때문에 수험자가 다국적 발음에 대해 크게 걱정할 필요는 없다.

쓰기 영역과 컴퓨터 자판

TOEFL® iBT의 쓰기 영역은 모든 답안을 컴퓨터 자판을 통해 작성해야 한다. 효율적인 답안 작성을 위해 평소에 영문 자판에 익숙해 있어야 한다.

인터넷을 통한 성적 확인

TOEFL® iBT는 수험자가 시험을 치른 후 15일 정도 지나서 시험 결과를 온라인으로 확인할 수 있다. 시험을 신청할 때 온라인 성적 확인과 함께 우편 확인까지 선택하면 차후에 우편으로도 성적표를 받아볼 수 있다.

TOEFL® iBT의 Writing Section 채점 기준

1. 통합형 문제 (Integrated Writing Task)

Score 5

강의의 내용을 명확하게 요약하고 강의 내용이 주어진 읽기 지문에서 나타난 주장과 어떻게 연관되는지를 명료하게 설명한다. 글의 구성이 우수하고 문법적인 실수가 거의 없기 때문에 그 의미가 모호하지 않다.

Score 4

강의 내용의 주제와 그 주제가 읽기 지문에서 나타나고 있는 주제와 어떻게 연관되는지를 잘 설명한다. 하지만 의미가 모호하거나 부정확한 경우가 간혹 있을 수 있다. 또한 이따금 눈에 띄는 문법적인 실수가 나타나서 의미가 모호해 지는 경우도 이 점수에 해당된다.

Score 3

전체적으로 강의의 주제와 그 주제가 읽기 지문에서 나타난 주제와 어떻게 연관되는지를 설명하나 그 의미가 모호하거나, 불명확하거나, 혹은 때때로 잘못되어 있다. 강의의 요점 중 한 가지를 빠뜨리는 경우도 이 점수에 해당된다. 문법적인 실수가 보다 많이 나타나서 강의 및 읽기 지문에서 나타난 주제들 간의 연관성을 알아보기가 힘들다.

Score 2

강의의 주제 중 일부만을 다루고 있으며 그 주제가 읽기 지문에서 나타난 정보와 어떻게 연관되는지를 설명하지 못한다. 또한 심각한 문법적 실수를 포함하고 있기 때문에 해당 주제를 접해본 적이 없는 독자라면 강의 및 읽기 지문의 주제를 이해할 수가 없게 된다.

Score 1

강의의 내용이 거의 다루어지지 않거나 전혀 다루어지지 않는다. 또한 언어 표현 능력이 매우 낮아서 그 의미를 전혀 이해할 수가 없다.

Score 0

단순히 읽기 지문의 내용을 복사해 쓰거나, 전혀 주제를 나타내지 못하거나, 영어 이외의 언어로 쓰여졌거나, 혹은 내용이 아예 없는 경우가 이 점수에 해당된다.

2. 독립형 문제 (Independent Writing Task)

Score 5

명확하게 주제를 전달한다. 글이 논리적으로 구성되어 있고, 아이디어와 단락이 적절하게 연관되어 있으며, 예들이 각 주제를 뒷받침해 준다. 자연스럽게 읽히고 문장 형식이 다양하며, 적합한 단어들이 사용되고, 관용적인 표현들도 올바르게 사용되었다. 사소한 문법적 실수가 있을 수 있으나, 읽는 사람의 이해를 방해하지는 않는다.

Score 4

주제를 잘 전달한다. 하지만 주장을 뒷받침하는 세부적인 내용이 불충분할 수 있다. 전반적으로 글의 구성은 좋으나 연결이 명확하지 않고, 장황하며, 그리고 혹은 관련이 없는 정보가 들어있을 수 있다. 또한 눈에 띄는 문법적인 실수 및 적절치 못한 단어들이 상대적으로 많을 수 있으나, 의미는 명확하게 전달된다.

Score 3

쉽게 이해할 수 없거나 불완전한 설명 및 예들을 사용하여 주제를 나타낸다. 글에 일관성은 있으나, 아이디어간의 연관성은 명확하지 않을 수 있다. 또한 정확하지만 문장 구조 및 어휘의 사용이 제한적일 수 있으며 문법적인 실수가 보다 자주 나타나기 때문에 때때로 그 의미가 모호해진다.

Score 2

주제를 명확하게 표현하지 못하고 글의 구성이 적절치 못하여 아이디어를 제대로 개진하지 못한다. 예들이 주제를 뒷받침하지 못하는 경우도 있고 보다 많은 문법적 실수로 인해 의미가 모호해지는 경우도 많다.

Score 1

주제를 표현하지 못하고 심각한 문법적 실수가 잦아 대체적으로 의미가 불명확하다.

Score 0

단순히 주제를 복사해 쓰거나, 전혀 주제를 나타내지 못하거나, 영어 이외의 언어로 쓰여졌거나, 혹은 내용이 아예 없는 경우 이 점수에 해당된다.

TOEFL® MAP
ACTUAL TEST
Writing 1

01

Thanks to modern technology, students can attend universities without ever setting foot on a physical campus. Instead of listening to lectures in classrooms, students can take online classes. Online degree programs are currently offered at both traditional colleges and cyber universities. However, when it comes to getting jobs, students with degrees from online programs are losing out to those with degrees from traditional schools.

First, the majority of managers are unfamiliar with online education. These individuals often grew up when computers were less prevalent than they are today. They also attended physical schools, which makes them somewhat suspicious of and biased against online programs. They often believe that online programs provide an education that is inferior to that attained at physical schools. This feeling is exacerbated since online programs are relatively new and have not yet established good reputations.

Additionally, many managers are concerned that online program graduates lack the social and interpersonal skills necessary to work alongside others. After all, students taking classes online study alone and do not interact with their professor or classmates. So there is a legitimate concern that these students have not learned how to work well with others and will therefore not make good team members.

Another concern is the ease with which students enrolled in online programs can cheat. For instance, professors cannot watch these students as they take their tests, so it is possible for them to cheat on their exams. Likewise, many online education students may utilize the Internet to submit plagiarized work as their own. Some managers are justifiably concerned that the possession of a diploma from an online program is not a sufficient measure of a person's ability. Resultantly, many are unwilling to risk hiring individuals with degrees from online programs.

🎧 01-01

Directions You have 20 minutes to plan and write your response. Your response will be judged on the basis of the quality of your writing and on how well your response presents the points in the lecture and their relationship to the passage. Typically, an effective response will be 150-225 words.

Question Summarize the points made in the lecture, being sure to explain how they challenge specific claims made in the reading passage.

(CUT) (PASTE) (UNDO) (REDO)   Hide Word Count : 0

Thanks to modern technology, students can attend universities without ever setting foot on a physical campus. Instead of listening to lectures in classrooms, students can take online classes. Online degree programs are currently offered at both traditional colleges and cyber universities. However, when it comes to getting jobs, students with degrees from online programs are losing out to those with degrees from traditional schools.

First, the majority of managers are unfamiliar with online education. These individuals often grew up when computers were less prevalent than they are today. They also attended physical schools, which makes them somewhat suspicious of and biased against online programs. They often believe that online programs provide an education that is inferior to that attained at physical schools. This feeling is exacerbated since online programs are relatively new and have not yet established good reputations.

Additionally, many managers are concerned that online program graduates lack the social and interpersonal skills necessary to work alongside others. After all, students taking classes online study alone and do not interact with their professor or classmates. So there is a legitimate concern that these students have not learned how to work well with others and will therefore not make good team members.

Another concern is the ease with which students enrolled in online programs can cheat. For instance, professors cannot watch these students as they take their tests, so it is possible for them to cheat on their exams. Likewise, many online education students may utilize the Internet to submit plagiarized work as their own. Some managers are justifiably concerned that the possession of a diploma from an online program is not a sufficient measure of a person's ability. Resultantly, many are unwilling to risk hiring individuals with degrees from online programs.

📝 NOTE-TAKING

READING

skepticism about online degree programs 온라인 학위 프로그램에 대한 회의

❶ relatively new + not yet established 비교적 새로움 + 아직 확립되지 못했음

- majority of managers attended school when computers were less prevalent
  대부분의 매니저들은 컴퓨터가 널리 보급되지 않았던 시절에 학교를 다녔음 → often biased 종종 편견을 가짐

 Online degree programs are comparatively novel, and their status has not yet been settled.

❷ lack social + interpersonal skills 사회적 + 대인 관계의 능력 결여

- no interaction w/profs / classmates 교수/급우와의 교류 없음 → good team members ✕ 훌륭한 팀 구성원 ✕

Paraphrasing Example Students are not proficient in social skills and interpersonal relationships.

❸ easy to cheat 부정 행위의 용이함

- no proctor 감독관 ✕
- exams / assignments 시험 / 과제
  ∴ insufficient to measure one's ability 개인의 능력을 측정하기에 불충분함

Paraphrasing Example Online programs create an environment where students can easily cheat.

WORD REMINDER

lose out 지다, 실패하다 suspicious 의심스러운 biased 편향된 inferior 열등한 exacerbate 악화시키다 interpersonal 대인 관계의
legitimate 정당한 ease 용이함 enroll 등록하다 plagiarize 표절하다 justifiably 정당하다고 인정할 수 있는

LISTENING

online university degrees: reliable 온라인 대학 학위: 믿을만함

❶ wrong belief 잘못된 믿음

- many of the best universities offer online programs 많은 우수한 대학이 온라인 프로그램을 제공함
  → administrators + profs: make sure students get good educational training
  행정관 + 교수: 학생들이 훌륭한 교육을 받는다는 것을 확실히 함

Paraphrasing Example Managers have mistaken ideas about online degree programs.

❷ interaction w/profs + classmates: not worrisome 교수 + 급우와의 교류: 우려되지 않음

- web conference: speak w/profs + classmates 온라인 미팅: 교수 + 급우들과 대화
- communicating, sharing information, doing group projects 의사소통, 정보 공유, 그룹 과제 수행

Paraphrasing Example The matter of students' interactions with professors and classmates is not worrisome.

❸ cheating: difficult 부정 행위: 어려움

- exam: requires proctor 시험: 감독관 요구
- plagiarism: profs (website) 표절: 교수들 (웹사이트)

Paraphrasing Example As there has to be a proctor every time a student takes an exam, cheating is almost impossible during the exam.

WORD REMINDER

shun 멀리하다 skeptical 회의적인 erroneously 잘못되게, 틀리게 administrator 관리자 interact 상호 작용하다 virtually 사실상
conferencing 회의의 개최 proctor 시험 감독관

The lecturer argues that managers should not be skeptical about hiring online university graduates. This directly challenges the reading passage's claim that some managers hesitate to hire graduates with online university degrees.

First, according to the professor, managers have mistaken ideas about online degree programs. He says many prestigious universities have online programs. This contradicts the reading passage's claim that online degree programs are comparatively novel and that their status has not yet been settled.

On top of that, the lecturer contends that the matter of students' interactions with their professors and classmates is not worrisome. Since web conferences are parts of these programs, communicating and sharing information with professors and classmates are mandatory. Moreover, students even do group projects together. This casts doubt on the reading passage's claim that students are not proficient in social skills and interpersonal relationships.

Finally, cheating has become difficult to do. As there has to be a proctor every time a student takes an exam, cheating is almost impossible during the exam. In addition, there are professors who carefully look if there is any plagiarized work. This goes against the reading passage's claim that online programs create environments where students can cheat easily.

WORD REMINDER

hesitate 망설이다   prestigious 일류의   comparatively 비교적   novel 새로운   mandatory 의무의   proficient 숙달한

TIPS for SUCCESS

GENIE

서론을 쓸 때에는 마법의 지니(GENIE)를 기억하자.

Generalize: 일반적인 큰 아이디어를 떠올리고
Elaborate: 그 아이디어를 조금 더 자세히 설명한 후
Narrow Down: 점점 좁혀 나가서
Introduce Thesis: 말하고자 하는 논제에 다다르며
Explain Reasons: 논제에 대한 이유에 대해 간략히 설명한다.

CUT   PASTE   UNDO   REDO   Hide Word Count : 0

Directions Read the question below. You have 30 minutes to plan, write, and revise your essay. Typically, an effective response will contain a minimum of 300 words.

Question

Do you agree or disagree with the following statement?

Grades encourage students to work harder at school.

Use specific reasons and examples to support your answer.

AGREE

● ***way to recognize effort + accomplishment*** 노력 + 성과를 인정하는 방법
  - motivated to work harder to maintain / improve 유지하기 위해 / 발전하기 위해 열심히 공부하도록 자극을 받음
    Ex ① grade: student not interested in subj → work hard → good grade → inspire student
    성적: 학생이 과목에 관심 없음 → 열심히 노력 → 좋은 성적 → 학생은 고무됨
    ② grade **X**: enjoy learning → evaluated **X** → worked hard **X** → performance: lower than average
    성적 x: 배움을 즐김 → 평가 x → 노력 x → 성과: 평균 이하

● ***set a goal*** 목표 설정
  - difficult to work for long-term goal 장기 목표를 위해 공부하는 것은 어려움
    Ex writing an essay: if not evaluated → lose motivation 에세이 작문: 만약 평가가 되지 않는다면 → 열정을 잃어버림
  - desire to reach goal → endeavor 목표에 도달하기 위한 바람 → 노력

INTRODUCTION

generalization: school → build knowledge + pursue academic goals
일반화: 학교 →지식을 쌓고 + 학구적 목표를 추구하는 곳
⬇
whether to give grades or not
성적을 줘야 하는가 아닌가
⬇
thesis: agree (way to acknowledge effort, self-motivation)
논제: 찬성 (노력을 인정하는 방법, 자발성 부여)

DISAGREE

● ***grade: stressful*** 성적: 스트레스
  - marking + scoring: discouragement + frustration → lose interest in the subj 채점 + 점수를 주는 것: 좌절 + 낙담
    Ex low grade in math → no way to recover and get an A 수학에서 낮은 성적 → 회복해서 A를 받을 가능성 x
    → lose motivation + give up 동기 부여 x + 포기

● ***chance to gain broad knowledge*** 폭넓은 지식을 습득할 수 있는 기회
  - objective of learning: should not be focused on a grade 배움의 목적: 성적에 초점을 맞춰서는 안됨
    Ex instead of acquiring knowledge, attention will be centered on parts that will be on exam
    지식을 얻으려는 것이 아닌, 관심이 시험에 나올 부분에만 맞춰질 것
    → once ready for test, not motivated to gain further knowledge
    일단 시험 준비가 되면, 더 이상의 지식을 얻을 열정 x

INTRODUCTION

generalization: school → build knowledge + pursue academic goals
일반화: 학교 →지식을 쌓고 + 학구적 목표를 추구하는 곳
⬇
whether to give grades or not
성적을 줘야 하는가 아닌가
⬇
thesis: disagree (stress+ pressure, takes motivation away)
논제: 반대 (스트레스 + 압박, 열정을 없앰)

School is where students build knowledge. According to student's effort and performance, grades are given. Some people say grades encourage students to work harder at school while others insist the grading system should be abolished. Though there are some advantages to learning without getting any grades, I strongly agree with the statement that grades encourage students to work harder at school. The reason is that grades provide motivation and goals for students.

First, a grading system is a tool for acknowledging students' efforts and accomplishments. For instance, a study was done at a school where one of the groups received grades while the other group did not. It was discovered that most students in the latter group were not motivated to work hard since they were not evaluated. However, in the former, even when students were not interested in a particular subject, they put a lot of effort into getting good grades and were inspired by the subject.

On top of that, it is crucial for individuals to set goals. At young ages, students find it difficult to set long-term goals and to work hard to pursue their dreams. For instance, if students are not evaluated on writing essays and simply must be satisfied with learning composition skills, those who worked hard will end up losing motivation and will not put much effort onto their following assignments.

It is true that the ultimate purpose of learning should be to accumulate knowledge rather than to get good grades. However, grades serve as tools for acknowledging people's endeavors and the time they have put in to their classes. Moreover, a desire to achieve an academic goal will get students to put more effort into their work. Therefore, I firmly believe that grades are necessary to encourage students to do their best.

WORD REMINDER

abolish 폐지하다　acknowledge 인정하다　accomplishment 성취　latter 후자의　evaluate 평가하다　former 전자의　particular 특정한 inspire 격려하다　pursue 추구하다　composition 작문　assignment 과제　ultimate 궁극적인　accumulate 축적하다, 모으다 endeavor 노력

▣ TIPS for SUCCESS

Triple E's (TEEE)

본론을 쓸 때에는 TEEE를 기억하자.

Topic Sentence: 본론 문단에서의 중요한 아이디어를 쓰고

Elaborate: 그 아이디어를 좀 더 자세히 설명한 후

Example: 예시를 제공하며

Explain: 주제와 연관시켜 결론을 맺는다.

School is where students build knowledge. According to students' effort and performance, grades are given. Some people say grades encourage students to work harder at school while others insist the grading system should be abolished. Though there are some advantages to grading students' work, I strongly disagree with the statement that grades encourage students to work harder at school. The reason is that students will experience pressure and possibly lose their motivation.

First of all, having to get good grades can be very stressful. Marking and scoring often discourage students and make them frustrated, leading them to lose interest in particular subjects. For instance, if a student does badly on a math test and gets a low grade, he might think there is no way to recover and to get an A. This might make him lose motivation and give up.

On top of that, getting grades hinders students from gaining more knowledge. Instead of acquiring in-depth knowledge on concepts they should learn, students' attention will be centered only on the parts that will be on their exams. Once they are ready for their tests, they will not be motivated to procure further knowledge on the content. Hence, rather than finding joy from learning the subject, the only goal the students have will be to get good grades.

It is true that setting a goal for good grades might make students work harder; however, that will only work for a certain period of time, and many will eventually lose motivation. The reason is that unless students can maintain good grades, they will get stressed out and may even give up. In addition, focusing on grades will inhibit students from learning various subjects. Therefore, I firmly believe that grades will rarely make students work harder but will only discourage students.

WORD REMINDER

pressure 압박   discourage 좌절시키다   frustrated 낙담한   hinder 막다   acquire 얻다   in-depth 철저한, 상세한   procure 얻다
inhibit 금지하다

TIPS for SUCCESS

PPR

결론을 쓸 때에는 PPR을 활용하자.

Present Contrary Opinion: 반대 의견의 관점에서 본 후
Point Out Reasons: 왜 반대 의견이 틀린지 설명하고
Restate Thesis: 논제를 다시 말하며 글을 마무리 짓는다.

RELATED TOPICS

1   Do you agree or disagree with the following statement? Sometimes it is better to be dishonest. Use specific reasons and examples to support your answer.

다음 명제에 찬성하는가 반대하는가? 가끔은 정직하지 않은게 낫다. 구체적인 이유와 예를 들어 자신의 입장을 뒷받침하시오.

AGREE	DISAGREE
- care for others (avoid hurting others' feelings) 타인에 대한 배려 (다른 이들의 기분을 다치게 하는 것을 피함) - provide hope and motivation (patients) 희망과 동기 부여를 주기 위함 (환자)	- lose trust between people 사람들 사이에서 신뢰를 잃음 - could become habit 습관이 될 수 있음

2   Do you agree or disagree with the following statement? People should keep trying to reach their goals even if their objectives seem impossible to achieve. Use specific reasons and examples to support your position.

다음 명제에 찬성하는가 반대하는가? 인간은 자신의 목표가 이루기 불가능해 보일지라도 목표에 도달하기 위해 계속 노력해야 한다. 구체적인 이유와 예를 들어 자신의 입장을 뒷받침하시오.

AGREE	DISAGREE
- procedure: more important 과정: 더 중요함 - able to discover something else related to the original goal 원래의 목표와 관련된 다른 것을 찾을 수 있음	- result is more important 결과가 더 중요함 - waste of time → can spend time on other things with more potential 시간 낭비 → 잠재력을 더 많이 가진 다른 것에 그 시간을 쓸 수 있음

3   Some students participate in school activities such as clubs and sports while other students spend more time on their studies. Which do you prefer and why? Use specific reasons and examples to support your position.

어떤 학생들은 공부에 더 많은 시간을 쏟는 반면 어떤 학생들은 클럽이나 스포츠 등의 학교 활동에 참여한다. 구체적인 이유와 예를 들어 자신의 입장을 뒷받침하시오. 당신은 어떤 것을 선호하고 그 이유는 무엇인가? 구체적인 이유와 예를 들어 자신의 입장을 뒷받침하시오.

CLUBS & SPORTS	STUDIES
- learn many factors: leadership, cooperation, time management 많은 요소를 배울 수 있음: 리더십, 협동심, 시간 관리 - extracurricular activities important for getting into college 대학교에 지원할 때 과외 활동이 중요함	- most colleges choose students based on academic grades 대부분의 대학들은 학업 성적으로 학생을 선택함 - able to develop and expand more knowledge and academic interests 지식과 학문적 흥미를 개발하고 넓힐 수 있음

TOEFL® MAP

ACTUAL TEST Writing 1

02

At some point, the Earth's supply of fossil fuels such as coal, petroleum, and natural gas is going to be exhausted. Then, humans are going to have to rely upon alternative energy sources to supply their electric needs. One of the most promising types is solar energy.

To begin with, solar energy does not harm the environment in ways that using coal or petroleum does. The burning of various fossil fuels releases contaminants into the atmosphere, which results in air pollution that can harm both the environment and also living organisms. Solar energy, on the other hand, is environmentally friendly. It does no harm to the environment or living organisms since it releases neither pollutants nor noxious materials.

Solar energy is an inexhaustible source of energy. So long as the sun is shining, it can be utilized. Of course, solar energy cannot be accessed at night or when weather conditions are less than optimal, yet there are still several hours a day when the power of the sun can be harnessed. As technology steadily improves, ways to store solar energy will be discovered, which will enable people to have access to solar energy twenty-four hours a day.

Finally, solar energy can be used from virtually anywhere on the planet. Most people are under the mistaken impression that it is viable only in hot deserts or in places that receive little cloud cover. However, this is not true. People can rely on solar energy even in remote areas such as mountains and thick forests. If the sun's rays can reach the solar panels, then people can create electricity from them. This makes solar energy the most convenient of all types of alternative energy resources, including wind, water, and geothermal power.

🎧 02-01

Directions You have 20 minutes to plan and write your response. Your response will be judged on the basis of the quality of your writing and on how well your response presents the points in the lecture and their relationship to the passage. Typically, an effective response will be 150-225 words.

Question Summarize the points made in the lecture, being sure to explain how they challenge specific arguments made in the reading passage.

CUT   PASTE   UNDO   REDO   Hide Word Count : 0

At some point, the Earth's supply of fossil fuels such as coal, petroleum, and natural gas is going to be exhausted. Then, humans are going to have to rely upon alternative energy sources to supply their electric needs. One of the most promising types is solar energy.

To begin with, solar energy does not harm the environment in ways that using coal or petroleum does. The burning of various fossil fuels releases contaminants into the atmosphere, which results in air pollution that can harm both the environment and also living organisms. Solar energy, on the other hand, is environmentally friendly. It does no harm to the environment or living organisms since it releases neither pollutants nor noxious materials.

Solar energy is an inexhaustible source of energy. So long as the sun is shining, it can be utilized. Of course, solar energy cannot be accessed at night or when weather conditions are less than optimal, yet there are still several hours a day when the power of the sun can be harnessed. As technology steadily improves, ways to store solar energy will be discovered, which will enable people to have access to solar energy twenty-four hours a day.

Finally, solar energy can be used from virtually anywhere on the planet. Most people are under the mistaken impression that it is viable only in hot deserts or in places that receive little cloud cover. However, this is not true. People can rely on solar energy even in remote areas such as mountains and thick forests. If the sun's rays can reach the solar panels, then people can create electricity from them. This makes solar energy the most convenient of all types of alternative energy resources, including wind, water, and geothermal power.

📝 NOTE-TAKING

READING

solar energy: one of the most promising types of alternative energy sources
태양 에너지: 가장 유망한 대체 에너지 원의 종류 중 하나

❶ *not harmful to environment* 환경에 해롭지 않음

- environmentally friendly (no pollutants / noxious materials) 친환경적 (오염 물질 / 유해한 물질 ✗)

 Solar energy is good for the environment because it does not release any pollutants.

❷ *inexhaustible* 무궁무진함

- sun's rays → able to be utilized as energy 태양 광선 → 에너지로 활용 가능
- tech ↑: way to store solar energy will be discovered 과학 기술의 진보: 태양 에너지의 저장 방법이 발견될 것임

 The supply of solar energy is unlimited as long as there is sunlight.

❸ *usable anywhere* 어느 곳에서도 사용이 가능함

- able to be used in remote areas 오지에서도 사용 가능
  - ∴ most convenient type of E resources 에너지원 중 가장 편리함

 Solar energy can be utilized anywhere.

WORD REMINDER

fossil fuel 화석 연료   petroleum 석유   exhaust 다 써버리다   alternative 대신의, 대안의   promising 전도유망한   contaminant 오염 물질
noxious 유해한   optimal 최적의   harness 이용하다   steadily 꾸준히   viable 실행 가능한   solar panel 태양 전지판   geothermal 지열의

LISTENING

solar energy: not as promising as it seems 태양 에너지: 보여지는 것처럼 유망하지는 않음

❶ *harmful to the environment* 환경에 해로움

- solar panels: made of many types of materials → harmful to environment
  태양 전지판: 많은 종류의 물질로 만들어졌음 → 환경에 유해
- process of manufacturing: noxious chemicals released 제작 과정: 유해한 화학 물질이 방출됨

 Solar energy is, in fact, harmful to the environment because of numerous kinds of toxic materials in solar panels.

❷ *limited* 한정되어 있음

- solar panels: inefficient at capturing sun's rays / converting to electricity
  태양 전지판: 태양 광선을 저장하고 전기로 변환시키는 것에 비효율적
  Ex power the U.S.: – enormous area needed for solar panels 미국에 전기 공급: 태양 전지판을 위해 거대한 지역이 필요
            – constant sun's rays 끊임없는 태양 광선

 There is only a certain amount of solar energy available.

❸ *breakdowns* 고장

- common ∵ panels are complex 흔함 ∵ 진지판이 복잡함
- remote cabin → panels not working 오지 → 전지판이 고장
  → can't fix on own / find a repairman easily 스스로 고침 ✗ / 수리공을 쉽게 찾는 것 ✗
  ∴ traditional energy sources: more convenient 기존의 에너지원: 더욱 편리함

 The malfunctioning of solar panels can be a serious problem.

WORD REMINDER

wean ~에서 떼어놓다   mine 채굴하다   free of ~을 떠나서   limited 한정된   inefficient 비능률적인   capture 획득하다   enormous 거대한
constant 지속적인   malfunction (기계 등이) 제대로 작동하지 않다   breakdown 고장   cabin 오두막집   repairman 수리공   convenient 편리한

The lecturer argues that solar energy is not as promising as it seems and provides three reasons why the energy source is inefficient. This directly refutes the reading passage's claim that solar energy is one of the most advantageous alternative energy sources that can be utilized easily.

Solar energy is, in fact, harmful to the environment because of numerous kinds of toxic materials in solar panels. Moreover, noxious chemicals are released during the process of manufacturing the panels. This contradicts the reading passage's claim that solar energy is good for the environment because it does not release any pollutants.

On top of that, there is only a certain amount of solar energy available. For example, huge solar panel arrays and a continuous supply of the sun's rays would be required to power the United States. This fact casts doubt on the reading passage's claim that the supply of solar energy is unlimited as long as there is sunlight.

Finally, the malfunctioning of solar panels can be a serious problem. As the panels are complicated structures, they often do not work, and people in remote areas would face disadvantages in fixing the panels once they break down. This contradicts the idea presented in the reading passage that solar energy can be utilized anywhere.

WORD REMINDER

unlimited 무한한   complicated 복잡한   face 직면하다

TIPS for SUCCESS

통합형 에세이: 본론

일부 학생들은 지문 내용에 나오는 단어를 약간 변형해서 이미 뼈대가 있는 지문의 문장을 제일 먼저 쓰며 안도감을 느끼는 것 같다. 하지만, 강의 내용이 에세이의 주된 부분을 차지해야 하기 때문에, 먼저 강의 내용에 대해 자세히 설명을 한 후, 그 내용이 지문의 특정 내용을 반박한다는 식으로 각 문단을 마무리짓는 것이 좋다. 다시 한 번 강조하지만, 통합형 에세이는 지문의 요점보다는 강의의 요점에 초점을 맞추어야 한다.

Hide Word Count : 0

Directions Read the question below. You have 30 minutes to plan, write, and revise your essay. Typically, an effective response will contain a minimum of 300 words.

Question

Do you agree or disagree with the following statement?

People in today's world have become too dependent on cars.

Use specific reasons and examples to support your answer.

ACTUAL TEST **02**

📝 NOTE-TAKING

- **work life balance: important** 워라벨: 중요해졌음
    → take at least one vacation /year 적어도 1번의 휴가 / 매년
       Ex road trips: 40%+ of vacations in the U.S. 장거리 자동차 여행: 미국 전체 휴가의 40% 차지함
          → demand ↑: shortage in market 수요 ↑: 시장에서 부족난

- **convenience** 편리함
    − drive cars to places w/in walking distance 걸어 다닐 수 있는 거리에 차를 가져감
       Ex 85% people drive cars to grocery stores 85% 사람들이 슈퍼마켓에 차를 가지고 감
          → spend time walking ✕ carry bags ✕ 걷는데 시간 ✕ 쇼핑백을 가지고 다닐 필요 ✕

INTRODUCTION

generalization: consumers: wide variety of choices of cars
일반화: 소비자: 다양한 자동차의 선택

⬇

# of cars ↑: new roads, parking buildings, gas stations
자동차 숫자↑ : 새로운 도로, 주차 건물, 주유소

⬇

thesis: agree (work-life balance, convenience)
논제: 찬성 (워라벨, 편리함)

DISAGREE

- **cars: greenhouse gases → global warming** 자동차: 온실 가스 →지구 온난화
    → many car companies: produce EVs 많은 자동차 회사: 전기차 생산
    − EV charging station: requires fossil fuels → still damaging to environment 전기차 충전소 → 여전히 환경 파괴
       → environmental awareness: public trans / bikes 환경 경각심: 대중 교통 / 자전거

- **most people drive to shops once a week** 대부분의 사람들은 일주일에 한 번 가게로 운전을 하고 감
    − switching to shop online 온라인 쇼핑으로 전환
       Ex Amazon: consumers find most products 아마존: 소비자들은 대부분의 물품들을 찾음
          → online shopping trend: save trips to and from store 온라인 쇼핑 유행: 가게로 이동 필요 ✕

INTRODUCTION

generalization: consumers: wide variety of choices of cars
일반화: 소비자:다양한 자동차의 선택

⬇

# of cars ↑: new roads, parking buildings, gas stations
자동차 숫자↑ :새로운 도로, 주차 건물, 주유소

⬇

thesis: disagree (environmental awareness, online shopping)
논제: 반대 (환경 경각심, 온라인 쇼핑)

Aiming to suit each individual's taste, car companies provide consumers with a wide variety of designs, options, and price points for cars. As the number of cars on the street is increasing every day, there are new roads, parking garages, and gas stations being built. Though many argue that people have become more aware of environmental concerns, most people have become too dependent on automobiles. The reasons are that work-life balance has become more important and that cars provide convenience.

First of all, as work-life balance has become important, numerous people choose to take at least one vacation per year, and many take trips by car to places such as national parks or beaches. For instance, a study has found that road trips represent more than 40% of vacations taken by travelers in the United States. Therefore, people have become more dependent on cars, and this soaring demand has even caused a shortage of cars on the market.

On top of that, people are used to the convenience that cars provide. A number of people drive cars even when they go to places that are within walking distance. According to recent research, more than 85% of people choose to drive their cars to grocery stores that are located in their neighborhood. By driving cars, they do not need to spend much time walking or carring heavy grocery items in their hands.

It is true that many people are worried about the environmental consequences of possessing cars. However, automotive companies are slowly switching from fossil fuel vehicles to electric ones that are environmentally friendly. Due to work-life balance, more people choose to take road trips. Moreover, many drive their cars to places due to the convenience. Therefore, I strongly agree with the statement that people in today's world have become too dependent on automobiles.

WORD REMINDER

suit 맞추다   taste 취향   national park 국립 공원   represent 나타내다   soaring 급상승하는   demand 수요   shortage 부족
consequence 결과   possess 소유하다   automotive 자동차의   fossil fuel 화석 원료

Aiming to suit each individual's taste, car companies provide consumers with a wide variety of designs, options, and price points for cars. As the number of cars on the street is increasing every day, there are new roads, parking garages, and gas stations being built. Though many contend that cars provide convenience, it is apparent that more people are becoming less dependent on their cars. This is due to people's environmental awareness and online shopping.

Climate change has become more serious than ever before, and cars produce tremendous amounts of greenhouse gases that contribute to global warming. Consequently, many automotive companies are striving to save the world from a catastrophic disaster and have started manufacturing electric vehicles. However, they are not free from being blamed for damaging the environment because electric vehicle charging stations themselves require fossil fuels. As a result, environmental awareness has caused people to use public transportation as well as bikes, which has led people to be less dependent on automobiles.

On top of that, most people drive to shopping malls or grocery stores at least once a week. However, thanks to online shopping, more people are switching to shopping at home instead of shopping at stores. For instance, Amazon is one of the biggest e-commerce companies in the United States, and consumers can find most products there. Therefore, this relatively new online shopping trend has let people avoid taking trips to stores.

It is true that many consumers are used to the convenience that cars provide. Nevertheless, online shopping provides even more advantages, including saving people from making trips to and from stores. In addition, more people are becoming aware of environmental issues and are deciding to take public transportation or to ride bikes. Therefore, I strongly disagree with the statement that people in today's world have become too dependent on their cars.

WORD REMINDER

apparent 명백한   awareness 경각심   tremendous 엄청난   greenhouse gas 온실 가스   contribute to 원인이 되다
global warming 지구 온난화   strive 노력하다   catastrophic 비극적인   disaster 재난   blame for ~에 대해 비난하다
e-commerce 전자 상거래   relatively 비교적으로   trend 유행

RELATED TOPICS

1 Do you agree or disagree with the following statement? Human activity is making the Earth a worse place to live. Use specific reasons and examples to support your answer.

다음 명제에 찬성하는가 반대하는가? 인간의 활동은 지구를 살기에 더 안좋은 곳으로 만들고 있다. 구체적인 이유와 예를 들어 자신의 입장을 뒷받침하시오.

AGREE	DISAGREE
- environmental damage 환경 피해 - extinction of many species: lots of species lose their lives or habitats 많은 종의 멸종: 수많은 종들이 생명이나 터전을 잃음	- restoration of environment 환경 복구 - more convenient 더욱 편리해짐

2 Do you agree or disagree with the following statement? In twenty years, there will be fewer cars in use than there are today. Use specific reasons and examples to support your answer.

다음 명제에 찬성하는가 반대하는가? 20년 후에 오늘날보다 더 적은 자동차가 사용될 것이다. 구체적인 이유와 예를 들어 자신의 입장을 뒷받침하시오.

AGREE	DISAGREE
- environment conservation movement: more people use bikes 자연 보호 운동: 더 많은 사람들이 자전거 이용 - our lives are focused more at home (work from home, online courses) 우리의 삶이 집에 좀 더 집중되어 있음 (재택근무, 온라인 수업)	- population keeps increasing 인구수가 계속 증가 - more cars with more affordable prices and functions 더 많은 자동차 들이 더 나은 가격과 기능을 가지고 있음

3 Do you agree or disagree with the following statement? It is almost impossible to restore nature since only a few people are trying to conserve the Earth. Use specific reasons and examples to support your answer.

다음 명제에 찬성하는가 반대하는가? 오직 일부만이 지구를 보호하기 위해 노력할 것이기 때문에 자연을 복구하는 것은 거의 불가능하다. 구체적인 이유와 예를 들어 자신의 입장을 뒷받침하시오.

AGREE	DISAGREE
- damage is done at a faster rate than restoration 손상이 복구보다 빠른 속도로 진행됨 - many people are still unaware of the potential disaster 많은 사람들이 잠재적인 재난에 대해 여전히 알지 못 함	- more people are aware of the need to protect nature 더 많은 사람들이 자연 보호의 필요성을 알고 있음 - technological developments to restore the environment 자연을 회복하기 위한 기술 개발

TOEFL® MAP
ACTUAL
TEST Writing 1

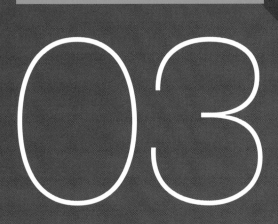

In several western regions of the United States, there are low-lying circular mounds. Called mima mounds, they are anywhere from three to fifty meters in diameter and stand around thirty centimeters to two meters in height. In the United States, there are three main areas and several minor areas where mima mounds are found. Despite their presence in many places, experts are not exactly sure how mima mounds were formed. There are, however, three main theories concerning their formation.

Some mima mound experts believe they were created by various Native American tribes during the past. The major and minor mima mound sites in the U.S. are all located in places where Native American tribes once flourished. These experts speculate that the mounds were created for ceremonial purposes. The tribe members might have used the mounds in various religious ceremonies, or they might have utilized them as burial mounds for deceased tribe members.

The second major theory concerning their formation centers on seismic activity. Two of the three major sites for mima mounds in the U.S. are in geologically active areas. This is also true of many minor sites. It is possible, some geologists claim, that earthquakes somehow changed the surface of the land and, in conjunction with other natural forces such as wind and water, formed mima mounds.

Additionally, there are a few experts who speculate that animals created mima mounds. They claim that gophers, which are small burrowing animals, were responsible for forming them. Simply put, the gophers built the mounds to live in. These individuals defend their argument by pointing out that many mima mounds serve as homes to gopher colonies. In their opinion, it is highly likely that gophers digging tunnels underground pushed up the soil from below and thereby created these mysterious mounds.

🎧 03-01

Directions You have 20 minutes to plan and write your response. Your response will be judged on the basis of the quality of your writing and on how well your response presents the points in the lecture and their relationship to the passage. Typically, an effective response will be 150-225 words.

Question Summarize the points made in the lecture, explaining how they challenge specific claims made in the reading passage.

In several western regions of the United States, there are low-lying circular mounds. Called mima mounds, they are anywhere from three to fifty meters in diameter and stand around thirty centimeters to two meters in height. In the United States, there are three main areas and several minor areas where mima mounds are found. Despite their presence in many places, experts are not exactly sure how mima mounds were formed. There are, however, three main theories concerning their formation.

Some mima mound experts believe they were created by various Native American tribes during the past. The major and minor mima mound sites in the U.S. are all located in places where Native American tribes once flourished. These experts speculate that the mounds were created for ceremonial purposes. The tribe members might have used the mounds in various religious ceremonies, or they might have utilized them as burial mounds for deceased tribe members.

The second major theory concerning their formation centers on seismic activity. Two of the three major sites for mima mounds in the U.S. are in geologically active areas. This is also true of many minor sites. It is possible, some geologists claim, that earthquakes somehow changed the surface of the land and, in conjunction with other natural forces such as wind and water, formed mima mounds.

Additionally, there are a few experts who speculate that animals created mima mounds. They claim that gophers, which are small burrowing animals, were responsible for forming them. Simply put, the gophers built the mounds to live in. These individuals defend their argument by pointing out that many mima mounds serve as homes to gopher colonies. In their opinion, it is highly likely that gophers digging tunnels underground pushed up the soil from below and thereby created these mysterious mounds.

CUT   PASTE   UNDO   REDO   Hide Word Count : 0

📝 NOTE-TAKING

READING

three major theories regarding formation of mima mounds
미마 둔덕의 형성에 관한 세 가지 주요 이론

❶ *formed by Native American tribes* 북미 원주민 부족에 의해서 형성
- mima sites found where tribes flourished 미마 장소가 부족들이 번성했던 장소에서 발견됨
- purpose: religious ceremonies / burial mounds 목적: 종교적 의식 / 매장 흙더미

Paraphrasing Example Mima mounds were made by Native Americans for ceremonial purposes.

❷ *formed by seismic activity* 지진 활동에 의해 형성
- 2 mounds + many mounds: in geologically active areas 2개의 대형 둔덕 + 많은 작은 둔덕: 지질학적으로 활성화된 지역에 위치함

Paraphrasing Example Mima mounds are the results of geological activity such as earthquakes.

❸ *formed by animals* 동물에 의해 형성
- gophers: built mounds to live in 땅다람쥐: 거주하기 위해 둔덕을 만듦
- digging tunnels underground → pushed up soil → formed mounds 지하에 터널을 팜 → 흙을 위로 밀어냄 → 둔덕 형성함

Paraphrasing Example Gophers should get credit for creating mima mounds.

WORD REMINDER

mound 흙무더기, 둔덕   diameter 지름   flourish 번성하다   burial 매장   deceased 사망한   seismic 지진의   in conjunction with ~와 함께
gopher 땅다람쥐   burrow (굴을) 파다   thereby 그 때문에

LISTENING

formation of mima mounds: no apparent evidence 미마 둔덕의 형성: 명확한 증거 ✕

❶ *no evidence of N. Americans making mounds* 북미 원주민이 둔덕을 만든 증거 ✕
- excavation → no artifacts / no human remains 발굴 → 유물 ✕ / 유골 ✕
- ∴ manmade ✕ 인공 ✕

Paraphrasing Example Mima mounds are artificially made.

❷ *mounds: found in other parts of country* 둔덕: 미국의 다른 지역에서도 발견됨
- ground: quite stable 지면: 꽤 안정적
- ∴ seismic activity ✕ 지진 활동 ✕

Paraphrasing Example Mima mounds have been spotted in various parts of the country.

❸ *no evidence of gophers making mounds* 땅다람쥐의 둔덕 형성에 관한 증거 ✕
- many live in the mounds 많은 땅다람쥐들이 둔덕에서 삶
- no one witnessed gophers building mima mounds 누구도 땅다람쥐가 미마 둔덕을 만드는 것을 목격한 적 없음

Paraphrasing Example Gophers have no relationship with mima mound building.

WORD REMINDER

feature 특징, 특색   prevalent 널리 퍼진   archaeologist 고고학자   excavate 발굴하다   artifact 인공 유물   human remains 사람의 유해
manmade 인공의   stable 안정된   authority 설득력, 권위   witness 목격하다 .

The lecturer argues that the cause of the formation of mima mounds in the United States is still unknown. This directly refutes the reading passage's claim that the formation of mima mounds can fit into one of the three major theories.

First, the professor says that mima mounds were artificially made. According to the professor, there are no artifacts or human remains found during the process of excavation. This casts doubt on the reading passage's claim that mima mounds were made by Native Americans for ceremonial purposes.

On top of that, the lecturer contends that mima mounds are located in various parts of the country. Those lands are geologically stable; in fact, they hardly experience any earthquakes. In that sense, it seems irrational to state that mima mounds are the results of geological activity such as earthquakes.

Finally, it turns out that gophers have no relationship with mima mound building. No one is sure whether gophers actually built the mounds or whether they moved into the mounds to dwell in them. In addition, the theory stating gophers built the mounds cannot be supported since no one has seen a gopher constructing a mound. This goes against the idea mentioned in the reading passage that gophers should get credit for creating mima mounds.

WORD REMINDER

fit into ~에 꼭 들어가다   artificially 인위적으로   spot 발견하다   irrational 불합리한   dwell 살다, 거주하다   get credit for ~의 공로를 인정받다

TIPS for SUCCESS

연결동사 Linking Verb

동작이나 상태를 표시하지 않고 문장의 주어와 보어만 연결하는 역할을 하는 동사를 연결동사라고 한다. 연결동사의 종류에는 become, seem, taste, appear, look, grow, get, go, turn, smell, remain, stay, sound, prove 등과 be동사(is, am, are, be, being, been, was, were)가 있다. 따라서 위의 동사들 다음에는 부사가 아닌 형용사 또는 명사가 오게 된다. 세 번째 단락의 문장을 살펴보자.

In that sense, it seems irrational to state that mima mounds are the results of geological activity such as earthquakes.

위의 문장에서 seem이라는 연결동사 다음에 irrational이 나와서 mima mounds are the results of geological activity such as earthquakes라는 이론(가주어 it에 대한 that절)과 irrational이라는 형용사를 연결시켜 준다.

CUT | PASTE | UNDO | REDO | Hide Word Count : 0

Directions Read the question below. You have 30 minutes to plan, write, and revise your essay. Typically, an effective response will contain a minimum of 300 words.

Question

Which do you prefer, traveling overseas alone or traveling with a tour guide?

Use specific reasons and examples to support your answer.

ACTUAL TEST **03**

📝 NOTE-TAKING

- *freedom* 자유
  - able to travel at one's own pace 본인의 속도에 맞춰서 여행을 할 수 있음
    - Ex France: interested in artwork 프랑스: 예술품에 흥미를 가짐
      - → changed the plan 계획 변경함

- *direct experience* 직접 경험
  - interacting w/local people / taking public transportation 현지인들과 교류 / 대중교통 이용
    - Ex friend: traveled to Hong Kong 친구: 홍콩으로 여행함
      - → restaurant famous with local people → experienced authentic tastes
      - 현지인들 사이에서의 유명한 식당 → 진정한 맛을 경험

INTRODUCTION

generalization: traveling: a common habit
일반화: 여행: 평범한 관습

two types of traveling: alone vs w/a tour guide
두 가지의 여행 방법: 홀로 vs 여행 가이드와 함께

thesis: alone (freedom, direct experience)
논제: 홀로 (자유, 직접 경험)

- *more organized* 보다 체계적임
  - take travelers to famous places / time saving 관광객들을 유명 장소로 데려감 / 시간 절약
    - Ex France: renowned museums 프랑스: 유명한 박물관들
      took shortest routes 최단 경로

- *safety* 안전함
  - familiar w/the place + culture including language, people, customs
    장소 + 언어, 사람들, 관습을 포함한 문화에 익숙함
    - Ex friend: traveled to Thailand 친구: 태국 여행함
      snake bit → prompt assistance from guide → able to get treatment quickly
      뱀에 물림 → 가이드의 신속한 도움 → 빨리 치료를 받을 수 있었음

INTRODUCTION

generalization: traveling: a common habit
일반화: 여행: 평범한 관습

two types of traveling: alone vs w/a tour guide
두 가지의 여행 방법: 홀로 vs 여행 가이드와 함께

thesis: w/a tour guide (more organized, safe)
논제: 여행 가이드와 함께 (보다 체계적, 안전)

As our lifestyles have improved over the years, it is not uncommon to see people traveling extensively overseas nowadays. The two most popular types of traveling are traveling with a tour guide and traveling alone, which has become feasible with the help of books and mass media. Though some prefer traveling with a tour guide, I strongly prefer traveling alone because I can enjoy more freedom that way. Moreover, I can experience a culture more closely in person.

For one, there is a lot of freedom when traveling alone. In other words, I can travel at my own pace without having to worry about others' schedules. For instance, when I made a journey to France, I got very interested in the artwork at the Orsay Museum. Thus, even though I had originally planned to visit Versailles in the afternoon, I changed my agenda. Instead, I stayed in the museum for the entire day and appreciated the works of great artists.

Furthermore, when traveling alone, I can experience a culture more closely. By interacting with local people and taking public transportation, I can gain first-hand experience. To illustrate, when my friend was traveling in Hong Kong, she asked a local person for a recommendation for a famous dim sum place. Though the restaurant was not as fancy as others popular with travelers, it was full of local people. Furthermore, she could also enjoy the authentic taste of dim sum. Had she traveled with a tour guide, she would not have dined at such an excellent restaurant.

Some say traveling with a tour guide would make a trip safer and more organized. However, making mistakes while traveling adds fun to a journey. Traveling alone gives me a chance to step aside from my daily routine. Thus I can relax and enjoy my freedom. In addition, there are more opportunities to experience the culture directly. For these reasons, I prefer traveling overseas alone to traveling with a tour guide.

ACTUAL TEST **03**

▎**WORD REMINDER**

extensively 널리 in person 본인이 직접 pace 속도 agenda 계획, 일정 appreciate 감상하다 ask for ~를 부탁하다 local (특정한) 지방의
dim sum 딤섬 authentic 진정한 routine 판에 박힌 일

■ **TIPS for SUCCESS**

Double Negative(이중 부정)

이중 부정은 강한 긍정, 즉 강조를 할 때 쓰이며 부정을 나타내는 단어 앞에 not을 붙여서 두 번의 부정으로 결국 긍정문을 만드는 것이다. 첫 문단의 문장을 살펴보자.

As our lifestyles have improved over the years, it is **not uncommon** to see people traveling extensively overseas nowadays.

(수년간 우리의 생활 방식이 향상됨에 따라, 근래에 사람들이 해외로 여행을 많이 하는 것을 보는 것은 드문 일이 아니다.)

아래의 문장은 위 문장의 이중 부정을 단순히 긍정의 단어를 사용하여 바꾼 것이다.

As lifestyles have improved over the years, it is **common** to see people traveling overseas a lot nowadays.

(수년간 생활 방식이 향상됨에 따라, 근래엔 사람들이 해외로 여행을 많이 하는 것을 보는 것은 흔한 일이다.)

즉, 맨 위의 문장은 '그만큼 흔한 일(common practice)'이 되었다는 점을 강조하기 위해 쓰였다.

As our lifestyles have improved over the years, it is not uncommon to see people traveling extensively overseas nowadays. The two most popular types of traveling are traveling with a tour guide and traveling alone, which has become feasible with the help of books and mass media. Though some prefer traveling alone, I strongly prefer traveling with a tour guide because it is more organized and safer.

For one, since guides know important sites and locations, they can take travelers to the most famous places at the right times. For example, I once had a chance to travel to France with a tour guide. The trip was excellent in that the guide showed me all the renowned art museums I wished to visit. Moreover, I was able to save time with the help of the guide. Because he was familiar with the locations, the guide always took me from place to place via the shortest routes. Conversely, if I had traveled alone, I might have wasted time roaming around from one end of the region to the other.

On top of that, guides are people who are comfortable with particular places. Consequently, travelers do not have to worry about language or local behavior, especially in cases of emergency. For instance, when my friend took a trip to Thailand, she was bitten by a snake. However, with prompt assistance from the guide, she was able to find a hospital and got treatment quickly. Therefore, for safety and in case of emergencies, having a tour guide will help one feel secure while traveling.

Some say traveling alone provides a chance to meet new people and to experience a culture in person. However, as most travelers are unfamiliar with the culture of a different country, they can encounter dangers while traveling. Hence, for a safer, more organized trip, I prefer traveling overseas with a tour guide to traveling alone.

WORD REMINDER

renowned 유명한   via ~을 거쳐   route 길   roam 배회하다   local behavior 현지 관습   in case of ~의 경우에는   prompt 신속한
assistance 도움   encounter 마주치다

TIPS for SUCCESS

'만약 ~했더라면, ~했을 것이다'와 같은 가정법에서 흔히 쓰이는 표현들을 살펴보자.

〈주어 + would (not) have p.p.〉 ~했을 (하지 않았을) 것이다
〈주어 + should (not) have p.p.〉 ~했어야 (하지 않았어야) 했다
〈주어 + could (not) have p.p.〉 ~할 수 있었을 (하지 못했을) 것이다
〈주어 + might (not) have p.p.〉 ~했을지도 (하지 않았을지도) 모른다

두 번째 단락의 끝부분을 살펴보자.

Conversely, if I had traveled alone, I might have wasted time roaming around from one end of the region to the other.
(반대로, 만약 홀로 여행을 했더라면, 나는 그 지역의 한쪽 끝에서 다른 쪽 끝으로 배회하느라 시간을 낭비했을지도 모른다.)

1 Traveling in one's own country provides more benefits than traveling abroad.

국내 여행은 해외 여행보다 더 많은 혜택을 준다.

AGREE	DISAGREE
- familiarity + comfort 친숙함 + 편안함 ex) custom 관습 - no language barrier 언어 장벽 X	- new culture + experience 새로운 문화 + 경험 - develop adaptation skills 적응 능력을 키움

2 Staying in one city or town for one's entire life is better than moving to other places.

한 곳의 도시나 마을에서 여생을 보내는 것이 다른 곳을 돌아다니는 것보다 낫다.

AGREE	DISAGREE
- stability + comfort 안정성 + 편안함 - save time / money 시간 / 돈 절약	- diverse experiences 다양한 경험 - meet new people: able to form broader interpersonal relationships 새로운 사람들과의 만남: 대인 관계를 넓힐 수 있음

3 When traveling abroad, it is important to follow the local customs even if they are different from that of one's own country. 해외 여행을 할 때, 자국의 관습과 다르더라도 현지 관습을 따르는 것이 중요하다.

AGREE	DISAGREE

- direct experience of new culture 새로운 문화에 대한 직접적인 경험
- respect toward the country + citizens that one is travel in 여행지 + 시민들에 대한 존중
	- religious matters 종교 문제
	  ex) Muslims: Ramadan 이슬람교도: 라마단
	- health-related routine for oneself 개인의 건강과 관련된 일상 생활
	  ex) wearing a hijab while jogging 조깅할 때 히잡을 두르는 것

TOEFL® MAP
ACTUAL
TEST Writing 1

04

When the Europeans arrived in the New World, they discovered that it was already populated with numerous tribes. Most experts have come to believe that these people's ancestors arrived in the Americas by crossing an ice bridge that connected Siberia in Asia with a part of North America. Over time, they spread out across North and South America. But there is now evidence suggesting that the Native Americans actually came from Europe, not Asia.

Around 13,000 years ago, there was a tribe in the Americas that archaeologists refer to as the Clovis people. The distinctive stone spear points they used have been found in several places across North America. Interestingly, these spear points are similar to those of a European people called the Solutreans. They lived in parts of France around 19,000 to 15,000 years ago. Some archaeologists believe that the Clovis people's spear points are based on Solutrean ones. They suggest that the Clovis people are either descendants of the Solutreans or were at least in contact with them.

Another similarity between early Americans and the Solutreans is their physical resemblance. Some ancient human remains exhumed in the Americas are similar in appearance with some Solutrean remains found in Europe. In particular, the shapes of the skulls are almost identical, which suggests a common ancestry between the two.

The Solutreans could have visited the Americas by sailing across the Atlantic Ocean. It would have been a difficult journey for them to accomplish, but they could have constructed ships strong enough to take them across the ocean. In just a matter of weeks, the Solutreans could have departed Europe and arrived in the Americas to start their new lives.

🎧 04-01

Directions You have 20 minutes to plan and write your response. Your response will be judged on the basis of the quality of your writing and on how well your response presents the points in the lecture and their relationship to the passage. Typically, an effective response will be 150-225 words.

Question Summarize the points made in the lecture, being sure to explain how they challenge specific arguments made in the reading passage.

CUT   PASTE   UNDO   REDO   Hide Word Count : 0

When the Europeans arrived in the New World, they discovered that it was already populated with numerous tribes. Most experts have come to believe that these people's ancestors arrived in the Americas by crossing an ice bridge that connected Siberia in Asia with a part of North America. Over time, they spread out across North and South America. But there is now evidence suggesting that the Native Americans actually came from Europe, not Asia.

Around 13,000 years ago, there was a tribe in the Americas that archaeologists refer to as the Clovis people. The distinctive stone spear points they used have been found in several places across North America. Interestingly, these spear points are similar to those of a European people called the Solutreans. They lived in parts of France around 19,000 to 15,000 years ago. Some archaeologists believe that the Clovis people's spear points are based on Solutrean ones. They suggest that the Clovis people are either descendants of the Solutreans or were at least in contact with them.

Another similarity between early Americans and the Solutreans is their physical resemblance. Some ancient human remains exhumed in the Americas are similar in appearance with some Solutrean remains found in Europe. In particular, the shapes of the skulls are almost identical, which suggests a common ancestry between the two.

The Solutreans could have visited the Americas by sailing across the Atlantic Ocean. It would have been a difficult journey for them to accomplish, but they could have constructed ships strong enough to take them across the ocean. In just a matter of weeks, the Solutreans could have departed Europe and arrived in the Americas to start their new lives.

Native Americans are descendants of the Solutreans 미대륙 원주민은 솔류트레인들의 후손임

❶ *distinctive stone spear points* 특유의 석창끝

– similar spear points → connection between the two 비슷한 창끝 → 둘 사이의 관련성

 The distinctive stone spear points prove that the two groups of people share a common ancestry.

❷ *physical resemblance* 신체적 유사함

– shapes of skulls: almost identical 두개골의 모양: 거의 동일

 The physical similarities add validity to the assertion that they had common antecedents.

❸ *the Solutreans: built ships* 솔류트레인: 배를 건조

→ sailed across the Atlantic → arrived in the Americas 대서양을 건너 항해 → 미대륙 도착

 The Solutreans probably built ships and sailed to the Americas by crossing the Atlantic.

WORD REMINDER

populate 거주시키다 ancestor 조상 archaeologist 고고학자 distinctive 구별이 있는 spear 창 descendant 자손 resemblance 유사
remain 유해 exhume 발굴하다 skull 두개골 identical 동일한

the theory on the origin of NA: erroneous 미대륙 원주민의 기원에 대한 이론: 잘못되었음

❶ *same spear points: mere coincidence* 동일한 창끝: 단순한 우연의 일치

– the Solutreans had died out thousands of years before the Clovis arose
솔류트레인은 클로비스인이 생기기 수천 년 전에 사라졌음

→ no connection between the two 둘 사이의 관련성 ✕

 Though the two groups of people had similar spear points, they did not share a relationship. The appearance of the Clovis people and the demise of the Solutreans happened thousands of years apart.

❷ *identical features of skulls: not enough to be evidence* 두개골의 유사한 특징: 증거로서 불충분함

– similarities in skull shapes of people from all around the world 전세계 사람들의 두개골 모양의 유사성

 It would be hasty to conclude a common ancestry only by looking at identical features in skull shapes.

❸ *the Solutreans sailing across the ocean: impossible* 솔류트레인의 대양을 건넌 항해: 불가능

– no one could make such ships back then 그 시대에 그러한 배를 만들 수 있는 사람 ✕
– Atlantic: rough weather 대서양: 거친 기후

 The contention that the Solutreans made it to the Americas by navigating across the Atlantic is irrational.

WORD REMINDER

nomad 유목민 herd 가축의 떼, 무리 subsequently 그 후에 erroneous 잘못된 unearth 발굴하다 die out 차차 소멸하다
mere 단지 ~에 불과한 coincidence 일치 prehistoric 선사의

The lecturer argues that the theory that the Solutreans were the ancestors of Native Americans is unreliable. This directly refutes the reading passage's claim that the notion that Native Americans are from Asia has been proved erroneous.

First, though the two groups had similar spear points, they did not share a relationship. This assertion is supported by the fact that the appearance of the Clovis people and the demise of the Solutreans happened thousands of years apart. This contradicts the reading passage's claim that the distinctive stone spear points prove that the two groups share a common ancestry.

Second, the lecturer contends that it would be hasty to conclude a common ancestry only by looking at identical features in skull shapes as there may be many similarities in skull figures between people with no relationship. This rebuts the reading passage's claim that the physical similarities add validity to the assertion that they had common antecedents.

The contention that the Solutreans made it to the Americas by navigating across the Atlantic is irrational. No one could make a ship with such capabilities during that time, and the rough weather would not have allowed anyone to cross the ocean. This contradicts the idea presented in the reading passage that the Solutreans probably built ships and sailed to the Americas by crossing the Atlantic.

WORD REMINDER

notion 개념   ancestry (집합적) 조상   hasty 성급한   figure 형상   validity 타당성   antecedent 선조   navigate 항해하다   irrational 불합리한

TIPS for SUCCESS

통합형 에세이를 쓸 때의 적절한 시간 분배

통합형 에세이는 독립형 에세이에 비해 짧은 시간(20분)이 주어진다. 하지만, 독립형 에세이에서는 아이디어와 그에 해당되는 예를 생각해야 하는 반면, 통합형 에세이는 이미 주어진 내용을 바탕으로 정리를 하듯 에세이를 쓰는 것이기 때문에 독립형에 비해 정리하는 시간이 짧게 걸린다. 리스닝을 다 들은 후 내용을 정리하는 것은 내용을 기억하는 일을 힘들게 할 뿐 아니라, 시간도 많이 낭비하게 만들기 때문에, 교수의 강의를 들으면서 동시에 노트를 적는 것이 중요하다. 최대한 빨리 정리를 한 후 에세이를 시작하여 독립형 에세이처럼 마지막 5분은 proof-reading을 하는 것이 좋다.

CUT   PASTE   UNDO   REDO   Hide Word Count : 0

Directions Read the question below. You have 30 minutes to plan, write, and revise your essay. Typically, an effective response will contain a minimum of 300 words.

Question

Do you agree or disagree with the following statement?

It is better for children to grow up in the countryside than in a large city.

Use specific reasons and examples to support your answer.

📝 NOTE-TAKING

AGREE

- ***health-related issues in big cities*** 대도시에서는 건강 관련 문제
  - population ↑ ‣ competition ↑ ‣ work harder 인구↑ → 경쟁↑ → 더욱 열심히 노력
    Ex study: 70%+ suffer from physical + emotional concerns 연구: 70% 이상 신체적 + 정서적 문제를 겪음
  - countryside: kids are happier ∵ learn cooperation + harmony while playing + running
    시골: 아이들이 더욱 행복함 ∵ 놀며 달리는 동안 협동 + 화합을 배움

- ***experience nature*** 자연을 경험
  - learn to interact w/others in a relaxed setting 느긋한 환경에서 다른 이들과 교류하는 것을 배움
    Ex direct experience w/nature → intrinsic motivation 자연과의 직접 경험 → 내재적 동기
  - more intrigued to gain deeper knowledge 더 깊이 있는 지식을 얻기 위한 흥미가 생김

INTRODUCTION

generalization: kids build + develop tools in many fields
일반화: 아이들은 많은 분야에서 필요한 도구를 개발 + 발전

⬇

surroundings ➜ where kids build tools
주위 환경 → 아이들이 도구를 개발하는 곳

⬇

thesis: agree (less stressful + grow up w/nature)
논제: 찬성 (적은 스트레스 + 자연과 함께 성장)

DISAGREE

- ***opportunities to learn + compete*** 배움 + 경쟁의 기회
  - educational institutions: variety of classes 교육 기관: 다양한 수업
  - get kids ready for the future 아이들을 미래를 위해 준비하게 함
  - events / contests / sports meets → discover + explore interests
    대회 / 콘테스트 / 스포츠 시합 → 관심사 발견 + 개발

- ***experience various parts of city*** 도시의 다양한 부분을 경험

  Ex city: wide selection of food vs countryside: limited selection 도시: 다양한 음식 vs 시골: 제한적인 메뉴
  - more exposed to cultural life (museums + concert halls) 문화 생활을 많이 경험 (박물관 + 콘서트 홀)
    → invaluable in forming fundamental basis for life 삶의 기본 토대를 형성하는데 있어 매우 귀중함

INTRODUCTION

generalization: kids build + develop tools in many fields
일반화: 아이들은 많은 분야에서 필요한 도구를 개발 + 발전

⬇

surroundings ➜ where kids build tools
주위 환경 → 아이들이 도구를 개발 하는 곳

⬇

thesis: disagree (more opportunities + lots of resources)
논제: 반대 (더 많은 기회 + 많은 자원)

Childhood is a critical period when children build and develop their social skills, knowledge of various topics, and personalities. Among the factors supporting this growth are the surroundings where they develop those skills and abilities. Though some people argue that children should grow up in a metropolis, I strongly agree with the statement that it is better for children to grow up in the countryside than in a large city. Two reasons are that they get less stress and that they can spend time in nature.

First, many children suffer from health-related issues in big cities. Numerous studies have shown that more than 70% of kids in metropolises suffer from physical as well as emotional concerns due to having too much stress and pressure. On the other hand, children tend to be happier in the countryside since kids learn to cooperate and harmonize with their peers while running and playing in many open spaces.

Furthermore, it is crucial to expose kids to a natural environment where they can learn in a relaxed setting. For instance, a study found that kids who had direct experiences with insects, plants, and animals showed intrinsic motivation in academic subjects. This happened because children's interactions with nature intrigued them to gain deeper knowledge. This is in contrast to kids who either had to be rewarded or had the pressure of learning in a classroom full of competitive students in order to be motivated.

It is true that there are many opportunities for children in big cities. However, more opportunities are often related to more competition and pressure. Learning in a relaxed environment will help kids build intrinsic motivation rather than make them motivated by such factors as grades or rewards. Furthermore, kids have more chances to play with their peers and to learn to cooperate and harmonize with others. Therefore, I firmly believe that it is better for children to grow up in the countryside than in a big city.

WORD REMINDER

harmonize 조화시키다   peers 친구   interaction 교류   intrinsic motivation 내재적 동기   intrigued 흥미를 불러일으키는
reward 보상하다; 대가, 상

ACTUAL TEST 04

Childhood is a critical period when children build and develop their social skills, knowledge of various topics, and personalities. Among the factors supporting this growth are the surroundings where they develop those skills and abilities. Though some people argue that children should grow up in a rural area, I strongly disagree with the statement that it is better for children to grow up in the countryside than in a large city. Two reasons are that they can have more opportunities in cities and that cities have lots of resources.

First, there are a number of opportunities to learn and compete in big cities. As cities have dense populations, there are many educational institutions that offer a variety of classes. It is necessary for children to learn to be competitive in order to be ready for the future. By actively engaging in diverse events, contests, and sporting events, not only are kids able to discover and explore their interests, but they can also learn to compete and cooperate with others.

Furthermore, cities give children a chance to experience a variety of cultures. For instance, big cities have many travelers and residents from different parts of the world; hence, one can find lots of restaurants with diverse food selections whereas food choices are limited in rural areas. Moreover, children are more exposed to cultural life by visiting museums and concert halls. These experiences are invaluable in forming the fundamental basis for life.

It is true that rural areas provide kids with more relaxed settings and less competition. However, competition, in fact, motivates kids to improve their skills. Besides, there are numerous opportunities for kids to take advantage of in a metropolis, and being exposed to cultural life will help them find their interests and goals for the future. Therefore, I firmly believe it is better for children to grow up in a big city than in the countryside.

WORD REMINDER
critical 중요한 personality 인성 surrounding 환경 resource 자원 institution 기관 actively engaging 적극적으로 참가하는
meet 운동 경기 resident 주민 limited 한정된 rural area 시골 지역 expose 경험하다 cultural life 문화 생활 invaluable 매우 귀중한
fundamental 기본이 되는 basis 기초, 원리 motivate 동기를 주다 metropolis 대도시

RELATED TOPICS

1 Do you agree or disagree with the following statement? My lifestyle is easier and more comfortable than the one my grandparents experienced when they were young. Use specific reasons and examples to support your answer.

다음 명제에 찬성하는가 반대하는가? 나의 조부모들께서 어릴 적 경험하셨던 삶에 비해 나의 삶은 더욱 쉽고 편안해졌다. 구체적인 이유와 예를 들어 자신의 입장을 뒷받침하시오.

AGREE	DISAGREE
- more convenient: technological improvements 더욱 편리해짐: 기술 개발 - more goods + services are available 더욱 많은 물품 + 서비스	- more competitive 더욱 치열한 경쟁 - environment: damaged → always need to be prepared for natural disasters 환경: 손상 → 자연재해에 항상 대비를 해야 함

2 Do you agree or disagree with the following statement? Every individual should spend at least one year living in a foreign country. Use specific reasons and examples to support your answer.

다음 명제에 찬성하는가 반대하는가? 모든 사람은 해외에서 최소 1년을 살아야 한다. 구체적인 이유와 예를 들어 자신의 입장을 뒷받침하시오.

AGREE	DISAGREE
- able to understand others with different backgrounds 다른 환경에서 온 다른 이들을 이해할 수 있음 - learn to adjust to new environment 새로운 환경에 적응하는 것을 배움	- waste of time 시간 낭비 - everyone has different personality: some feel comfortable staying in hometown 모두 다른 성향을 갖고 있음: 어떤 이들은 고향에 머무는 것에 편안함을 느낌

3 Which would you prefer, going to a small university in the countryside or a large university in a city? Use specific reasons and examples to support your choice.

다음 중 어떤 것을 선호하는가, 시골에서 작은 대학교를 다니는 것 혹은 도시에서 큰 대학을 다니는 것? 구체적인 이유와 예를 들어 자신의 입장을 뒷받침하시오.

A SMALL UNIVERSITY IN THE COUNTRYSIDE	A LARGE UNIVERSITY IN A CITY
- fewer students → know one another → able to form community w/strong bond 적은 학생 수 → 서로 알고 지냄 → 탄탄한 유대감의 단체를 형성할 수 있음 - less competition → able to enjoy college life w/out stress 경쟁이 덜함 → 스트레스 없이 대학 삶을 즐길 수 있음	- more competition → become more competent 더 많은 경쟁 → 더욱 유능해짐 - many opportunities for experiences 경험에 대한 많은 기회

4 Which would you prefer, attending a large university with many students or a small university with few students? Use specific reasons and examples to support your choice.

다음 중 어떤 것을 선호하는가, 적은 숫자의 학생이 있는 작은 대학교를 다니는 것 혹은 많은 학생들이 있는 큰 대학을 다니는 것? 구체적인 이유와 예를 들어 자신의 입장을 뒷받침하시오.

A LARGE UNIVERSITY WITH MANY STUDENTS	A SMALL UNIVERSITY WITH FEW STUDENTS
- strong alumni 탄탄한 동문 - many majors available 많은 전공 학과가 있음	- more chances to interact w/professors 교수와 교류할 기회가 더 많아짐 - less competition → able to enjoy college life w/out stress 경쟁이 덜함 → 스트레스 없이 대학 생활을 즐길 수 있음

TOEFL® MAP

ACTUAL TEST

05

Forestry officials in the United States once sought to prevent even small forest fires from breaking out. But in recent decades, many forestry services have enacted policies permitting controlled burnings, also called prescribed burns. In a controlled burn, parts of a forest are allowed to burn, but care is taken to ensure that the fire does not spread too much. While prescribed burns are popular nowadays, there is mounting evidence that they do more harm than good.

One of the greatest negative effects of a prescribed burn is its impact on a region's wildlife. Prescribed burns frequently directly cause the deaths of forest denizens such as deer, bears, squirrels, and rabbits. Additionally, the fires destroy the homes of most animals that survive. Having lost their habitats, these animals must move to new areas. This negatively affects the wildlife native to those areas since more animals are forced to compete for a finite supply of food.

Prescribed burns in national parks do not just take a day or two. They often last for days at a time. These burns therefore produce large amounts of air pollution in the form of smoke from burning trees and other vegetation. This smoke is extremely thick and full of ash. It is not only hazardous to those nearby who breathe it, but it can also flow through the atmosphere, where it decreases the air quality in areas far from the burning region.

Many forestry officials claim that prescribed burns are necessary since they prevent large-scale forest fires. Yet forest fires often simply bypass the burned areas and spread to other places instead. In some cases, prescribed burns have gotten out of control and transformed into major forest fires. Thus, forestry officials themselves have been the cause of widespread destruction in some forested areas.

ACTUAL TEST 05

🎧 05-01

Directions You have 20 minutes to plan and write your response. Your response will be judged on the basis of the quality of your writing and on how well your response presents the points in the lecture and their relationship to the passage. Typically, an effective response will be 150-225 words.

Question Summarize the points made in the lecture, being sure to explain how they cast doubt on specific points made in the reading passage.

CUT   PASTE   UNDO   REDO   Hide Word Count : 0

Forestry officials in the United States once sought to prevent even small forest fires from breaking out. But in recent decades, many forestry services have enacted policies permitting controlled burnings, also called prescribed burns. In a controlled burn, parts of a forest are allowed to burn, but care is taken to ensure that the fire does not spread too much. While prescribed burns are popular nowadays, there is mounting evidence that they do more harm than good.

One of the greatest negative effects of a prescribed burn is its impact on a region's wildlife. Prescribed burns frequently directly cause the deaths of forest denizens such as deer, bears, squirrels, and rabbits. Additionally, the fires destroy the homes of most animals that survive. Having lost their habitats, these animals must move to new areas. This negatively affects the wildlife native to those areas since more animals are forced to compete for a finite supply of food.

Prescribed burns in national parks do not just take a day or two. They often last for days at a time. These burns therefore produce large amounts of air pollution in the form of smoke from burning trees and other vegetation. This smoke is extremely thick and full of ash. It is not only hazardous to those nearby who breathe it, but it can also flow through the atmosphere, where it decreases the air quality in areas far from the burning region.

Many forestry officials claim that prescribed burns are necessary since they prevent large-scale forest fires. Yet forest fires often simply bypass the burned areas and spread to other places instead. In some cases, prescribed burns have gotten out of control and transformed into major forest fires. Thus, forestry officials themselves have been the cause of widespread destruction in some forested areas.

NOTE-TAKING

READING

prescribed burns: more harm than good 처방화입: 이득보다는 해를 더 끼침

❶ *direct cause of deaths of forest animals* 숲 속 동물들 죽음의 직접적인 원인
- destroy homes of animals 동물들의 보금자리 파괴
  → moving to a new area → competition for food 새로운 곳으로 이주 → 식량에 대한 경쟁

> **Paraphrasing Example** Forest animals die from prescribed burns and suffer from finding food.

❷ *causes air pollution* 공해 유발
- PB: takes days → smoke → air pollution 처방화입: 수일이 걸림 → 연기 → 대기 오염

> **Paraphrasing Example** Since many prescribed burnings take several days, smoke coming from the burning causes air pollution.

❸ *spreads to other areas* 다른 곳으로 번짐
- getting out of control → major forest fires 속수무책 → 큰 산불

> **Paraphrasing Example** Prescribed burns can change into major forest fires by spreading unexpectedly.

WORD REMINDER

forestry official 삼림 관리자   prevent 예방하다   break out 발생하다   enact 규정하다   controlled 관리된   prescribed 규정된
spread 퍼지다   mount 늘다   wildlife 야생 생물   denizen 생물   finite 한정된   vegetation 식물   hazardous 위험한   atmosphere 공기
bypass 우회하다

LISTENING

prescribed burns: prevent major forest fires 처방화입: 큰 산불 예방

❶ *animals: fast enough to escape from the burns* 동물: 산불에서 도망가기에 충분히 빠름
- Yellowstone National Park: no problem w/animals finding new homes
  옐로우스톤 국립 공원: 동물들이 새로운 보금자리를 찾는 것에 문제 ✕
  ∵ enormous size of forest 숲의 거대한 크기

> **Paraphrasing Example** Only a few animals die from the burns because there is enough time for animals to escape.

❷ *PB: prevents larger fires* 처방화입: 더 큰 산불을 예방
- larger fires → more smoke 큰 산불 → 더 많은 연기
  ∴ less harmful 덜 해로움

> **Paraphrasing Example** Prescribed burns produce smoke; however, the amount of smoke is much less than the amount of smoke generated during major forest fires.

❸ *very carefully monitored* 매우 신중하게 감독됨
- forestry officials: cautious 삼림 관리인: 주의 깊음
  → no PB until conditions are right 조건이 맞을 때까지 인위적 산불 ✕

> **Paraphrasing Example** Prescribed burns are deliberately carried out.

WORD REMINDER

authority 당국   put out 끄다   arsonist 방화범   take place (사건 등이) 일어나다   opponent 반대자   unfounded 근거 없는   flee 달아나다
displaced 추방된   encounter 마주치다   enormous 거대한   release 방출하다   rare 드문   precaution 예방 조치   ensure 확실하게 하다
flame 화염   raging 맹렬한, 극심한   inferno 지옥   slim 매우 적은

The lecturer contends that prescribed burns prevent larger forest fires. This directly contradicts the reading passage's claim that there are more disadvantages than advantages.

First, only a few animals die from the burns because there is enough time for animals to escape. Moreover, the professor cites the example of Yellowstone National Park, where animals have no difficulties finding new habitats because of the park's huge size. This refutes the reading passage's claim that forest animals die from prescribed burns and suffer from finding food.

On top of that, the lecturer says there has been a misunderstanding about the environmental damage of prescribed burns. It is true that prescribed burns produce smoke; however, the amount of smoke is much less than the amount of smoke generated during major forest fires. This rebuts the reading passage's claim that since many prescribed burns take several days, smoke coming from the burning causes air pollution.

Finally, prescribed burns are deliberately carried out. Forest officials put a lot of thought and effort into the burns before they intentionally set a forest on fire; accordingly, it is less feasible that the forest officials would conduct the burns if the conditions are not suitable. This contradicts the idea mentioned in the reading passage that prescribed burns can change into major forest fires by spreading unexpectedly.

WORD REMINDER

cite 언급하다   misunderstanding 오해   generate 발생시키다   deliberately 신중하게   carry out 실행하다   set on fire ~에 불을 지르다
feasible 가능한   conduct 수행하다   suitable 적절한   unexpectedly 돌연히

TIPS for SUCCESS

부사절접속사 I

부사절은 시간, 원인, 또는 장소 등에 대한 보다 자세한 정보를 제공해 줌으로써 읽는 사람의 이해를 돕는 절이다. 접속사의 종류에 대해서 알아보자.

시간	원인	결과	장소
after (~ 후에)	as (~ 때문에)	so ~ that (너무 ~해서 ~하다)	where (~하는 곳에)
as (~하면서)	because (~ 때문에)	such ~ that (너무 ~해서 ~하다)	wherever (~하는 곳마다)
as long as (~하는 동안)	in that (~라는 점에서)		
as soon as (~ 하자마자)	now that (이제 ~하니까)		
before (~ 전에)	since (~ 때문에)		
by the time (~할 때)			
since (~한 이래로)			
until / till (~할 때까지)			
when (~할 때)			
whenever (~할 때마다)			
while (~ 동안)			

cf. for는 원인을 나타낼 때 쓰이지만 종속접속사가 아닌 등위접속사이다. (TEST 05 참고)

CUT PASTE UNDO REDO

Hide Word Count : 0

Directions Read the question below. You have 30 minutes to plan, write, and revise your essay. Typically, an effective response will contain a minimum of 300 words.

Question

Do you agree or disagree with the following statement?

People who organize their rooms neatly have a higher chance of succeeding at achieving their goals.

Use specific reasons and examples to support your answer.

ACTUAL TEST **05**

📝 NOTE-TAKING

- ***organizing skill: essential in most fields of work*** 정돈 능력: 대부분의 일터에서 중요함
  - learns to categorize things: importance + frequency of use 물건을 분류하는 것을 배움: 중요도 + 이용의 빈도
    Ex people classifying books by genre → organize tasks effectively
    장르별로 책을 분류하는 사람들 → 업무를 효율적으로 정리함
    ∴ better management + productivity 뛰어난 관리 + 생산성

- ***strong sense of responsibility*** 강한 책임감
  - organize on a regular basis 정기적으로 정돈함
    Ex cousin: organizes her room every 2 days 사촌: 이틀에 한 번씩 방을 정리함
    → recognized + promoted to manager at work 회사에서 인정을 받고 매니저로 승진

INTRODUCTION

generalization: : room → place where one's day begins
일반화: 방 → 하루가 시작하는 곳
⬇
diff. ways of managing rooms
방을 관리하는 여러 가지 방법
⬇
thesis: agree (habit of organization, responsibility)
논제: 찬성 (정리하는 습관, 책임감)

- ***diff. values to diff. kinds of work*** 다른 일에 대해 다른 가치를 부여
  - harder to put extra effort into organizing a room 방을 정리하는데 별도의 노력을 하기 힘듦
    Ex get off work late: no time to clean my room 늦게 퇴근: 방을 정리할 시간 ✗
    ∴ hired a maid 도우미 고용

- ***some jobs require other skills*** 일부 직업은 다른 능력을 필요로 함
    Ex athletes: workout 〉 organizing skills 운동선수들: 연습 〉 정리하는 능력
    ∴ no correlation 상관관계 ✗

INTRODUCTION

generalization: room → place where one's day begins
일반화: 방 → 하루가 시작하는 곳
⬇
diff. ways of managing rooms
방을 관리하는 여러 가지 방법
⬇
thesis: disagree (diff. in priority, no correlation in some jobs)
논제: 반대 (우선도의 차이, 일부 직업에서의 상관관계 ✗)

The bedroom is the place where one's day begins. People have different ways of managing their rooms. Some people decorate their rooms in a specific theme, some organize their rooms according to practicality, and some do not bother arranging their belongings since they feel they should have complete comfort in their rooms. Though some deny that there is a correlation between organizing skills and success, I strongly believe that people who organize their rooms neatly have a higher chance of succeeding at achieving their goals because they can develop a habit of organization and have a strong sense of responsibility.

First, having organizing skills is essential in most fields of work. By arranging one's belongings in order, one learns how to categorize things in order of importance and frequency of use. For example, people who are used to classifying their own books by genre tend to organize their tasks effectively, resulting in better management and productivity.

Secondly, people who tend to keep their rooms tidy have a sense of responsibility because they must organize their rooms on a regular basis, and the discipline that they develop helps them fulfill their duties at work. To illustrate, my cousin organizes her room every two days even if she is very tired. This sense of responsibility is reflected at work. She was recognized as a responsible employee and promoted to manager of her team.

It is true that sometimes it is difficult for people to organize their rooms since most people are busy with work and want to relax while at home. However, leaving one's personal items in a mess can cause inconveniences. Having good organizing skills is useful at work. Furthermore, tidying their rooms regularly helps people become responsible. For the above reasons, I firmly agree with the statement that people who organize their rooms neatly have a higher chance of succeeding at achieving their goals.

WORD REMINDER

theme 주제   practicality 실용성   bother 걱정하다   arrange 정리하다   belonging 소유물   complete 완전한   deny 부인하다
correlation 상관관계   organize 정리하다   essential 필수적인   in order 순서대로   frequency 빈도   classify 분류하다   task 직무
productivity 생산성   on a regular basis 정기적으로   discipline 훈련법   fulfill 이행하다   duty 임무   reflect 반영하다   recognize 인정하다
promote 승진시키다   mess 난잡   inconvenience 불편   tidy 정리하다

TIPS for SUCCESS

every와 each는 단수명사를 동반한다는 것을 언제나 명심하자. '모든'이라는 뜻을 가졌기 때문에 복수명사를 쓰는 학생들이 생각보다 많다. 단, every가 기수를 동반할 경우, 복수명사가 온다. 세 번째 단락의 문장을 살펴보자.

To illustrate, my cousin organizes her room **every two days** even if she is very tired.

서수가 오는 경우 즉, every second day일 때는 반드시 단수명사를 써야 하지만, 위의 문장처럼 '~ 마다'라는 뜻을 가지며 기수를 동반할 경우에는 복수명사를 써야 한다.

CUT PASTE UNDO REDO

The bedroom is the place where one's day begins. People have different ways of managing their rooms. Some people decorate their rooms in a specific theme, some organize their rooms according to practicality, and some do not bother arranging their belongings since they feel they should have complete comfort in their rooms. Though some contend that people who organize their rooms neatly have a higher chance of succeeding at achieving their goals, I disagree. Priorities differ among people, and the correlation between organizing skills and success applies only to certain jobs.

First, everyone assigns different values to different kinds of work. As our society has become demanding and people have become too busy at work, it has become harder to put extra effort into organizing one's room. To illustrate, I always get off work late. By the time I get home, I am extremely tired and have no time to put my belongings in order. Because I find my work to be more important than cleaning my room, I hired a maid instead.

Secondly, although keeping one's room tidy teaches organizing skills, some jobs require other skills in order for a person to succeed. For instance, it is more crucial for athletes to spend their time working out than developing organizing skills in that there is no correlation between winning an athletic competition and having an ability to keep one's room in order.

It is true that building skills in keeping one's room clean could contribute to success. Conversely, there are many other factors that are needed to succeed; therefore, it is hasty to say that an ability to arrange one's belongings helps one get ahead. People who are busy with their work have difficulty finding the time to tidy their rooms. Furthermore, having organizing skills is helpful only in certain jobs. For the above reasons, I firmly disagree with the statement that people who organize their rooms neatly have a higher chance of succeeding at achieving their goals.

▶ WORD REMINDER

priority 우위   apply 적용되다   assign 할당하다   value 가치   demanding 큰 노력을 요하는   get off 퇴근하다   extremely 극히   hire 고용하다   maid 하녀, 가정부   crucial 중요한   athlete 운동선수   contribute 기여하다   factor 요소   hasty 성급한   get ahead 나아가다

■ TIPS for SUCCESS

because vs. for

because와 바꾸어 쓸 수 있는 표현들로 since, as, due to, 그리고 in that이 있다. 이들 중 due to 다음에는 명사, 명사구, 명사절은 쓸 수 있으나, 〈주어+동사〉의 형태는 쓸 수 없다. 다만, due to the fact that ~ 형태로 주어, 동사를 쓸 수는 있다.

for를 가끔 because 대신 쓰는 학생들이 있지만 차이점을 확실히 알고 쓰는 것이 좋다. because는 직접적인 원인이 될 때 쓴다. 두 번째 단락의 문장을 살펴보자.

Because I find my work to be more important than cleaning my room, I hired a maid instead.

'내가 도우미를 고용한 직접적인 원인은 일이 방을 정리하는 것보다 중요하기 때문이다'에서 볼 수 있듯이, 일의 중요성이 도우미 고용에 직접 영향을 끼쳤음을 알 수 있다. 반면, 다음의 문장을 살펴보자.

It must be summer now, **for** there are lots of ads for air conditioners.

'에어컨에 대한 광고가 많기 때문에 여름이 온 것이 확실하다'는 것은 정확한 사실이 아닌 추측, 판단에 의한 것이므로 because가 아닌 for를 쓴다.

또한, for는 종속접속사가 아닌 등위접속사이므로 앞 절과 대등한 관계를 유지할 때 쓴다. for 앞에는 쉼표가 쓰이며 because, as, 또는 since는 문장의 맨 앞에 올 수 있는 반면 in that이나 for는 문장의 처음에 올 수 없다.

1 In order to succeed, should people do the same things as others, or should they do different things? 성공하기 위해서는 다른 사람들과 같은 것을 해야 하는가 다른 것을 해야 하는가?

SAME	DIFFERENT
- less risk → many previous case studies 위험 부담이 적음 → 많은 전례 - many people to get advice from 조언을 얻을 수 있는 사람들이 많이 있음	- innovator 혁신자 - less competitive 경쟁이 덜함

2 In order to be well informed, a person must get information from many different news sources.
정보에 밝기 위해서는 여러 다양한 뉴스 매체로부터 정보를 얻어야 한다.

AGREE	DISAGREE
- validity 타당성 - different views on the same topic 같은 주제에 관한 다른 관점	- repetitive → waste of time 반복 → 시간 낭비 - many sources → not reliable 많은 자료 → 근거 ✗

3 Computer games should be banned since they are a waste of time.
컴퓨터 게임을 하는 것은 시간 낭비이기 때문에 금지되어야 한다.

AGREE	DISAGREE
- addictive 중독성 있음 - cannot apply the skills to work / study 게임 능력을 일 / 공부에 적용할 수 없음	- release stress 스트레스 해소 - helpful 도움이 됨 ex) quiz 퀴즈

4 It is better to have a positive attitude after a failure than to have a negative attitude.
실패 후 부정적인 태도를 갖는 것보다 긍정적인 태도를 갖는 것이 낫다.

AGREE	DISAGREE
- motivator 자극 - learn from failure 실패로부터 배움	- need to be critical / objective of oneself 자신에게는 더욱 비판적 / 객관적일 필요가 있음 - too positive → no motivation to put in more effort 너무 긍정적 → 더욱 노력할 자극 ✗

TOEFL® MAP
ACTUAL
TEST Writing **1**

Along the east coast of the United States from Delaware to northern Florida, there is a series of around half a million depressions commonly called Carolina bays. They are mostly oval in shape and are typically dry, yet some are lakes. An elevated rim of sand is often found surrounding them, too. The origin of Carolina bays is uncertain, but one theory suggests that objects from space struck the Earth and created them.

The impact theory proposes that an asteroid exploded above the Great Lakes in the Midwestern United States. Then, fragments from the asteroid, as well as the shock wave from the explosion, created the Carolina bays. The shape of the bays is one clue as to their origin. They are oval and stretch from the northwest to the southeast with their southeast ends being more pointed than rounded. This suggests that the objects struck the Earth from the northwest, which is where the Great Lakes are found.

Geologists have dug core samples from some of the bays. They discovered a few traces of rocks and minerals that are commonly found at other well-known impact sites. There is also an uncommon lack of iron in the sand of these samples. Some experts postulate that the iron may have been destroyed by the pressure of the asteroid fragments hitting the Earth.

Another oddity is the presence in some Carolina bays of buckyballs, a rare form of carbon. Buckyballs were first discovered in 1985 during an experiment in outer space. Thus many scientists feel that the presence of buckyballs in Carolina bays indicates that an extraterrestrial object struck the planet. Taken together, all of these factors lend weight to the notion that an impact event created Carolina bays.

ACTUAL TEST **06**

🎧 06-01

Directions You have 20 minutes to plan and write your response. Your response will be judged on the basis of the quality of your writing and on how well your response presents the points in the lecture and their relationship to the passage. Typically, an effective response will be 150-225 words.

Question Summarize the points made in the lecture, being sure to explain how they challenge specific arguments made in the reading passage.

CUT PASTE UNDO REDO   Hide Word Count : 0

Along the east coast of the United States from Delaware to northern Florida, there is a series of around half a million depressions commonly called Carolina bays. They are mostly oval in shape and are typically dry, yet some are lakes. An elevated rim of sand is often found surrounding them, too. The origin of Carolina bays is uncertain, but one theory suggests that objects from space struck the Earth and created them.

The impact theory proposes that an asteroid exploded above the Great Lakes in the Midwestern United States. Then, fragments from the asteroid, as well as the shock wave from the explosion, created the Carolina bays. The shape of the bays is one clue as to their origin. They are oval and stretch from the northwest to the southeast with their southeast ends being more pointed than rounded. This suggests that the objects struck the Earth from the northwest, which is where the Great Lakes are found.

Geologists have dug core samples from some of the bays. They discovered a few traces of rocks and minerals that are commonly found at other well-known impact sites. There is also an uncommon lack of iron in the sand of these samples. Some experts postulate that the iron may have been destroyed by the pressure of the asteroid fragments hitting the Earth.

Another oddity is the presence in some Carolina bays of buckyballs, a rare form of carbon. Buckyballs were first discovered in 1985 during an experiment in outer space. Thus many scientists feel that the presence of buckyballs in Carolina bays indicates that an extraterrestrial object struck the planet. Taken together, all of these factors lend weight to the notion that an impact event created Carolina bays.

NOTE-TAKING

origin of Carolina Bays: the impact theory 캐롤라이나 만의 유래: 충돌 이론

❶ asteroid explosion 소행성의 폭발
- fragments + shock wave = Carolina bays 파편 + 충격파 = 캐롤라이나 만
- shape: object struck from NW (Great Lakes) 형상: 북서쪽(5대호)에서부터 물체가 충돌

   The shape of the bays is that of an asteroid crater, indicating that extraterrestrial objects struck from northwest of the United States.

❷ core samples: rocks + minerals found at impact sites 핵심 샘플: 암석 + 광물이 충돌 지역에서 발견됨
- lack of iron: destroyed by pressure of asteroid fragments 철의 결핍: 소행성 파편의 압력에 의해 파괴됨

   Core samples have shown similarities with other impact sites, and iron was destroyed by the pressure of the asteroid fragments.

❸ presence of buckyballs 버키볼의 존재
- extraterrestrial object struck Earth 지구 밖의 물체가 지구에 충돌

   The existence of buckyballs proves that extraterrestrial objects struck the Earth.

WORD REMINDER

depression 함몰된 땅   bay 만(灣)   oval 타원형의   rim 가장자리   asteroid 소행성   shock wave 충격파   postulate 가정하다   oddity 이상한 점
buckyball 버키볼(fullerene를 구성하는 공 모양의 분자)   extraterrestrial 지구 밖의

the impact theory: doubtful 충돌 이론: 의심스러움

❶ shape 형상
- not all share the same shape 모든 만이 같은 형상을 가지고 있지는 않음
  → some: almost circular 일부: 거의 원형
- not made simultaneously → thousands of years apart 동시에 만들어지지 않았음 → 수천 년의 차이

   The shapes of Carolina bays prove that the impact theory is invalid.

❷ no common materials / known impact craters 일반적인 물질 × / 충돌 구덩이 ×

Ex shocked quartz not found 충격 석영 ×
- lack of iron: result of chemical process 철의 결핍: 화학 작용의 결과

   No one could find common materials or known impact craters at the sites.

❸ buckyballs: can be made by lightning strikes 버키볼: 번개에 의해 생길 수 있음
- regions w/Carolina bays: severe thunderstorms 캐롤라이나 만이 있는 지역: 극심한 뇌우

   It is feasible that buckyballs are created by lightning strikes.

WORD REMINDER

impact 충돌   simultaneously 동시에   date 날짜를 매기다   disprove 반박하다   crater 분화구, 구멍   quartz 석영   cite 언급하다

ACTUAL TEST **06**

The lecturer argues that the impact theory, which some experts postulate to explain the origin of Carolina bays, is doubtful. This directly refutes the reading passage's claim that Carolina bays are created by objects from space striking the Earth in the past.

First, the professor says the shapes of Carolina bays prove that the impact theory is invalid. According to the lecturer, not all Carolina bays share the same shape. This fact casts doubt on the reading passage's claim that the shape of the bays is that of an asteroid crater, indicating that extraterrestrial objects struck from northwest of the United States.

Next, the lecturer contends that no one has found common materials or known impact craters at the sites. For example, shocked quartz, which is generally found at impact sites, has not been spotted at all. Moreover, the absence of iron can be explained as a result of a chemical process. This contradicts the reading passage's assertion that core samples have shown similarities with other impact sites, and iron was destroyed by the pressure of the asteroid fragments.

Finally, it is feasible that buckyballs are created by lightning strikes. This can be explicated by looking at the regions with Carolina bays where severe thunderstorms often occur. This argument counters the reading passage's argument that the existence of buckyballs proves that extraterrestrial objects struck the Earth.

WORD REMINDER

invalid 타당하지 않은   absence 부재   core 핵심   feasible 가능한   explicate 확실히 하다

■ TIPS for SUCCESS

by + -ing

〈by + -ing〉는 '~을 함으로써'라고 해석이 되며 방법을 나타낼 때 쓰이는 표현이다.
네 번째 단락의 문장을 살펴보자.

This can be explicated **by looking** at the regions with Carolina bays where severe thunderstorms often occur.

'살펴봄으로써'라는 방법이 앞의 버키볼의 형성에 관한 이론을 뒷받침해 주는 방법으로 쓰였다. 이와 비슷한 표현들로는 〈in + -ing〉(~하는데 있어: 2권 TEST 03 참고)와 〈on/upon + -ing〉(~하자마자: Test 11 참고) 등이 있다.

Hide Word Count : 0

Directions Read the question below. You have 30 minutes to plan, write, and revise your essay. Typically, an effective response will contain a minimum of 300 words.

Question

Do you agree or disagree with the following statement?

It is better to spend money for vacation and travel than to save it for the future.

Use specific reasons and examples to support your answer.

ACTUAL TEST **06**

📝 NOTE-TAKING

- ***free from stress*** 스트레스 ✕
  - – beautiful scenery + special moments 아름다운 경관 + 특별한 순간
    - **Ex** pressure of new task → trip to a few villages 새로운 일의 압박 → 몇몇 마을로 여행
      - → food + hot springs + environment → felt rejuvenated 음식 + 온천 + 환경 → 다시 원기 회복을 한 느낌

- ***broaden perspectives*** 견해를 넓힘
  - – learn new customs + expand scope of thinking 새로운 관습을 배움 + 견해를 넓힘
    - **Ex** cousin: diff country each year 사촌: 해마다 다른 나라
      - → new culture + unfamiliar customs → learn to understand + respect others
      - 새로운 문화 + 익숙지 않은 관습 → 다른 이들을 이해하고 존중하는 것을 배움

> **INTRODUCTION**
>
> **generalization**: : lifestyle: improved → how to spend money: evolved in various ways
> 일반화: 삶의 방식: 향상 → 돈의 소비: 여러 가지 방법으로 진화
>
> ⬇
>
> traveling, learning, saving
> 여행, 배움, 저축
>
> ⬇
>
> **thesis**: agree (release stress, broaden perspectives)
> 논제: 찬성 (스트레스 해소, 견해를 넓힘)

- ***long-term goals (buying house, paying for tuition)*** 장기 목표 (주택 구입, 학비 지불)
  - – more meaningful 더 의미가 있음
    - **Ex** save money to buy house 집을 사기 위해 저축
      - → spend money on vacation → take longer to buy house 휴가 비용으로 지출 → 집을 사는데 더 오래 걸림

- ***unanticipated situations*** 예기치 못한 상황
  - – financially stable + prepared 재정적으로 안정 + 준비됨
    - **Ex** friend: accident / hospitalized 친구: 사고 / 입원
      - → could get operation w/the money saved 저축한 돈으로 수술을 받을 수 있었음

> **INTRODUCTION**
>
> **generalization**: lifestyle: improved → how to spend money: evolved in various ways
> 일반화: 삶의 방식: 향상 → 돈의 소비: 여러 가지 방법으로 진화
>
> ⬇
>
> traveling, learning, saving
> 여행, 배움, 저축
>
> ⬇
>
> **thesis**: disagree (long-term goals, financial security)
> 논제: 반대 (장기 목표, 재정적 안정)

As lifestyles have improved over the years, the question of how to spend one's money has evolved in various ways. Some people spend money on traveling, some spend it on exploring a new hobby, and others save it for the future. Although it is always wise to save money for the future or for unexpected circumstances, I strongly believe one should spend it on vacations and travel because one can release stress while taking a trip. Moreover, one can broaden one's perspective by traveling.

Firstly, traveling helps one relieve stress from hard days at work. With the breathtaking scenery and special moments that a journey can provide, a person can get away from his or her daily routine. For instance, last summer, I was feeling anxious from the pressure of a new task given to me at work. Hence, I decided to go on a trip to a few small villages in Korea. During the trip, I enjoyed traditional food and hot springs in towns full of fresh air and wonderful landscapes. As a result, I felt rejuvenated and was able to successfully initiate the new project.

Second, one can learn and broaden one's perspectives while traveling in other places. By meeting different people and having diverse experiences, one can learn new customs and explore the unknown. To illustrate, my cousin travels to a different country on vacation each year. Every time she visits a new place, she experiences a new culture and tries to grasp the unfamiliar customs of the region. It opens up her mind and builds understanding of others. Had she not learned such skills, she could have had difficulty dealing with certain types of people or situations.

It is true that saving money for the future makes ones feel secure. However, gaining invaluable memories and experiences is just as crucial. Through taking a journey, a person can escape from stressful work and motivate oneself to work harder. In addition, one can learn from direct experiences and widen his or her range of thinking. For the above reasons, I firmly agree with the statement that it is better to spend money for vacation and travel than to save it for the future.

WORD REMINDER
evolve 진화하다, 진화시키다 wise 현명한 unexpected 예기치 못한 circumstance 상황 release 방출하다 broaden 넓히다
perspective 견해 relieve 완화하다 breathtaking 숨막히 daily routine 평범한 일상 anxious 걱정하는 pressure 압박 hot spring 온천
landscape 경치 rejuvenate 원기를 회복하다 initiate 시작하다 custom 관습 unknown 미지의 grasp 이해하다 invaluable 매우 귀중한
crucial 중요한 motivate ~에게 동기를 주다

TIPS for SUCCESS

독립형 에세이를 쓸 때의 적절한 시간 분배

5분: brainstorming
20분: writing
5분: proofreading

마지막의 5분간 proofreading을 할 때에는 내용을 보며 논리상의 문제나 빈약한 예 등의 이유로 에세이를 다시 고치다가는 자칫 시간에 쫓겨 incomplete essay를 제출할 수 있다. 시간의 여유가 별로 없을 때에는 내용보다는 문법(주어-동사 일치, 스펠링, 대문자, 시제 등)을 위주로 체크하자. 본인이 쓴 에세이라고 생각하고 볼 때는 완벽해 보이고 실수가 눈에 띄지 않는 경우가 대부분이기 때문에, 타인의 에세이를 검토한다는 생각으로 보는 것이 도움이 될 수 있다.

As lifestyles have improved over the years, the question of how to spend one's money has evolved in various ways. Some people spend money on traveling, some spend it on exploring a new hobby, and others save it for the future. Although traveling gives one invaluable experiences, I strongly believe one should save money for the future because money can support the long-term goals people strive for. Moreover, saving always makes one feel financially secure even in cases of emergency.

Firstly, there are many fundamental goals one needs to pursue, such as buying a house or paying for tuition. It is true that traveling is exciting; however, saving money for the future is more meaningful. For instance, instead of spending money on a vacation, I save it in order to buy my own house in the future. While the money spent on traveling is gone after a vacation, a house will remain as long as I keep it. Moreover, if I spend money on a trip, it will take much longer until I can purchase a house.

Second, one should always save money for unanticipated situations, including emergencies. That way, one can feel financially stable and prepared. For example, my friend had a car accident and was hospitalized for two weeks. Though he needed a lot of money for a big operation, he could have the operation without having to worry about the money required thanks to his habit of saving. Had he not saved the money, he would have had to borrow it from other people or a financial institution, which could have delayed the surgery.

It is true that traveling helps one feel rejuvenated after coming back to work. On the other hand, a person cannot solely follow his or her desire to enjoy life because there are many unexpected circumstances. It is important that one try hard to accomplish long-term goals. In addition, it is always wise to save money for emergencies. In this way, one can feel reassured in terms of finance. For the above reasons, I firmly disagree with the statement that it is better to spend money for vacation and to travel than to save it for the future.

WORD REMINDER

strive 노력하다   financially 재정적으로   in cases of ~의 경우에는   fundamental 기본적인   pursue 추구하다   meaningful 의미 있는
remain 남다   unanticipated 예기치 않은   stable 안정된   hospitalize 입원시키다   operation 수술   thanks to ~의 덕택으로   borrow 빌리다
financial institution 금융 기관   delay 지체시키다   surgery 수술   solely 혼자서   accomplish 성취하다   reassure 안심시키다

TIPS for SUCCESS

결합력 cohesion

문장과 문장 사이의 결합력을 위해 접속사, signal word, 또는 transition phrase를 적절히 사용하는 것이 좋으며 moreover, in other words, to be specific 등을 다양하게 사용할 수 있다. 그리고 fortunately, perhaps, for the most part, under these circumstances 등의 표현들 역시 이전의 문장과 다음 문장을 자연스럽게 연결해 주며 문장들 사이의 결합력을 높여 준다. 또한, 시간을 나타내 주는 표현들로 는 then, later, next 등이 있다.

RELATED TOPICS

1

People would be happier if they had fewer possessions. 사람들은 소유물이 거의 없을 때 더욱 행복해질 것이다.

AGREE	DISAGREE
- greed ↓: pressure ↓ 욕심 ↓: 압박 ↓ - less stress of keeping them (security) 재산을 지켜야 하는 스트레스가 적음 (보안)	- more possessions: convenient + comfortable 더 많은 소유물: 편리 + 편안함 ex) electronic devices 전자 기기 - accomplishment 성취감

2

People often buy products not because they really need them but because others have them.
사람들은 종종 필요에 의해서가 아닌 타인이 가지고 있다는 이유로 물건을 산다.

AGREE	DISAGREE
- people often judge others according to what they have 사람들은 종종 다른 이들을 소유하고 있는 것에 따라 판단함 - trend: often a topic of conversation → socialize w/other people 유행: 종종 대화의 주제 → 사람들과 어울림	- reason for others having products: b/c they need them 다른 이들이 물건을 소유하는 이유: 필요하기 때문 - rationality: most people know how to manage their budgets 합리성: 대부분의 사람들은 자기 예산을 관리하는 법을 알고 있음

3

Most businesspeople are motivated only by a desire to make money.
대부분의 사업가들은 오직 돈을 벌려는 바램에 의해서만 자극을 받는다.

AGREE	DISAGREE
- objective of business: making money 사업의 목적: 이윤 창출 - accomplishment / recognition: through profits 성취 / 인정: 이윤을 통해서 보여짐	- participate in campaigns + donations 캠페인 + 기부 참여 - accomplishment: more important than making profits 성취: 이윤 창출보다 더욱 중요함 ex) many CEOs w/tremendously low salaries 상당히 적은 연봉을 받는 다수의 최고 경영인들

4

Athletes do not deserve as much money as they earn nowadays. 운동선수들은 지금처럼 돈을 벌 만한 가치를 가지고 있지 않다.

AGREE	DISAGREE
- other employees putting in a similar amount of effort: huge salary difference 비슷한 노력을 하는 다른 직장인들: 막대한 연봉 차이 - chance of injury / downfall of abilities → waste of salary 부상이나 실력 저하의 가능성 → 연봉 낭비	- make a lot of profits for sponsors 후원자에게 많은 이득을 가져다 줌 ex) advertisement in the Super Bowl 슈퍼볼의 광고 - risk of injury / death 부상 / 죽음의 위험

5

It is rare to see people with enough money and no work being happy.
충분한 돈이 있지만 일이 없는 사람들은 행복한 경우가 드물다.

AGREE	DISAGREE
- no goals / no accomplishments 목표 / 성취감 ✕ - no chance of feeling responsibility + cooperation in workplace 일터에서의 책임감 + 협동심을 느낄 기회 ✕	- able to enjoy hobbies 취미 생활을 즐길 수 있음 ex) traveling 여행 - no stress from work 일의 스트레스 ✕

TOEFL® MAP

ACTUAL TEST Writing **1**

In the early twentieth century, many explorers were vying to reach the North Pole. Several subsequently claimed to have reached their objective, which has made the question of who got there first somewhat controversial. One explorer, American Robert E. Peary, made the best case for having reached the North Pole by an overland route on April 9, 1909, however, since his claim is supported by a variety of evidence.

When Peary returned from his trip to the Arctic, he learned that another explorer, Fredrick Cook, was claiming to have reached the North Pole the previous year. Peary submitted his evidence to the National Geographic Society, a highly respected organization. After a close examination of his records, the society concluded that Peary had reached the North Pole while Cook had not.

In his report, Peary stated that it took him approximately thirty-seven days to reach the North Pole from his last base camp. Many Arctic experts believe that was much too fast considering the harsh conditions Peary endured on his trek. However, in 2005, another explorer, Tom Avery, repeated Peary's journey. His team used replicas of 1909 dogsleds and mirrored the conditions Peary faced as best as they could. Avery's team reached the North Pole in just under thirty-seven days, which proved Peary's claim was valid.

Peary himself was a skilled navigator and took many sightings as he traveled, so he was cognizant of when he reached the North Pole. He also took some photographs while there. By examining the sun's position in the sky and the lengths of the shadows on the ice on the dates when the photos were taken, experts at the National Geographic Society determined that Peary was indeed standing at the North Pole when he took those photographs.

🎧 07-01

Directions You have 20 minutes to plan and write your response. Your response will be judged on the basis of the quality of your writing and on how well your response presents the points in the lecture and their relationship to the passage. Typically, an effective response will be 150-225 words.

Question Summarize the points made in the lecture, being sure to explain how they challenge specific arguments made in the reading passage.

| CUT | PASTE | UNDO | REDO | Hide Word Count : 0

In the early twentieth century, many explorers were vying to reach the North Pole. Several subsequently claimed to have reached their objective, which has made the question of who got there first somewhat controversial. One explorer, American Robert E. Peary, made the best case for having reached the North Pole by an overland route on April 9, 1909, however, since his claim is supported by a variety of evidence.

When Peary returned from his trip to the Arctic, he learned that another explorer, Fredrick Cook, was claiming to have reached the North Pole the previous year. Peary submitted his evidence to the National Geographic Society, a highly respected organization. After a close examination of his records, the society concluded that Peary had reached the North Pole while Cook had not.

In his report, Peary stated that it took him approximately thirty-seven days to reach the North Pole from his last base camp. Many Arctic experts believe that was much too fast considering the harsh conditions Peary endured on his trek. However, in 2005, another explorer, Tom Avery, repeated Peary's journey. His team used replicas of 1909 dogsleds and mirrored the conditions Peary faced as best as they could. Avery's team reached the North Pole in just under thirty-seven days, which proved Peary's claim was valid.

Peary himself was a skilled navigator and took many sightings as he traveled, so he was cognizant of when he reached the North Pole. He also took some photographs while there. By examining the sun's position in the sky and the lengths of the shadows on the ice on the dates when the photos were taken, experts at the National Geographic Society determined that Peary was indeed standing at the North Pole when he took those photographs.

READING

Robert E. Peary: first to reach the North Pole 로버트 피어리: 북극에 처음 도달

❶ *approval from the NGS* 국립 지리 협회(National Geographic Society) 로부터의 승인
  - records: under close examination 기록: 면밀한 조사

    Paraphrasing Example Peary's records were examined deliberately and approved by the National Geographic Society.

❷ *experts → 37 days: too short* 전문가들 → 37일: 너무 짧음
  - Avery repeated the journey → just under 37 days 에이버리가 여정을 반복 → 37일이 조금 못 되었음

    Paraphrasing Example Experts were skeptical that Peary's journey took only thirty-seven days until Avery repeated it in less time.

❸ *took pictures* 사진 촬영
  - sun's position in the sky + lengths of the shadows on the ice 하늘의 태양 위치 + 얼음 위의 그림자 길이
    → indeed standing at the North Pole 실제 북극에 서 있었음

    Paraphrasing Example His pictures showing the sun's position and the lengths of shadows led the National Geographic Society to assert that Peary had truly gotten to the North Pole.

WORD REMINDER

vie 경쟁하다 subsequently 그 후에 objective 목표 controversial 논쟁의 overland 육로의 submit 제출하다 harsh 혹독한
endure 견디다 trek 길고 고된 여행 replica 복제, 복제품 mirror 반영하다 navigator 항해자 sighting 목격 cognizant 알고 있는

LISTENING

many experts are not convinced by the claim 많은 전문가들이 그 주장에 납득하지 않음

❶ *The NGS: impartial observers ✕* 국립 지리 협회: 공정한 감독관 ✕
  - examiners: P's friends 검사관들: 피어리의 친구들
  - P: big donor 피어리: 중요한 기부자
    → took only 2 days to examine the evidence 증거를 검사하는데 단 이틀 소요

    Paraphrasing Example The inspectors at the National Geographic Society rushed through his records in only two days before determining that Peary was the first explorer at the North Pole.

❷ *navigation records* 항해 기록
  - P: the only member skilled in navigation → no one could confirm his figures
    피어리: 항해에 숙련된 유일한 구성원 → 어느 누구도 그의 수치를 직접 확인할 수 없었음
  - 37 days: too short 37일: 너무 짧음
  - Avery's journey: different from P's 에이버리의 여정: 피어리의 여정과 다름
  - weather conditions / weights on sled loads 기후 조건 / 썰매 짐의 무게
    → inaccurate test 부정확한 실험

    Paraphrasing Example As Peary was the only skilled member of the expedition, there was no one to corroborate his presence at the North Pole, making Peary's navigation records unpersuasive.

❸ *camera: fit 6 diff. lenses* 카메라: 6개의 다른 렌즈를 설치함
  - lengths of shadows vary depending on the lens 렌즈에 따라서 그림자의 길이가 달라짐
    → cannot trust photographic evidence 사진 증거는 신뢰할 수 없음

    Paraphrasing Example Since the camera could mount six different lenses that could show dissimilar images, the photographic evidence is unreliable.

WORD REMINDER

shaky 불확실한 impartial 공평한 donor 기부자 lone 혼자의 school 훈련[단련]시키다 site 장소 confirm 확인하다 figure 수치, 숫자
duplicate 재현하다, 되풀이하다 feat 위업 flawed 결함이 있는 load 짐 accurate 정확한 manufacture 제작하다 vary 바뀌다

The lecturer argues that many experts are not convinced that Robert E. Peary was the first person to successfully reach the North Pole. This directly refutes the reading passage's claim that there are many pieces of evidence to verify the assertion.

First, Peary's claim is invalid in that examiners at the National Geographic Society were his fellows. Furthermore, the inspectors rushed through his records in only two days before determining that Peary was the first explorer at the North Pole. This contradicts the reading passage's claim that Peary's records were examined deliberately and approved by the society.

Next, the lecturer contends that as Peary was the only skilled member of the expedition, there was no one to corroborate his presence at the North Pole, making Peary's navigation records unpersuasive. Moreover, the different conditions make it hard to compare with journeys by others. This casts doubt on the reading passage's claim that experts were skeptical that Peary's journey took only thirty-seven days until Tom Avery repeated it in less time.

Finally, since the camera could mount six different lenses that could show dissimilar images, the photographic evidence is unreliable. This contradicts the reading passage's claim that his pictures showing the sun's position and the lengths of shadows led the National Geographic Society to assert that Peary had truly gotten to the North Pole.

WORD REMINDER

verify 증명하다   inspector 검사관   deliberately 신중히   approve 승인하다   corroborate 확증하다   presence 존재   persuasive 설득력 있는
expert 전문가   skeptical 회의적인   dissimilar 다른   unreliable 신뢰할 수 없는

TIPS for SUCCESS

부사절이 주절 앞에 올 경우
부사절과 주절 사이에 comma(쉼표)를 반드시 붙인다.
마지막 단락의 문장을 살펴보자.
Since the camera could mount six different lenses that could show dissimilar images라는 부사절이 주절 앞에 있으므로 comma를 붙인 후 the photographic evidence is unreliable를 쓴다.

부사절이 주절 뒤에 올 경우
comma가 필요 없다.
두 번째 단락의 문장을 살펴보자.
First, Peary's claim is invalid라는 주절과 in that examiners at the National Geographic Society were his fellows라는 부사절 사이에는 comma가 붙지 않는다.

   Hide Word Count : 0

Directions Read the question below. You have 30 minutes to plan, write, and revise your essay. Typically, an effective response will contain a minimum of 300 words.

Question

Do you agree or disagree with the following statement?

People learn more by watching television than by reading books.

Use specific reasons and examples to support your answer.

ACTUAL TEST 07

📝 NOTE-TAKING

AGREE

- **saving time** 시간 절약
  - summarize: vast amount of info 요점 정리: 상당한 분량의 정보
  - Ex cousin: only a month to learn about philosophers of 17th c 사촌: 단 한 달 동안 17세기 철학자들에 대해 배워야 했음
    - → able to manage learning by watching TV TV를 시청함으로써 배울 수 있었음

- **visual effects** 시각적 효과
  - – able to understand better 좀 더 잘 이해할 수 있음
    - Ex friend: couldn't understand an experiment → watched a prof's demonstration on TV
      친구: 실험 이해 못했었음 → TV에서 교수의 실연을 시청
    - → could perform one on his own 스스로 실험을 할 수 있게 되었음

INTRODUCTION

generalization: many ways of learning
일반화: 배움의 여러 가지 방식

⬇

attending class / using mass media / reading books
수업 참여 / 대중 매체 사용 / 독서

⬇

thesis: agree (visual effects, saving time)
논제: 찬성 (시각적 효과, 시간 절약)

DISAGREE

- **greater details** 더 깊은 세부 사항
  - – in-depth knowledge 심도 있는 지식
    - Ex cousin: volcanoes on TV (general info) 사촌: TV에서 화산 시청 (전반적인 정보)
      - → could fully understand after reading books 독서 후 완전히 이해할 수 있었음

- **many skills (analyze, imagine, interpret)** 많은 능력 (분석, 상상, 해석)
  - – TV: interpretation can be different TV: 해석이 달라질 수 있음
    - Ex dolphins at Sea World Sea World의 돌고래
      - → TV: biased TV: 편견
      - → books: keep species / inform people 책: 종 보존 / 사람들에게 전달

INTRODUCTION

generalization: many ways of learning
일반화: 배움의 여러 가지 방식

⬇

attending class / using mass media / reading books
수업 참여 / 대중 매체 사용 / 독서

⬇

thesis: disagree (details, skills)
논제: 반대 (세부 사항, 능력)

There are many ways to learn: Some learn by attending class; some learn by using mass media, including television; and others learn by reading books. Though each method has disadvantages as well as advantages, I strongly believe that learning by watching TV is the most effective of all. There are two reasons I have this belief: Learning by watching TV saves time, and visual lessons can help people understand better.

To begin with, people can save time acquiring knowledge by watching television because TV usually offers a summary of topics in such areas as history, astronomy, and geology. This lets people gain a vast amount of information in a short period of time. To illustrate, my cousin had to study the great philosophers of the seventeenth century. Though she was given only a month to fulfill the assignment, she managed to do so. This achievement was possible through her viewing of TV programs, which provided her with a summary of the matter at hand. Had she tried to study these philosophers by reading books, it would have taken much longer.

In addition, television provides visual effects that aid people in gaining information more effectively. In other words, viewers can grasp difficult concepts better when they see them illustrated in sequential images. For instance, my friend had a hard time understanding an experiment. However, he could grasp the process without much of a struggle when he learned it through a TV program in which a professor demonstrated the procedure. Hence, my friend could follow the directions and could in fact conduct the experiment on his own after watching the instructor performing it.

It is true that people can get numerous details by reading books; nevertheless, it would take too long for those who wish to gain comprehensive information in various fields. In this sense, viewers can save time while getting a vast amount of knowledge by watching TV. Furthermore, television assists viewers in grasping a subject more effectively. For the above reasons, I firmly agree with the statement that learning by watching TV is better than learning by reading books.

WORD REMINDER

mass media 대중 전달 매체   acquire 얻다   fulfill 수행하다   achievement 성취   at hand 가까이에   illustrate 설명하다   sequential 연속적인   grasp 이해하다   struggle 애쓰다   demonstrate 실제로 해 보이다   procedure 순서   conduct 이행하다   comprehensive 포괄적인   in this sense 이러한 점에서   assist 돕다

TIPS for SUCCESS

세미콜론 Semicolon(;) **l**

절과 절 사이를 마침표로 끊기에는 두 절의 내용이 연관되어 있거나, 쉼표로 끊기에는 두 절의 무게가 다소 다른 경우 사용한다. 뒤의 절은 앞 절의 내용에 대해 보충 설명을 해 주기도 하고, 앞 내용을 반박 혹은 바꾸기도 하며, 앞 내용의 원인에 대한 결과를 제시해 주기도 한다.

네 번째 단락의 문장을 살펴보자.

It is true that people can get numerous details by reading books; nevertheless, it would take too long for those who wish to gain comprehensive information in various fields.

두 절은 독서에 관해 반대되는 내용을 담고 있으며 접속부사인 nevertheless로 연결되어 있다. 접속사의 생략이 가능하고, 두 절의 관계를 좀 더 명확히 표현하고자 할 때에는 위의 문장에서처럼 부사절접속사(TEST 05, 06 참고)나 등위접속사(2권 TEST 05 참고) 등을 사용할 수 있다.

There are many ways to learn: Some learn by attending class; some learn by using mass media, including television; and others learn by reading books. Though each method has disadvantages as well as advantages, I strongly believe that learning by reading books is the most effective of all. There are two reasons I have this belief: Books provide more detailed information, and by reading books, people can gain such skills as analysis and interpretation.

To begin with, books provide readers with rich insights and details. In other words, readers can get in-depth knowledge through books. To illustrate, my cousin watched a television program about volcanoes around the world. While she learned general information about volcanoes, she was not able to gain specific knowledge about them. Subsequently, she found books on the topic and was able to more fully understand volcanoes. This example illustrates that even though it takes more time to read a book than to watch TV, reading is a more effective way of learning.

In addition, people learn skills in analysis and interpretation by reading books. For instance, when I watched a show on TV about dolphins at Sea World, it seemed as if the dolphins in captivity were spending their entire lives preparing to perform well in the shows. However, as I read about them in books, I realized that the TV program was produced only from an environmentalists' point of view. By reading many books on the topic, I've learned to think from different perspectives. Had I only watched the dolphins on TV, I would have been biased against Sea World.

It is true that TV can help viewers comprehend better by providing them with images. However, many books contain pictures that can aid readers' understanding of concepts. Books offer readers greater details. Furthermore, readers get a chance to develop their skills in imagination, analysis, and interpretation. For the above reasons, I firmly disagree with the statement that learning by watching TV is better than learning by reading a book.

WORD REMINDER

analysis 분석   interpretation 해석   insight 통찰력   in-depth 심층의   subsequently 그 후에   illustrate 설명하다   captivity 포로   perform 상연하다   point of view 관점, 입장   comprehend 이해하다

TIPS for SUCCESS

세미콜론 Semicolon(;) **II**

세미콜론은 또한, 나열하고자 하는 항목들이 중간에 쉼표를 가지고 있거나, 숫자를 포함해 혼란을 초래할 수 있을 때 사용한다. 다음의 문장을 살펴보자. 참고로, 나열된 항목들 사이에 세미콜론이 포함되어 있을 경우 나열하기 전 나열의 의미를 나타내 주는 콜론(:)을 쓴다.
중간에 쉼표가 있을 때) I've been to the following places in the United States: Palo Alto, California; Manhattan, New York; and Saint Louis, Missouri.
숫자를 포함할 때) The call numbers for those books are: 45,000; 32,805;1,102; and 529.

나열하고자 하는 항목들이 절일 경우, 너무 길어지면 이해가 어렵거나 무종지문(run-on sentence)에 빠질 염려가 있기 때문에 세미콜론을 사용한다. 다음 첫 단락의 문장을 보자.

There are many ways of learning: Some people learn by attending class; some learn by using mass media, including TV; and others learn by reading books.

마찬가지로 포괄의 의미를 담고 있는 절이 나온 후 콜론을 쓰고, 그 뒤로 절을 나열한다. 절과 절 사이에의 세미콜론은 일반 문장에서의 쉼표 역할을 한다.

RELATED TOPICS

1 TV has more negative influences than positive influences on children.

TV는 어린이들에게 긍정적인 영향보다는 부정적인 영향을 더 끼친다.

AGREE	DISAGREE
- violence / coarse language → imitating 폭력 / 거친 언어 → 모방 - addictive 중독성 있음	- informative: getting broad knowledge in a relatively short period of time 정보 제공: 폭넓은 지식을 비교적 짧은 시간 안에 습득 - entertainment: releasing stress 기분 전환: 스트레스 해소

2 Advertisements are responsible for unhealthy eating habits. 광고는 건강하지 못한 식습관에 대해 책임이 있다.

AGREE	DISAGREE
- exaggerated: only advantages are advertised 과장됨: 장점만 광고됨 - children: immature → unable to control themselves from buying junk food 어린이들: 미숙함 → 불량 식품을 사는 것으로부터 자신을 절제하지 못함	- informs consumers of various products through ads 광고를 통해서 소비자에게 다양한 제품을 알려줌 - directions, ingredients, side effects: properly indicated 방법, 성분, 부작용: 올바르게 표기되어 있음

3 Movies are worth watching as long as they teach us something about real life.

삶에 대해 가르쳐 주는 한, 영화는 볼 가치가 있다.

AGREE	DISAGREE
- teach people lessons 사람들에게 교훈을 줌 - opportunities for discussion 토론의 기회를 줌	- for entertainment purposes 기분 전환의 목적 ex) comedy: worth watching even if they don't teach about life 코미디: 삶에 대해서 가르쳐 주지 않더라도 볼 가치가 충분함 - composite art: other elements to be considered as art 종합 예술: 예술로 고려되기 위해서는 다른 요소들도 필요함 ex) visual effects, music 시각적 효과, 음악

4 Reading a book a second time is more interesting. 책은 두 번째 읽을 때 더욱 흥미롭다.

AGREE	DISAGREE
- more details 더 자세한 내용 - reader: able to enjoy amusing or inspiring parts of the book again 독자: 책의 흥미롭거나 감동적인 부분을 다시 즐길 수 있음	- getting bored → no expectations since one already knows the conclusion 지루해짐 → 결말을 이미 알기 때문에 기대감 ✕ - simple information → no need to review 간단한 정보 → 복습할 필요 ✕

5 Most advertisements exaggerate about the products they promote.

대부분의 광고들은 광고되는 제품들을 과장하고 있다.

AGREE	DISAGREE
- purpose: to get a lot of profits 목적: 많은 이득 창출 - only advantages are displayed 이점만 보여짐	- proper regulations from organizations 단체로부터의 올바른 규정 - informative 정보 제공 ex) new products / trends 새로운 제품 / 유행

TOEFL® MAP

ACTUAL TEST Writing 1

08

Music has a history of about 40,000 years. It has served recreational and ceremonial purposes as well as artistic expression. Because music has always been around us, learning musical instruments from an early age is often considered compulsory. However, is it really necessary to be able to play an instrument in order to appreciate music? A lot of studies have found that playing a musical instrument during childhood may not be as helpful as one might think.

It is easy to suffer physical injuries when playing instruments. When a person is young, pain can develop and cause serious problems in the future. For instance, many children suffer from neck or shoulder pain since some instruments make kids tilt their heads while playing. Another common physical challenge musicians often encounter is dry mouth. Wind instruments typically require a lot of breath control and support, making mouths extremely dry. In this sense, it is irrational to push a child to play an instrument.

Another concern about making kids play instruments when they are young is that they can suffer emotional difficulties. Amateurs and even professional musicians suffer a lot of stress while preparing for concerts or certificate exams. Some children may not be able to handle all of the pressure while others may feel frustrated when they make mistakes during important events like recitals or auditions.

Besides physical and emotional challenges, learning musical instruments at a young age can be time consuming. Not every kid can handle the commitment and the responsibility that are necessary to learn to play a musical instrument. Learning an instrument requires everyday practice, making it easy for many children to give up. This may be a waste of time in that unless a student has grasped the basics of the instrument, it is highly likely he will lose most of the knowledge he has gained.

🎧 08-01

ACTUAL TEST **08**

Directions You have 20 minutes to plan and write your response. Your response will be judged on the basis of the quality of your writing and on how well your response presents the points in the lecture and their relationship to the passage. Typically, an effective response will be 150-225 words.

Question Summarize the points made in the lecture, being sure to explain how they challenge specific claims made in the reading passage.

CUT   PASTE   UNDO   REDO   Hide Word Count : 0

Music has a history of about 40,000 years. It has served recreational and ceremonial purposes as well as artistic expression. Because music has always been around us, learning musical instruments from an early age is often considered compulsory. However, is it really necessary to be able to play an instrument in order to appreciate music? A lot of studies have found that playing a musical instrument during childhood may not be as helpful as one might think.

It is easy to suffer physical injuries when playing instruments. When a person is young, pain can develop and cause serious problems in the future. For instance, many children suffer from neck or shoulder pain since some instruments make kids tilt their heads while playing. Another common physical challenge musicians often encounter is dry mouth. Wind instruments typically require a lot of breath control and support, making mouths extremely dry. In this sense, it is irrational to push a child to play an instrument.

Another concern about making kids play instruments when they are young is that they can suffer emotional difficulties. Amateurs and even professional musicians suffer a lot of stress while preparing for concerts or certificate exams. Some children may not be able to handle all of the pressure while others may feel frustrated when they make mistakes during important events like recitals or auditions.

Besides physical and emotional challenges, learning musical instruments at a young age can be time consuming. Not every kid can handle the commitment and the responsibility that are necessary to learn to play a musical instrument. Learning an instrument requires everyday practice, making it easy for many children to give up. This may be a waste of time in that unless a student has grasped the basics of the instrument, it is highly likely he will lose most of the knowledge he has gained.

 **NOTE-TAKING**

music: artistic expression, recreational + ceremonial purposes
음악: 예술적 표현, 기분 전환 + 의식의 목적

❶ *physical injuries* 신체 부상

- neck / shoulder pain, dry mouth (wind instrument) 목 / 어깨 통증, 마른 입 (관악기)

 Learning an instrument during early childhood can cause injuries.

❷ *emotional challenge* 감정 고통

- a lot of stress from pressure + frustration 압박 + 좌절로 인한 많은 스트레스

 Learning an instrument can put a lot of pressure on children and cause them stress.

❸ *time consuming* 시간 낭비

- not every kid has commitment + responsibility → easy to quit 모든 아이가 의지 + 책임을 갖고 있지는 않음 → 중단하기 쉬움

 Since learning an instrument is quite demanding, it might turn out to be a waste of time if a student decides to quit.

WORD REMINDER

serve 제공하다   recreational 기분 전환의   ceremonial 의식의   compulsory 필수의   appreciate 감상하다   injury 부상   tilt 기울이다
encounter 직면하다   breath 호흡   irrational 불합리한   concern 우려   amateur 비전문가   certificate 자격증   frustrated 좌절된
time consuming 시간을 낭비하는   commitment 책무, 헌신   demand 요구하다   in that ~하므로, ~이므로   grasp 이해하다

crucial to provide kids with stimulating environment
아이들에게 자극을 주는 환경을 제공하는 것은 중요함

❶ *injury: more common while playing sports* 부상: 스포츠를 할 때 더 흔함
- music: help patients get treatment or surgery (↓ BP, ↓ ♥, ↓ stress hormones) → helps body heal
음악: 환자들이 치료를 받거나 수술을 받을 때 도움이 됨 (혈압 ↓, 심장 박동수 ↓, 스트레스 호르몬 ↓) → 몸이 회복하는데 도움을 줌

 Learning a musical instrument yields many advantages, such as reducing blood pressure and lowering the amount of stress hormones during treatment or surgery.

❷ *overcome emotional challenges* 정서적 어려움을 극복함
- pleasing music → ↑ dopamine (related to cognitive, behavioral, and emotional functioning)
유쾌한 음악 → 도파민 ↑ (인지, 행동, 감정의 기능과 연관됨)

 Learning music can help kids overcome emotional problems.

❸ *learning instrument → invaluable lesson* 악기를 배우는 것 → 귀중한 교훈
- responsibility + dedication + patience 책임 + 헌신 + 인내
- even if quit: commitment + discipline gained during lessons, practices, and performance
만약 그만 두더라도: 레슨, 연습 그리고 연주 할 때 얻은 의지 + 훈련

 Children learn to become disciplined while building creativity and confidence when learning a musical instrument.

WORD REMINDER

stimulating 자극을 주는   conduct 실행하다   pleasurable 유쾌한   reinforcement 강화   fracture 골절   sprain (손, 발목 등을) 삐기
undergo 겪다   treatment 치료   blood pressure 혈압   heal 낫다   overcome 극복하다   primary 주된   neurotransmitter 신경 전달 물질
associated 연관된   cognitive 인지의   function 기능하다   dedication 헌신, 노력   discipline 훈련

ACTUAL TEST 08

The lecturer contends that learning musical instruments at an early age is necessary in order to provide kids with a stimulating environment. This directly refutes the idea mentioned in the reading passage that learning musical instruments is not ideal.

First, injuries can happen even when kids are sitting still, and music can, in fact, help the body heal. To be specific, learning a musical instrument yields many advantages, such as reducing blood pressure and lowering the amount of stress hormones during treatment or surgery. This directly rebuts the assertion that learning an instrument during early childhood can cause injuries.

On top of that, the lecturer contends that learning music can help kids overcome emotional problems. According to him, playing and listening to pleasant music secretes high levels of dopamine, which is related to cognitive, behavioral, and emotional functioning. This goes against the idea that learning an instrument can put a lot of pressure on children and cause them stress.

Lastly, children learn to become disciplined while building creativity and confidence when learning a musical instrument. The commitment and the effort that kids put in are never in vain even when they quit playing the instrument. This goes against the idea presented in the reading passage that since learning an instrument is quite demanding, it might turn out to be a waste of time if a student decides to quit.

WORD REMINDER

stimulating 자극을 주는, 활기를 주는   ideal 이상적인   yield 가져오다   overcome 극복하다   secrete 분비하다

TIPS for SUCCESS

부사절 접속사 II

대조	비교 / 방법	조건	목적
although (비록 ~할지라도)	as (~ 만큼)	as long as (~하는 한)	lest (~하지 않도록)
even if (비록 ~일지라도)	than (~ 보다)	if (~라면)	in order that (~하도록)
even though (~하는데도)	as (~처럼)	in case (~하는 경우에)	so that (~가 되도록)
though (~에도 불구하고)		once (일단 ~하면)	
while (~하는 반면에)		provided (만일 ~라면)	
whereas (~하는 반면에)		providing (만일 ~라면)	
whether (~이던지 아니던지)		unless (~하지 않으면)	

provided와 providing을 과거형 동사 또는 형용사 등으로 잘못 해석하는 학생들이 종종 있는데 부사절접속사로도 쓰일 수 있다는 점을 유의하자. provided나 providing 앞에 독립절이 나오는 경우 부사절 접속사로 쓰였음을 예상해 볼 수 있다. in order that과 so that 다음에는 〈주어 + can/could/may/might/will/would ~〉 형태가 온다. (부사절과 주절의 순서에 따른 쉼표 위치에 대해서는 TEST 18 참고)

CUT   PASTE   UNDO   REDO   Hide Word Count : 0

Directions Read the question below. You have 30 minutes to plan, write, and revise your essay. Typically, an effective response will contain a minimum of 300 words.

Question

Do you agree or disagree with the following statement?

People learn more by watching television than by reading books.

Use specific reasons and examples to support your answer.

📝 NOTE-TAKING

AGREE

- ***socialize w/people who have different occupations*** 다른 직업을 가진 사람들과 어울림
  - **Ex** cousin (scientist): rock climbing every weekend 사촌 (과학자): 매 주말마다 암벽등반
    - → release stress (being away from office + meeting people w/various backgrounds)
    - 스트레스 해소 (사무실에서 x + 다양한 배경을 가진 사람들과 만남)

- ***gain diverse experiences*** 다양한 경험을 얻음
  - **Ex** friend (archaeologist) → workplace: suburban areas 친구 (고고학자) → 일터: 교외
    - → started learning flamenco dance 플라멩코 춤을 배우기 시작
    - → new skill + experience Spanish culture 새로운 능력 + 스페인 문화 경험

> ### INTRODUCTION
>
> **generalization**: most people experience stress from work
> 일반화: 대부분의 사람들이 일에서 스트레스를 겪음
> ⬇
> take time off + relax w/hobbies / physical activities
> 시간을 내서 취미 / 운동을 하며 쉼
> ⬇
> **thesis**: agree (meeting w/new people, experiencing diverse fields)
> 논제: 찬성 (새로운 사람들과의 만남, 다양한 분야 경험)

DISAGREE

- ***jobs: based on interests*** 직업: 관심사에 바탕을 둠
  - – higher chance to enjoy activities related to work 일과 관련된 활동을 즐길 가능성 ↑
    - **Ex** 95% of workers at Nature Conservation Society 환경 보호 단체의 95%의 직원
      - → unwilling to enjoy hobbies harmful to environment 환경에 해로운 취미를 즐기는 것을 꺼림
      - → participate in activities related to green campaigns 환경 보호 운동과 연관된 활동에 참여

- ***save time + money in learning a new activity*** 새로운 활동을 배우는데 시간 + 돈 절약
  - – more opportunities to enjoy a pastime 취미를 즐길 수 있는 더 많은 기회
    - **Ex** travel agent: more chances to take trips at discounted prices
    - 여행사 직원: 할인된 가격으로 여행을 할 수 있는 더 많은 기회
      - → musical instrument: no talent → stress → waste of time + money
      - 악기: 소질 x → 스트레스 → 시간 + 돈 낭비

> ### INTRODUCTION
>
> **generalization**: most people experience stress from work
> 일반화: 대부분의 사람들이 일에서 스트레스를 겪음
> ⬇
> take time off + relax w/hobbies / physical activities
> 시간을 내서 취미 / 운동을 하며 쉼
> ⬇
> **thesis**: disagree (jobs: related to interests, saving time + money)
> 논제: 반대 (직업: 관심사와 연관 있음, 시간 + 돈 절약)

CUT　PASTE　UNDO　REDO

Though there is a difference in degree, most people experience stress as a result of their work. Accordingly, they take some time off from work and relax by doing hobbies or physical activities. Some contend that people should enjoy hobbies or physical activities that are similar to what they do at work. However, I disagree with this idea because by trying new things, people get chances to meet others with different backgrounds. Moreover, they can experience diverse fields.

First off, trying different hobbies provides people with opportunities to socialize with others who have different backgrounds. For example, my cousin, who is a scientist, goes rock climbing every weekend. He says that he can release his stress not only by being away from his office and by doing a physical activity but also by meeting people with various jobs.

Secondly, by doing an activity that is dissimilar to one's job, one can partake in diverse experiences. To illustrate, my friend works as an archaeologist, and she works mostly in suburban areas where she and her coworkers unearth artifacts or remains. However, she has started to learn flamenco dance. By learning it, my friend has both gained a new skill and had chances to experience Spanish culture, including the food.

It is true that by doing a hobby that is similar to one's work, one does not have to take the risk of trying a hobby which one later discovers to be not so fascinating, a situation which could cause stress and waste time and money. Conversely, challenges often open up a new world for people in which they find opportunities to meet people with different occupations. Furthermore, one can enjoy diverse experiences by choosing an activity that is unrelated to one's job. Therefore, I firmly agree with the statement that people should take time off from work to relax with hobbies or physical activities that are very different from what they do at work.

WORD REMINDER

diverse 다양한　field 분야　release 방출하다　various 다양한　archaeologist 고고학자　suburban 교외의　unearth 발굴하다
artifact 인공 유물　remain 유골　fascinating 매우 재미있는　challenge 도전

TIPS for SUCCESS

쉼표 comma

수많은 쉼표에 관한 용법 중 하나는 절과 절을 나누는 것이다. 단어, 구, 절을 동등하게 잇는 역할의 등위접속사(and, but, so, for, yet, or, as well as, nor)가 절이 아닌, 단어나 구를 연결해 줄 경우 쉼표를 쓰지 않지만, 절 즉, 접속사 다음 주어부터 다시 쓸 경우에는 반드시 쉼표를 붙인다. 세 번째 단락의 문장을 살펴보자.

To illustrate, my friend works as an archaeologist**,** and she works mostly in suburban areas.

위의 문장에서 my friend works as an archaeologist라는 절과 she works mostly in suburban areas라는 절을 등위접속사 and가 연결해 주고 있기 때문에 앞에 쉼표를 붙인다. 세 번째 단락의 문장 하나를 더 살펴보자.

My friend has both gained a new skill and had chances to experience Spanish culture.

반면, 위의 문장에서는 주어인 My friend가 and 뒤에 생략되면서 gained a new skill이라는 구와 had chances to experience Spanish culture라는 구가 연결되고 있으므로 쉼표를 붙이지 않는다.

Though there is a difference in degree, most people experience stress as a result of their work. Accordingly, they take some time off from work and relax by doing hobbies or physical activities. Some contend that people should enjoy hobbies or physical activities that are very different from what they do at work. However, I disagree with this idea because people tend to have jobs that are related to their interests. Moreover, doing activities similar to their work saves time and money.

First off, most people choose their job based on their field of interest. Thus, there is a greater chance of them enjoying activities that have a close relationship to their work. To illustrate, more than ninety-five percent of people working at the Nature Conservation Society have stated that they are unwilling to play golf or other kinds of hobbies that would harm the natural environment. Instead, many of them participate in activities, including acting in plays and creating paintings, which deal with campaigns to protect nature.

Secondly, trying a new hobby can create stress rather than provide fun experiences. For example, travel agents who like to travel around the world encounter lots of chances to take trips at discounted prices. Conversely, if a travel agent tries to learn a musical instrument and later finds out he is not talented at it, he will have wasted his time and money, not to mention enduring stress, too.

It is true that participating in a new activity can give one a chance to meet new people; however, broadening interpersonal relationships is not necessary in life. Since most people's jobs are related to their interests, they would enjoy activities that are similar to their jobs. Furthermore, doing hobbies that have a close relationship to their work can save people time and money. Therefore, I firmly believe that it is pointless to try hobbies that are very different from one's own work.

WORD REMINDER

degree 정도   tend to ~하는 경향이 있다   unwilling 마음 내키지 않는   participate 참여하다   deal with ~를 다루다   travel agent 여행사 직원
encounter 마주치다   mention 언급하다   endure 견디다   broaden 넓히다   interpersonal relationship 대인 관계
pointless 무의미한, 가치가 없는

■ TIPS for SUCCESS

퍼센트가 나올 경우 단순히 숫자가 오면 단수동사를 쓰지만, 퍼센트 다음 복수명사가 올 경우 복수동사를 쓴다. 두 번째 단락의 문장을 살펴보자.

To illustrate, more than ninety-five percent of people working at the Nature Conservation Society **have** stated that they are unwilling to play golf or other kinds of hobbies that would harm the natural environment.

위의 문장에서 만약 ninety-five percent만 쓰였다면 has가 오는 것이 맞다. 하지만 ninety-five percent 다음 people이라는 복수명사가 왔기 때문에 여기에서는 have가 쓰였다.

1 Twenty years from now, people will have more time for leisure activites.

지금으로부터 20년 후, 사람들은 여가 활동을 위한 시간이 더 많아질 것이다.

AGREE	DISAGREE
- work: automated 일: 자동화됨 - people will put more value on enjoying life → less stress 사람들은 삶을 즐기는 것에 더 많은 가치를 둘 것임 → 스트레스 ↓	- busier w/work 일로 더 바빠질 것임 - values may change 가치가 바뀔 수 있음 ex) more time for family gatherings 가족 모임에 더 많은 시간을 소비

2 It is better to spend money on things that will last a long time than on things that will provide short-term fun. 단기간의 즐거움보다 오래 지속될 수 있는 것에 돈을 쓰는 것이 더 낫다.

AGREE	DISAGREE
- more useful / practical 더 유용 / 실용적 ex) buying a camera 카메라 구입 - more meaningful / valuable 더욱 의미가 있음 / 가치 있음 ex) present: remembers the person who gave it 선물: 준 사람을 기억함	- release stress 스트레스 해소 ex) traveling 여행 - better way to celebrate special moments 특별한 순간을 축하하는 더 좋은 방법 ex) birthday party 생일 파티

3 Jobs with a lot of vacation time are better than jobs with high salaries.

더 많은 휴가를 주는 직업이 더 많은 연봉을 주는 직업보다 좋다.

AGREE	DISAGREE
- less stressful 스트레스를 덜 받음 - able to concentrate on work better → greater chance of promotion → higher salary 일에 더 집중할 수 있음 → 승진의 기회 ↑ → 더 높은 연봉	- save more money → prepare for the future → feel secure 더 많은 돈을 저축 → 미래에 대한 준비 → 안정감 - feel more accomplished 더 뿌듯함

TOEFL® MAP
ACTUAL TEST Writing 1

For much of the twentieth century, the American federal government, as well as various state and city governments, controlled the country's infrastructure, particularly the power, water management, and transportation industries. Yet in the past three decades, many industries in the United States have been privatized. The results have been mostly positive.

Governments have reaped enormous profits from selling various infrastructure industries and projects. For instance, in 1987, Conrail, a railroad, was sold for $1.7 billion. In 1997, the Elks Hill Petroleum Reserve was privatized for $3.7 billion. In many northern states, governments have sold the rights to manage their toll roads for billions of dollars. During a time when most state governments are facing budget shortfalls, these injections of cash from the private sector are much needed.

Private companies typically manage infrastructure projects better than the government. First, they are focused on turning a profit, so they eliminate inefficiencies that existed under the government-run regimes. For instance, they eliminate unnecessary departments and fire unproductive workers while rewarding and promoting productive ones. Countless studies have proven that employee productivity dramatically rises whenever government entities are privatized. Through superior management, the companies become more efficient.

Private companies are more likely to introduce new technology than government-owned companies are. One example is in Texas. There, private industry is leading the way in energy production. Several multibillion-dollar power projects, particularly ones utilizing green energy such as wind power, are either currently being implemented or are in the developmental stages. As a result, Texas, an industrial powerhouse, produces so much energy that it not only creates enough for its own companies but also exports electricity to nearby states. It is Texas's reliance on new technology that has made it possible for the state to produce so much energy.

🎧 09-01

Directions You have 20 minutes to plan and write your response. Your response will be judged on the basis of the quality of your writing and on how well your response presents the points in the lecture and their relationship to the passage. Typically, an effective response will be 150-225 words.

Question Summarize the points made in the lecture, being sure to explain how they challenge specific claims made in the reading passage.

For much of the twentieth century, the American federal government, as well as various state and city governments, controlled the country's infrastructure, particularly the power, water management, and transportation industries. Yet in the past three decades, many industries in the United States have been privatized. The results have been mostly positive.

Governments have reaped enormous profits from selling various infrastructure industries and projects. For instance, in 1987, Conrail, a railroad, was sold for $1.7 billion. In 1997, the Elks Hill Petroleum Reserve was privatized for $3.7 billion. In many northern states, governments have sold the rights to manage their toll roads for billions of dollars. During a time when most state governments are facing budget shortfalls, these injections of cash from the private sector are much needed.

Private companies typically manage infrastructure projects better than the government. First, they are focused on turning a profit, so they eliminate inefficiencies that existed under the government-run regimes. For instance, they eliminate unnecessary departments and fire unproductive workers while rewarding and promoting productive ones. Countless studies have proven that employee productivity dramatically rises whenever government entities are privatized. Through superior management, the companies become more efficient.

Private companies are more likely to introduce new technology than government-owned companies are. One example is in Texas. There, private industry is leading the way in energy production. Several multibillion-dollar power projects, particularly ones utilizing green energy such as wind power, are either currently being implemented or are in the developmental stages. As a result, Texas, an industrial powerhouse, produces so much energy that it not only creates enough for its own companies but also exports electricity to nearby states. It is Texas's reliance on new technology that has made it possible for the state to produce so much energy.

 **NOTE-TAKING**

 READING

the privatization of infrastructure: advantageous 기반 시설의 민영화: 이로움

❶ *government: a lot of profits from selling* 정부: 매각으로 많은 이득 남김

- helpful when state governments suffer from budget difficulties 주정부가 자금난을 겪을 때 도움이 됨

> Paraphrasing Example The privatization of infrastructure can provide financial aid for governments, particularly those going through economic crises.

❷ *better management* 더 나은 경영

- profit-oriented → eliminate inefficiencies 이윤 지향적 → 비효율성 제거
  ∴ productivity ↑ 생산성 ↑

> Paraphrasing Example Liquidation for the purpose of making revenue would improve productivity.

❸ *technological improvements* 과학 기술의 향상

- Texas: wind power 텍사스: 풍력
  ∴ a lot of E → exports electricity to nearby states 많은 에너지 → 근접해 있는 주에 전기 수출

> Paraphrasing Example The continuous implementation of up-to-date technology, as shown in Texas with the successful wind power system, is needed.

WORD REMINDER

federal government 연방 정부   infrastructure 기반 시설   privatize 민영화하다   reap (성과, 이익 등을) 거두다   rights 공민권   toll 요금
shortfall 부족   injection 주입   eliminate 없애다, 제거하다   inefficiency 비능률   regime 체제   productive 생산적인   entity 자주 독립체
utilize 이용하다   implement 실행하다   powerhouse 발전소   export 수출하다

 LISTENING

better to have governments manage infrastructure industries
기반 시설 사업은 정부가 관리하는 것이 더 나음

❶ *purpose of government: NOT profit-making* 정부의 목적: 이윤 목적 ✕

- operation: for citizens 운영: 시민을 위함
- private company: monopoly 사기업: 독점
  → may impose exorbitant rates 과대한 요금을 부과할 수 있음

> Paraphrasing Example The purpose of government is not profit-making but rather the benefit of its own citizens.

❷ *employment opportunities ↓* 취업 기회 ↓

Ex power company: fired 300 workers (20%) 전력 회사: 300명의 노동자 해고 (20%)
  → many: still unemployed 다수: 여전히 실직된 상태
- government: source of income for the workers 정부: 노동자에게 수입의 원천

> Paraphrasing Example Many workers lost their jobs at a power company after it was privatized.

❸ *new tech: many unexpected problems* 새로운 과학 기술: 많은 예상치 못한 문제

  → breakdown / poor performance 고장 / 작동이 제대로 되지 않음

> Paraphrasing Example The speedy introduction of new technology could bring about problems, including serious ones.

 WORD REMINDER

waterworks 급수 시설   in control 관리하는   influx 유입   utility 공익 설비   net ~의 순익을 올리다   monopoly 독점   exorbitant 과대한
lay off 해고하다   income 수입   innovator 혁신자   adopt 도입하다   plethora 과다   awful 끔찍한, 지독한   incorporate 통합시키다

ACTUAL TEST **09**

The lecturer argues that it is better to have governments manage infrastructure industries rather than to have organizations in the private sector do that. She supports her contention with three disadvantages to private management. This directly refutes the reading passage's claim that the privatization of infrastructure would result in many benefits.

First, the purpose of government is not profit-making but rather the benefit of its own citizens. If a private company were to abuse its monopoly and impose excessive rates, it would be the citizens who suffered from the system. This fact contradicts the claim from the reading passage that the privatization of infrastructure can provide financial aid for governments, particularly those going through economic crises.

In addition, the lecturer contends that the privatization of infrastructure would reduce employment opportunities. As shown in the example, many workers lost their jobs at a power company after it was privatized. This contradicts the reading passage's claim that liquidation for the purpose of making revenue would improve productivity.

Finally, the lecturer asserts that the speedy introduction of new technology could bring about problems, including serious ones. Thus the relatively unhurried adoption of innovative systems would reduce the possibility of trouble. This goes against the idea presented in the reading passage that the continuous implementation of up-to-date technology, as shown in Texas with the successful wind power system, is needed.

WORD REMINDER
abuse 남용 impose 부과하다 excessive 과도한 crisis 위기 liquidation 청산 revenue 수익 unhurried 신중한 innovative 혁신적인 up-to-date 최신의

TIPS for SUCCESS

타자를 치는데 익숙하지 않은 경우, 시간을 정해 놓고 컴퓨터에 에세이를 쓰는 연습을 자주 하도록 하자.
Microsoft Word에서는 보통 문장의 첫 번째 단어나, I 등의 일반화되어 있는 대문자, 또는 오타가 종종 자동 수정이 되기 때문에 'Word 옵션'에서 자동 입력 체계를 바꾸어 놓고 항상 스펠링이나 대문자 등을 체크하는 습관을 기르는 것이 중요하다.

CUT | PASTE | UNDO | REDO | Hide Word Count : 0

Directions Read the question below. You have 30 minutes to plan, write, and revise your essay. Typically, an effective response will contain a minimum of 300 words.

Question

Many people welcome the opening of shopping areas near their homes. On the other hand, some people are strongly opposed to the construction of such facilities. If the opening of a large shopping center in your neighborhood were announced, would you support or oppose its construction?

Use specific reasons and examples to support your answer.

 **NOTE-TAKING**

AGREE

- *security: reinforced / cleaner environment* 보안: 강화 / 더 깨끗한 환경
    - private security company + local police + surveillance cameras 사설 경보 업체 + 현지 경찰 + 감시 카메라
      Ex studies: areas w/new shopping malls: crime ↓ 90% 연구: 새로운 쇼핑몰이 들어선 지역: 범죄 90% ↓
        → cleaner + safer environment → more consumers 더욱 깨끗 + 안전한 환경 → 더 많은 소비자

- *economic growth: more retail stores + service business* 경제 성장: 더 많은 가게 + 서비스업
      Ex research: 75% consumers purchased meal / drink after shopping
      연구: 75%의 소비자들이 쇼핑 후 식사 / 음료 구입
        → visit more than 1 store → end up spending more money → economic benefits
      2개 이상의 가게 방문 → 더 많은 지출을 하게 됨 → 경제 이득
    - job opportunities 취업 기회

INTRODUCTION

generalization: cities: continuous development + improvement
일반화: 도시: 끊임없는 개발 + 발전

⬇

demand for shopping ↑ → more shopping centers → where to be built?
쇼핑에 대한 수요 ↑ → 더 많은 쇼핑센터 → 어디에 지어져야 할까?

⬇

thesis: support (security + econ. advantages)
논제: 찬성 (안전 + 경제 이점들)

DISAGREE

- *high rate of crime* 높은 범죄율
    - megamalls: movie theaters / sports arenas / hotels → possibility of crime
      대형몰: 극장 / 스포츠 경기장 / 호텔 → 범죄 가능성
    - vandalism + shoplifting + public disturbance → bother residents 파괴, 절도, 그리고 대중 소란 → 주민들에게 방해
    - lots of waste 많은 쓰레기

- *traffic-related issues* 교통 관련 문제
      Ex more shoppers drive cars → more parking spaces needed 더 많은 사람들이 차를 가져옴 → 더 많은 주차 공간이 필요
        → a lot of stress for residents 주민들 사이에서 높은 스트레스
    - more traffic violations, car accidents, and noise 더 많은 교통 위반, 자동차 사고, 소음

INTRODUCTION

generalization: cities: continuous development + improvement
일반화: 도시: 끊임없는 개발 + 발전

⬇

demand for shopping ↑ → more shopping centers → where to be built?
쇼핑에 대한 수요 ↑ → 더 많은 쇼핑센터 → 어디에 지어져야 할까?

⬇

thesis: oppose (crime + traffic issues)
논제: 반대 (범죄 + 교통 문제)

As cities go through continuous development and improvement, it is not uncommon to see construction sites around a town. Among the newly constructed buildings are shopping malls. Though people want more stores, some people are against the idea of having malls in the area where they reside. If I had a choice, I would like to have a shopping area in the neighborhood where I live. The reasons are that they provide increased security and economic advantages.

First, security would be reinforced thanks to the companies that run businesses in the area. When a large shopping center is built, there is a private security company that takes care of the overall safety of the buildings on top of local police and surveillance cameras providing extra safety. For instance, studies show that neighborhoods where new shopping centers were just built have a decreased crime rate by up to 90%.

Furthermore, having a big shopping mall will result in economic growth since there will be other types of service businesses, including hair salons, yoga centers, and restaurants. For example, research conducted at the Stanford Shopping Center found that more than 75% of consumers purchased either a meal or a drink after visiting other stores, resulting in more spending. Convenience and diverse options attract many consumers and provide numerous job opportunities, eventually bringing economic benefits to the community.

It is true that a large shopping center causes heavy traffic with a lot of people and cars. However, that only happens during holiday seasons which, in fact, add holiday vibes to the town. A big shopping center provides extra security to the area with security patrol services. In addition, attracting more shoppers can improve the economic situation. Therefore, I would definitely support the construction of a large shopping center in my neighborhood.

WORD REMINDER

site 현장   reside 거주하다   reinforce 강화하다   overall 전반적으로   surveillance 감시   crime 범죄   rate 비율   service business 서비스업
consumer 소비자, 고객   spending 지출   vibe 분위기   patrol 순찰, 경비   definitely 분명히

As cities go through continuous development and improvement, it is not uncommon to see construction sites around a town. Among the newly constructed buildings are shopping malls. Though people want more stores, some people are against the idea of having a mall in the area where they reside. If I had a choice, I would like to have a shopping area far from where I live. The reasons have to do with crime and traffic-related problems.

First, there is always a higher rate of crime in areas with lots of shops. Megamalls can include movie theaters, sports arenas, and even hotels, and it is inevitable for crimes to happen at those places. For example, studies show that areas around big shopping malls are always exposed to vandalism, shoplifting, and public disturbances. Furthermore, an influx of shoppers will produce more waste, and cleaning up might take more time than throwing trash away.

Furthermore, residents of the area will suffer from traffic-related issues. For instance, more shoppers will drive more cars to a mall; thus, there will be a higher demand for parking spaces. Unless the shopping center provides a vast area or a huge parking structure, which usually requires a lot of money, especially in cities, there will be parking problems. To add to the trouble, there will be more traffic violations, car accidents, and noise.

It is true that having a large shopping center will be convenient. However, nothing can be compared to the safety of a town. With a high possibility of an increased crime rate, the whole neighborhood could be exposed to constant danger. Moreover, residents around a mall will have to cope with traffic-related concerns such as parking problems, traffic violations, and noise. Therefore, I would definitely oppose the construction of a large shopping center in my neighborhood.

WORD REMINDER

sports arena 운동 경기장 inevitable 불가피한 expose 노출하다 vandalism 파괴 shoplifting 가게 물건을 슬쩍하기 disturbance 소란
influx 유입 vast 광대한 to add to ~에 더하여 traffic violation 교통 위반

1 Imagine you could improve the town where you live by changing one important thing about it. Which of the following would you choose to do? Use specific reasons and examples to support your choice.

당신이 사는 곳에서 하나의 중요한 것을 바꿈으로써 마을을 발전시킬 수 있다고 생각해 보자. 다음 중 어느 것을 고를 것인가? 구체적인 이유와 예를 들어 자신의 선택을 뒷받침하시오.

- Build additional parks
- Construct more libraries
- Improve public transportation

BUILD ADDITIONAL PARKS

- environment 환경
- places for people to rest 사람들에게 휴식 공간을 제공

CONSTRUCT MORE LIBRARIES

- education: full of resources 교육: 자료가 풍부함
- spaces for people to enjoy reading / studying
  사람들에게 독서 / 공부를 즐길 수 있는 공간을 제공

IMPROVE PUBLIC TRANSPORTATION

- environment 환경
- less traffic 교통 감소

2 You are going to have a new roommate next semester. Which of the following qualities is the most important to you? Use specific reasons and examples to support your choice.

당신에게 다음 학기에 새로운 룸메이트가 생길 것이다. 당신에게는 다음 중 어느 요소가 가장 중요한가? 구체적인 이유와 예를 들어 자신의 선택을 뒷받침하시오.

- Cleanliness
- A sense of humor
- Politeness

CLEANLINESS

- sanitation has become one of most important factors 위생은 가장 중요한 요소 중 하나가 되었음
- cannot rest / study in filthy place
  지저분한 곳에서 휴식 / 공부를 할 수 없음

A SENSE OF HUMOR

- always encouraging and cheerful → necessary, especially when going through difficulties / stressful moments
  항상 격려해 주고 응원해 주는 것 → 어려움 / 스트레스를 받는 순간을 겪을 때 특히나 필요함
- able to get rest in comfortable environment w/out hearing constant complaints
  끊임없는 불평을 듣지 않고 편한 환경에서 쉴 수 있음

POLITENESS

- respect others with polite words 예의 있는 언어로 타인을 존중
- respect privacy 사생활 존중

TOEFL® MAP
ACTUAL TEST Writing 1

10

The question of how the ancient Egyptians built the pyramids has long baffled historians and archaeologists. Each pyramid is comprised of massive stone blocks. In some cases, a single pyramid may contain millions of them. Yet the Egyptians somehow managed to move and hold these blocks in place without modern equipment. The answer to how they accomplished this feat seems to lie in three aspects of engineering: ramps, cranes, and concrete.

First, the Egyptians employed earthen ramps around the pyramids to move the stones to higher levels. As construction proceeded, the ramps were built higher. Each block was rolled on logs or dragged up by teams of men and animals. Then, the blocks were pushed into place. The Egyptians used either a single long, high ramp built on one side or a series of shorter ramps on both sides that wound their way to the top.

Second, the Egyptians used cranes with ropes and pulleys to move some stones into hard-to-reach positions. These devices were made of wood and used leather straps to hold the blocks. Then, workers pulled on long ropes to lift and subsequently lower the blocks into place. The usage of cranes explains how the Egyptians could lift enormous stone blocks—some weighing as much as sixty tons—into place in some internal chambers.

Finally, it is likely that the Egyptians possessed some form of concrete. Made of limestone and other materials, the concrete was used to fill the spaces between the blocks. This strengthened the overall structure and permitted the pyramids to be built to great heights. Without the use of concrete, it is likely that the pyramids would have collapsed upon themselves due to their enormous weight.

🎧 10-01

Directions You have 20 minutes to plan and write your response. Your response will be judged on the basis of the quality of your writing and on how well your response presents the points in the lecture and their relationship to the passage. Typically, an effective response will be 150-225 words.

Question Summarize the points made in the lecture, being sure to explain how they cast doubt on specific points made in the reading passage.

CUT PASTE UNDO REDO   Hide Word Count : 0

The question of how the ancient Egyptians built the pyramids has long baffled historians and archaeologists. Each pyramid is comprised of massive stone blocks. In some cases, a single pyramid may contain millions of them. Yet the Egyptians somehow managed to move and hold these blocks in place without modern equipment. The answer to how they accomplished this feat seems to lie in three aspects of engineering: ramps, cranes, and concrete.

First, the Egyptians employed earthen ramps around the pyramids to move the stones to higher levels. As construction proceeded, the ramps were built higher. Each block was rolled on logs or dragged up by teams of men and animals. Then, the blocks were pushed into place. The Egyptians used either a single long, high ramp built on one side or a series of shorter ramps on both sides that wound their way to the top.

Second, the Egyptians used cranes with ropes and pulleys to move some stones into hard-to-reach positions. These devices were made of wood and used leather straps to hold the blocks. Then, workers pulled on long ropes to lift and subsequently lower the blocks into place. The usage of cranes explains how the Egyptians could lift enormous stone blocks—some weighing as much as sixty tons—into place in some internal chambers.

Finally, it is likely that the Egyptians possessed some form of concrete. Made of limestone and other materials, the concrete was used to fill the spaces between the blocks. This strengthened the overall structure and permitted the pyramids to be built to great heights. Without the use of concrete, it is likely that the pyramids would have collapsed upon themselves due to their enormous weight.

📝 NOTE-TAKING

READING

the Egyptians used three aspects of engineering in building the pyramids
이집트인들은 피라미드의 건설에 공학의 세 가지 측면을 사용했음

❶ *earthen ramps* 흙으로 만들어진 경사로
- stone block: rolled on logs / dragged by men + animals → pushed into place
  돌덩어리: 사람과 동물에 의해 통나무 위에서 굴려짐 / 끌어올려짐 → 제자리로 이동시킴

   The Egyptians could carry stone blocks to higher places with the use of earthen ramps.

❷ *cranes w/ropes + pulleys* 밧줄 + 도르래가 있는 기중기
- made of wood / used leather straps 나무로 만들어졌음 / 가죽 끈을 사용했음
  → Egyptians could lift huge stone blocks 이집트인들은 거대한 돌덩어리들을 들어올릴 수 있었음

   Cranes allowed the Egyptians to lift huge stone blocks.

❸ *concrete* 콘크리트
- used to fill spaces btwn blocks 돌덩어리들 사이의 공간을 메우기 위해 사용되었음
  → strengthen overall structure 전체적인 구조를 강화시킴
  ∴ pyramids: could be built at greater heights 피라미드: 더 높게 지어질 수 있었음

   Concrete was used by the Egyptians to fill in the cracks in the pyramids.

WORD REMINDER

baffle 좌절시키다   comprise of ~을 구성하다   feat 위업   aspect 관점   ramp 경사로   crane 기중기   proceed 나아가다   log 통나무
drag 끌다   wind 나선상으로 나아가다   pulley 도르래   device 장치   strap 가죽 끈   usage 사용   internal 내부의   chamber 방
limestone 석회암   collapse 무너지다

LISTENING

none of the theories concerning the Great Pyramid of Giza is satisfactory
기자의 거대 피라미드에 관한 이론들은 어떤 것도 만족스럽지 않음

❶ *no evidence for ramps* 경사로에 관한 증거 ✕
- pyramids: too tall to construct ramps 피라미드: 경사로를 건설하기에는 너무 높음
  → ramps would've collapsed due to their heaviness 무게 때문에 경사로는 무너졌을 것임

   The use of ramps in the construction of the pyramids cannot be proven.

❷ *cranes: irrational* 기중기: 불합리함
- no cranes / record found 크레인 / 기록 발견 ✕
- wood: scarce 나무: 드물었음

   Neither any actual cranes nor any record of their use has been found in Egypt.

❸ *concrete: not from Egyptians* 콘크리트: 이집트인으로부터 온 것이 아님
- Egyptians: no knowledge of using it 이집트인: 콘크리트의 사용에 관한 지식 ✕
- Romans used it for repairing 보정을 위해 로마 사람들이 사용

   It has been verified that the Egyptians had no knowledge of the use of concrete.

WORD REMINDER

estimate 추정하다   satisfactory 만족스러운   plausible 그럴듯한   reach ~에 도달하다   scarce 드문   gap 갈라진 틈   occupy 차지하다
repair 수리[보수]하다   utilize 이용하다

The lecturer argues that none of the theories concerning the Great Pyramid of Giza seems reliable. This assertion directly refutes the reading passage's claim that the Egyptians could move and hold stone blocks in place successfully by using three aspects of engineering.

First, the use of ramps in the construction of the pyramids cannot be proven. According to the lecturer, it would have been impossible to build ramps since the pyramids were so high. This contradicts the reading passage's claim that the Egyptians could carry stone blocks to higher places with the use of earthen ramps.

On top of that, the lecturer contends that another theory concerning the use of cranes is unrealistic. Neither any actual cranes nor any record of their use has been found in Egypt. Furthermore, wood was scarce in the time when the pyramids were built. This casts doubt on the reading passage's claim that cranes allowed the Egyptians to lift huge stone blocks.

Finally, it has been verified that the Egyptians had no knowledge of the use of concrete. Since the Romans had control over Egypt, they probably used concrete to fix the pyramids. This goes against the idea presented in the reading passage that concrete was used by the Egyptians to fill in the cracks in the pyramids.

WORD REMINDER
reliable 믿을 수 있는　engineering 공학　earthen 흙으로 만든　verify 증명하다　have control over ~을 관리하고 있다　crack 갈라진 금, 틈

▌TIPS for SUCCESS

통합형 에세이: 형식
통합형 에세이는 질문에 나와있듯이, 강의의 내용이 어떻게 지문의 내용과 연관되었는지에 대해 간략히 정리하는 것이다. 지문이 화면에 뜬후 강의를 듣는 동안 지문이 사라지는데, 강의가 끝나면 쓰는 시간이 주어지는 동안 지문이 다시 뜨기 때문에 지문의 노트테이킹에서는 중요한 단어들만 써도 된다. 강의와 지문의 연관성을 첫 번째 단락에, 세부적인 요점들을 각각의 세 단락에 걸쳐 쓰는 것이 보통이다.

CUT   PASTE   UNDO   REDO   Hide Word Count : 0

Directions Read the question below. You have 30 minutes to plan, write, and revise your essay. Typically, an effective response will contain a minimum of 300 words.

Question

Do you agree or disagree with the following statement?

Professors should focus on teaching rather than doing research.

Use specific reasons and examples to support your answer.

AGREE

- *purpose of education: help students fulfill goals* 교육의 목적: 학생들이 목표를 이루기 위해 도와줌
  - high school: form fundamental basis of knowledge in many subjects 고등학교: 많은 과목들에 기본 토대를 형성
  - college: deeper knowledge in particular field 대학교: 특정 분야에 대해 더 깊은 지식
  - learning on own → affect standard + reputation of school 독학 → 학교의 기존 + 명성에 영향을 끼침

- *diff position: research prof* 다른 직책: 연구 교수
  - focus on research / no obligation to teach 연구에 집중 / 가르쳐야 할 의무 없음
  - start a new project → need funding from government / private companies → need time + effort for presentation 새로운 프로젝트 → 정부나 사기업으로부터의 지원금 필요 → 알리기 위한 시간 + 노력 필요
  - sabbatical year available → encourage for research 안식년 가능 → 연구 장려

INTRODUCTION

generalization: universities: higher education + research ➡ pursue academic goals
일반화: 대학교: 고등 교육 + 연구 → 학구적 목표 추구

⬇

prof's also spend time in + effort on research while teaching
교수들도 가르치면서 연구에 시간 + 노력

⬇

thesis: agree (purpose of learning, diff. position)
논제: 찬성 (배움의 목적, 다른 직책)

DISAGREE

- *necessary for prof's personal + academic growth* 교수의 개인적 + 학문적 성장에 필요함
  - research → bring and share knowledge 연구 → 지식을 가져와서 나눔
  - research → raises new Q's → form a professional community 연구 → 새로운 질문을 불러일으킴 → 전문 단체 형성
  - crucial to take part in research projects for improvement of teaching tech + qualities → footmark
    가르치는 방법 + 질의 향상을 위해 연구 프로젝트에 참여하는 것은 중요함 → 발자취

- *funding: necessary in conducting research* 지원금: 연구를 실행하는데 필요함
  - comes from gov't / private companies 정부 / 사기업에서 지원
    Ex new research → enough financial support for lab + team
    새로운 연구 → 연구실과 팀을 꾸리기 위해 충분한 자금 지원이 필요함
  - need previous research to prove ability + scheme 능력과 계획을 증명하기 위한 이전의 연구 이력이 필요함

INTRODUCTION

generalization: cities: universities: higher education + research ➡ pursue academic goals
일반화: 대학교: 고등 교육 + 연구 → 학구적 목표 추구

⬇

prof's also spend time + effort on research while teaching
교수들도 가르치면서 연구에 시간 + 노력

⬇

thesis: disagree (academic improvement, funding)
논제: 반대 (학구적 발전, 지원금)

Colleges and universities are institutions of higher education where students pursue their own academic goals. Although colleges are where students learn, professors also spend a lot of time and effort on their research. Though some people contend that professors should dedicate themselves to doing research, I strongly believe they should focus on teaching. I feel this way due to the purpose of learning and the availability of different positions for those who would like to concentrate on research.

First of all, the purpose of an educational institute is to help students fulfill their academic goals. To be specific, after graduating from high school, where they have formed a fundamental basis of knowledge in a variety of subjects, students enter college in order to get deeper knowledge in a particular field they are intrigued by. However, if a professor spends most of his time researching and working on his own project, he might be able to accomplish work himself, but the students will end up researching and learning on their own. This will also affect the overall academic standards and reputation of the school. Thus, being able to pass his knowledge onto students should be the professor's top priority at school.

On top of that, there is a position called a research professor that allows a professor to focus solely on his research without any obligation to teach. In order to start a research project, a professor needs to get funding from a government or companies and will have to spend a lot of time and effort on preparation. A professor can also take a sabbatical year and put more emphasis on his research. The objective of providing a professor with a sabbatical is to encourage him to do research.

It is true that research encourages professors to develop and improve their knowledge in their field of expertise. On the other hand, the objective of educational institutions is to educate students. Passing knowledge onto students should be the top priority for professors. It is the responsibility of professors to provide students with a deeper knowledge in a specific major so that students can pursue their academic goals during their college years. Furthermore, professors can apply for a research position or take a sabbatical. Therefore, I firmly agree with the statement that professors should focus on teaching rather than doing research.

WORD REMINDER

institution 기관 pursue 추구하다 take place 일어나다 fundamental 근본적인 basis 토대 intrigue 호기심을 돋우다
accomplish 성취하다 end up ~게 되다 reputation 명성, 이미지 priority 우선 solely 오로지 obligation 의무 funding 지원, 투자
sabbatical year 안식년 objective 목표 expertise 전문 지식

Colleges and universities are educational institutions of higher education and research where students pursue their own academic goals. Although colleges are where students' learn, professors also spend a lot of time and effort on their research. Some people think teaching should be a priority for professors while others contend that professors should rather dedicate themselves to doing research. In my opinion, professors should focus on researching. I feel this way because instructors themselves need to develop and improve academically, and continuous research makes it easier to get funding for projects.

First of all, doing research is necessary for professors' personal as well as academic growth and development. During class, professors share the knowledge they have gained through research. Research usually raises new questions, which eventually form a professional community. For instance, there are new research studies released every day, and engaging with the studies is crucial for professors to improve their teaching techniques and abilities. Moreover, as scholars, professors will have chances to leave their marks on their academic fields.

On top of that, it is necessary to have a history of conducting research for professors to get funding from the government or companies. For example, if a professor wants to conduct research on finding a new DNA structure, the professor needs enough financial support to form a lab and a team to work with. However, if the professor does not have any previous research history to prove his abilities and ideas, neither the government nor companies will be willing to take a risk and invest very much money.

It is true that there are sabbaticals that professors can take. However, that particular year is not just for conducting research, but it is a period when professors can develop new pedagogy, programs, and curricula for students. Conducting research throughout the years provides professors with academic development. Furthermore, getting enough funding to do projects or research is necessary. Therefore, I strongly believe that professors should focus on researching.

WORD REMINDER
raise 제기하다 release 발표하다 scholar 학자 mark 흔적 particular 특정한 pedagogy 교육 curriculum 교과 과정

RELATED TOPICS

ACTUAL TEST **10**

1 In a classroom, some people learn best when a lesson is presented in an entertaining and enjoyable way while others learn best when a lesson is presented in a serious and formal way. Which do you prefer and why? Use specific reasons and examples to support your answer.

교실에서, 어떤 이들은 진지하고 형식적인 방법으로 수업을 받을 때 가장 잘 배우는 반면, 어떤 이들은 유쾌하고 즐거운 방법으로 수업을 받을 때 가장 잘 배운다. 당신은 어떤 것을 선호하고 그 이유는 무엇인가? 구체적인 이유와 예를 들어 자신의 입장을 뒷받침하시오.

AN ENTERTAINING AND ENJOYABLE WAY	A SERIOUS AND FORMAL WAY
- no stress / pressure 스트레스 / 압박 ✗ - more motivated to get deeper knowledge 더욱 깊은 지식을 얻기 위해 동기 부여를 받음	- possible only for younger kids or only for introductory lessons 어린 아이들에게 혹은 입문 단계에서만 가능함 - able to progress lesson at faster pace 더 빠른 속도로 배울 수 있음

2 Do you agree or disagree with the following statement? It is better to buy books than to borrow them from libraries or from other people. Use specific reasons and examples to support your answer.

다음 명제에 찬성하는가 반대하는가? 책을 구입하는 것이 도서관이나 다른 사람들로부터 빌리는 것보다 낫다. 구체적인 이유와 예를 들어 자신의 입장을 뒷받침하시오.

BUYING	BORROWING FROM LIBRARIES OR OTHER PEOPLE
- keep and read again anytime 보관하고 언제든 다시 읽을 수 있음 - no need to hurry to keep due date 반납일을 지키기 위해 서두를 필요가 없음	- save space: no need to store 공간 절약: 보관할 필요 없음 - economical: save money 경제적: 돈을 절약

3 Which of the following do you prefer, working or studying at night or working or studying during the day? Use specific reasons and examples to support your answer.

다음 중 어떤 것을 선호하는가, 일하거나 공부를 밤에 하는 것 혹은 일하거나 공부를 낮에 하는 것? 구체적인 이유와 예를 들어 자신의 입장을 뒷받침하시오.

AT NIGHT	DURING THE DAY
- nocturnal: able to focus better at night 야행성: 밤에 좀 더 집중을 할 수 있음 - quiet environment: no distractions 조용한 환경: 방해 ✗	- getting enough sleep at night: important 밤에 충분한 숙면을 갖는 것: 중요함 - able to get prompt help from others (coworkers / teachers) when needed 필요하면 다른 이들로부터 (동료들 / 교사들) 바로 도움을 받을 수 있음

TOEFL® MAP
ACTUAL TEST Writing **1**

11

Most people sleep every night and sometimes even during the day. One question that researchers in the field of medicine have often tried to answer is why people need sleep. It appears as though there are three reasons for this. The first is that sleep improves people's memory functions. Next, people sleep in order to conserve energy. Finally, people sleep to flush the body—particularly the brain—of harmful toxins.

For several decades, scientists have conducted experiments focusing on sleep and memory functions. Through these experiments, they have learned that people who sleep regularly and for long enough—usually six or seven hours a night—have much better cognitive abilities and memory retention than those who fail to get enough sleep. Additionally, people who have more dreams, which occur during REM sleep, typically have better memories than those who get less REM sleep.

When people sleep, their bodies are restored, and their energy is replenished. Sleep allows a person's body to repair itself while simultaneously letting it conserve energy. When a person is sleeping, that individual's body uses less energy; therefore, that person has more energy upon awaking. This helps explain why some animals, such as bears, hibernate: They can survive on little stored energy for a long period of time.

Experiments conducted on humans have proven that, after prolonged periods of sleep, their brains have fewer toxins than when they were awake. By cleansing the brain of toxins, people can think more clearly. Moreover, after getting a sufficient amount of sleep, they feel more refreshed upon waking. This permits people to engage in everyday functions with a clear mind. Contrarily, the less sleep a person gets, the more toxins remain in that individual's brain. As a result, the person is both fuzzy headed and less productive.

🎧 11-01

Directions You have 20 minutes to plan and write your response. Your response will be judged on the basis of the quality of your writing and on how well your response presents the points in the lecture and their relationship to the passage. Typically, an effective response will be 150-225 words.

Question Summarize the points made in the passage, being sure to explain how they cast doubt on specific points made in the reading passage.

| CUT | PASTE | UNDO | REDO | | Hide Word Count : 0 |

Most people sleep every night and sometimes even during the day. One question that researchers in the field of medicine have often tried to answer is why people need sleep. It appears as though there are three reasons for this. The first is that sleep improves people's memory functions. Next, people sleep in order to conserve energy. Finally, people sleep to flush the body—particularly the brain—of harmful toxins.

For several decades, scientists have conducted experiments focusing on sleep and memory functions. Through these experiments, they have learned that people who sleep regularly and for long enough—usually six or seven hours a night—have much better cognitive abilities and memory retention than those who fail to get enough sleep. Additionally, people who have more dreams, which occur during REM sleep, typically have better memories than those who get less REM sleep.

When people sleep, their bodies are restored, and their energy is replenished. Sleep allows a person's body to repair itself while simultaneously letting it conserve energy. When a person is sleeping, that individual's body uses less energy; therefore, that person has more energy upon awaking. This helps explain why some animals, such as bears, hibernate: They can survive on little stored energy for a long period of time.

Experiments conducted on humans have proven that, after prolonged periods of sleep, their brains have fewer toxins than when they were awake. By cleansing the brain of toxins, people can think more clearly. Moreover, after getting a sufficient amount of sleep, they feel more refreshed upon waking. This permits people to engage in everyday functions with a clear mind. Contrarily, the less sleep a person gets, the more toxins remain in that individual's brain. As a result, the person is both fuzzy headed and less productive.

 **NOTE-TAKING**

 READING

reasons for sleeping 수면의 이유

❶ *improve memory functions* 기억력 향상
- people sleeping regularly + for long enough 규칙적으로 + 충분히 수면을 취한 사람들
  → better cognitive abilities + memory retention 더 나은 인지 능력 + 기억력

> **Paraphrasing Example** People who got enough sleep had better cognitive and memory skills compared to those who did not sleep enough.

❷ *body: restored / E: replenished* 신체: 회복됨 / 에너지: 보충됨
- → body: repair + conserve E 신체: 회복함 + 에너지 유지함
- → use less E while sleeping (hibernation) 수면 시 적은 에너지 사용함 (동면)

> **Paraphrasing Example** People's bodies are rejuvenated during sleep because their energy is supplemented during that time.

❸ *brains: fewer toxins after sleeping* 뇌: 수면 후 더 적은 양의 독소를 가짐
- → sufficient sleep → feeling more refreshed 충분한 수면 → 더욱 상쾌한 기분

> **Paraphrasing Example** People's brains get rid of toxins during sleep.

WORD REMINDER

improve 개선하다 function 기능 conserve 보존하다 flush 씻어 내리다 cognitive 인식의 retention 유지 typically 전형적으로
restore 회복시키다 replenish 보충하다 repair 회복하다 simultaneously 동시에 awake 깨어나다 hibernate 동면하다
prolonged 오래 끄는 cleanse 정화하다 sufficient 충분한 refresh 상쾌하게 하다 engage in ~에 참여하다 remain 남다
fuzzy headed 머리가 멍한 productive 생산적인

 LISTENING

why people sleep → uncertain 사람들이 잠자는 이유 → 불확실함

❶ *REM sleep doesn't improve memory* 렘수면은 기억력을 향상시키지 않음
- people w/little / no REM → still had good memories 적은 양 또는 렘수면 x 사람들 → 여전히 좋은 기억력 유지

> **Paraphrasing Example** There is no correlation between REM sleep and memory improvement.

❷ *improving bodily conditions: doubtful* 몸 상태 향상: 의심스러움
- living things get E from food 생명체는 음식으로부터 에너지를 얻음
- people eat immediately after waking up 사람들은 일어나자마자 식사

> **Paraphrasing Example** It is inaccurate to say that people's energy is restored while they sleep.

❸ *diff amount of toxins / diff amount of absorption* 다양한 양의 독소 / 다른 양의 흡수
- experiment → no sleep → sleep for a longer per. of time → toxin lev ↓ 실험 → 수면 x → 장시간의 수면 → 독소 수치 ↓
  → not conducted under a normal sleep pattern 정상적인 수면 패턴 하에 진행 x
  ∴ inconclusive 결론 x

> **Paraphrasing Example** The amount of toxins that people are exposed to and that their bodies take in is different for every individual.

WORD REMINDER

uncertainty 불확실성 expert 전문가 subject 피실험자 contradictory 모순된 essential 필수적인 retention 유지
bodily condition 몸 상태 injured 부상한 immediately 즉각 as far as ~ be concerned ~에 관한 한 remove 제거하다
expose 노출시키다 absorb 흡수하다 be deprived of ~을 빼앗기다 afterward 그 후에 inconclusive 결정적이 아닌

The lecturer argues that it is unclear why people sleep. She makes three statements regarding the reasons for sleep. These assertions directly contradict the claim in the reading passage that there are definite reasons why people need sleep.

First, the professor asserts that there is no correlation between REM sleep and memory improvement. Those who had little or no REM sleep did not show any difference in terms of memory. This refutes the reading passage's contention that people who got enough sleep had better cognitive and memory skills compared to those who did not sleep enough.

Secondly, she emphasizes that it is inaccurate to say that energy is restored while people sleep. Living organisms gain energy by ingesting food, a statement that is proved by the fact that they eat immediately upon waking up. This rebuts the idea presented in the reading passage that our bodies are rejuvenated during sleep because their energy is supplemented during that time.

Lastly, the amount of toxins that people are exposed to and that their bodies take in is different for every individual. In addition, the experiment was conducted under a rare sleep pattern. Hence, nobody is certain about whether sleep allows the elimination of toxins. This challenges the reading passage's argument that people's brains get rid of toxins during sleep.

WORD REMINDER

regarding ~에 관해서　definite 명확한　correlation 상관관계　improvement 향상　in terms of ~에 관하여　emphasize 강조하다　ingest 섭취하다　rejuvenate 원기 회복하다　supplement 보충하다　rare 드문, 희박한　elimination 제거　get rid of 제거하다

TIPS for SUCCESS

upon/on + -ing

〈upon/on + -ing〉는 '~ 하자마자'라고 해석하며 시간적 의미를 나타낼 때 쓰인다. 세 번째 단락의 문장을 살펴보자.

Living organisms gain energy by ingesting food, a statement that is proved by the fact that they eat immediately **upon waking** up.

위의 문장에서 upon waking up은 '일어나자마자'라는 뜻이며 앞의 immediately는 upon waking up를 강조하기 위해 쓰여 '일어나자마자 바로'라고 해석한다.

cf. 이와 비슷한 표현들로는 〈in + -ing〉(~하는데 있어: 2권 Test 03 참고)와 〈by + -ing〉(~함으로써: Test 06 참고) 등이 있다.

TOEFL® MAP **ACTUAL TEST**

VOLUME

HELP

NEXT

WRITING | Question 2 of 2

00:30:00 ⊝ HIDE TIME

ACTUAL TEST **11**

CUT   PASTE   UNDO   REDO   Hide Word Count : 0

Directions Read the question below. You have 30 minutes to plan, write, and revise your essay. Typically, an effective response will contain a minimum of 300 words.

Question

In general, people live longer now. Which of the following do you think accounts for this phenomenon?

- Technological improvements
- Changes in education systems
- Improvements in people's diets

Use specific reasons and examples to support your answer.

Technological Improvements

- *robots: perform surgery* 로봇: 수술 집행
  - many patients: new life 많은 환자들: 새로운 삶
    - Ex cancer: meant death in the past 암: 과거에는 죽음을 의미함
      - → now: highly likely to be cured 현재: 치료 확률이 높아짐

- *people: knowledgeable* 사람들: 지식이 풍부해짐
  - past: hard to get advice on symptoms → miss golden window for treatment
    과거: 증상에 대해 조언을 얻는 것이 힘들었음 → 골든 타임을 놓쳤음
    - Ex stroke: resulted in death most of the time in the past 뇌졸중: 과거에는 거의 죽음을 초래했음
      - → now: searching for signs on the Internet + taking immediate action
        현재: 인터넷으로 징후를 검색 + 즉시 조치를 취함

INTRODUCTION

generalization: many cultures: celebrated 50th birthday
일반화: 부모: 많은 문화: 50세 생일 잔치

⬇

life expectancy now: 70+
현재 평균 수명: 70 이상

⬇

thesis: technological improvement (medical equipment, Internet)
논제: 기술 향상 (의료 도구, 인터넷)

Changes in Education Systems

- *past: lack of knowledge on health → hard to diagnose oneself*
  과거: 건강에 대한 지식 부족 → 스스로 진단하기 어려움
  - proper education system: more aware of common diseases 올바른 교육 제도: 흔한 질병에 대해 좀 더 알게 됨
    - Ex immunization → given information + ways to handle side effects
      예방 접종 → 정보 + 부작용을 해결할 수 있는 방법이 주어짐
      - → decrease in deaths 치사율 ↓

- *# of medical labs ↑* 의료 연구소 # ↑
  Ex past: many deaths caused by measles 과거: 홍역으로 많이 사망
  - government: allocated budgets + built labs → vaccine 정부: 많은 예산을 할당 + 연구소 설립 → 백신
    - → what used to be fatal can now be treated 치명적이었던 병이 이젠 치료 가능

```
━━━━━━━━━━━━━ INTRODUCTION ━━━━━━━━━━━━━

generalization: many cultures: celebrated 50th birthday
일반화: 부모: 많은 문화: 50세 생일 잔치
⬇
life expectancy now: 70+
현재 평균 수명: 70 이상
⬇
thesis: changes in education systems (knowledge on general health ➡ research on disease ↑)
논제: 교육 제도 변화 (일반적 건강에 대한 지식 → 병균에 대한 연구 ↑)
```

Improvements in People's Diets

- *health-related issues: unbalanced diets* 건강 관련 문제: 불균형한 식단

  - healthy diet: nutrients + energy 건강한 식단: 영양분 + 에너지
    Ex calcium↓: sudden cardiac arrest↑ 칼슘↓: 갑작스런 심장마비↑
    ➡ intake food w/calcium (yogurt + fish w/bones) 칼슘이 있는 음식 섭취 (요구르트 + 가시 있는 생선)

- *dietary supplements* 건강 보조 식품

  Ex easy to find vitamin shops 비타민 가게를 찾기 쉬움
    ➡ manage health conditions + improve overall health 건강 상태 관리 + 전반적인 건강 개선
  - many shops: specific categories (age, gender, function) 많은 가게들: 세분화된 항목 (나이, 성별, 기능)

```
━━━━━━━━━━━━━ INTRODUCTION ━━━━━━━━━━━━━

generalization: many cultures: celebrated 50th birthday
일반화: 부모: 많은 문화: 50세 생일 잔치
⬇
life expectancy now: 70+
현재 평균 수명: 70 이상
⬇
thesis: improvements to diet (balanced diets + dietary supplements)
논제: 식생활 개선 (균형 잡힌 식단 + 건강 보조 식품)
```

Many decades ago, people in lots of cultures celebrated when a person reached fifty years of age because the life expectancy in many countries was around forty-five. Thanks to improvements in people's lifestyles, global life expectancy nowadays averages more than seventy. Of the many factors that have contributed to the increase in life expectancy, I strongly believe that technological improvements account for this phenomenon the most. The main reasons are the development of medical equipment and the advent of the Internet.

First, compared to the time when medical equipment was not as developed, there are even robots which can perform surgery today. This has made it feasible for many patients to live longer. For instance, getting cancer almost always meant death in the past; however, today, if detected at an early enough stage, it is highly likely for someone to survive most cancers. Therefore, the development of medical technology has made it possible for humans to live longer than before.

Furthermore, people have broad knowledge on how to prevent themselves from getting certain diseases. In the past, it was hard to get any advice on the symptoms people had; thus, people often missed the golden window for treatment. For example, strokes used to be neglected and even resulted in death. On the other hand, many people have saved their lives by searching for the signs of strokes on the Internet and by taking immediate action.

Some contend that people live longer due to improvements in their diets; nevertheless, the same food was available in the past. It was the Internet which made it feasible for people to find out what kinds of food are the best for their health. In addition, medical technology has saved numerous lives over the years. Hence, I firmly believe technological improvements accounts for the increase in people's life expectancy.

▶ **WORD REMINDER**

decade 십 년간   life expectancy 평균 수명   contribute to 원인이 되다   account for 설명하다   phenomenon 현상   advent 등장
perform 수행하다   feasible 실행할 수 있는   detect 발견하다   broad 넓은   prevent 방지하다   symptom 증상   stroke 뇌졸중
neglect 방치하다   immediate 즉각적인   diet 음식, 식단

Many decades ago, people in lots of cultures celebrated when a person reached fifty years of age because the life expectancy in many countries was around forty-five. Thanks to improvements in people's lifestyle, global life expectancy nowadays averages more than seventy. Of the many factors that have contributed to the increase in life expectancy, I strongly believe that changes in education systems account for this phenomenon the most. The main reasons are due to people's knowledge about health in general and research on incurable diseases.

First of all, in the past, ordinary people hardly had any knowledge on health, making it hard for people to diagnose themselves. However, with proper education, people have become more aware of common diseases, including their symptoms and prevention methods. For instance, when children get immunized, the parents are given printed sheets with all the information about the immunization as well as how to handle any side effects that may occur. This has led to decreases in deaths and increased life expectancy.

On top of that, a growing number of medical laboratories have contributed greatly to saving people's lives. For instance, many died from measles a long time ago; however, governments allocated a lot of funds to build more laboratories, and researchers developed vaccines to prevent others from being infected with measles. Thus, there are many diseases which used to be fatal in the past but which are now easily treated and no longer considered life threatening, therefore resulting in greater longevity.

Some contend that people live longer due to improvements in their diets; nevertheless, the same food was available in the past. Without proper education, people would not have the knowledge to find out what they need to do or eat in order to maintain their health. Moreover, endless research on diseases and germs has led to scientists finding treatments for some diseases that used to be incurable. Therefore, people's increased life expectancy can be attributed to education systems.

WORD REMINDER

general 전반적인   incurable 불치의   ordinary 일반적인   diagnose 진단하다   immunization 예방 접종   handle 처리하다, 다루다
side effect 부작용   allocate 할당하다   infect 감염시키다   fatal 치명적인   life threatening 생명을 위협하는   longevity 장수   germ 세균
attribute to A를 B의 탓으로 돌리다

Many decades ago, people in lots of cultures celebrated when a person reached fifty years of age because the life expectancy in many countries was around forty-five. Thanks to improvements in people's lifestyles, global life expectancy nowadays averages more than seventy. Of the many factors that have contributed to the increase in life expectancy, I strongly believe that improvements in diets account for this phenomenon the most. The main reasons are that people are eating more balanced and nutritious meals and that they are taking dietary supplements.

First of all, many health-related issues were caused by improper diets due to a lack of knowledge or food shortages. Healthy diets provide people with the nutrients and the energy they need to survive and to stay healthy. For instance, low levels of calcium in blood may put a person at a greater risk of sudden cardiac arrest. This can be easily prevented by consuming food with a lot of calcium. Therefore, having different kinds of foods in the right proportions has resulted in longevity.

On top of that, there are many dietary supplements available. For example, people can easily find vitamin shops with a wide range of brands. There are many kinds of vitamins specifically categorized according to age, gender, and function. This has helped people manage and improve their health. Thus, with the aid of dietary supplements, it is possible for people to maintain their health and to live longer.

Some contend that people live longer due to changes in education systems. However, books were widely available in the past, and most people had a basic knowledge about health, making it hard to believe that a lack of education would have caused low life expectancy. Instead, a balanced diet and dietary supplements, including vitamins, have allowed people's bodies to work more effectively. Therefore, the reasons mentioned above helped bodies overcome diseases, eventually leading to increased life expectancy.

WORD REMINDER

nutritious 영양분이 풍부한   dietary supplement 건강 보조 식품   cardiac arrest 심장 마비   consume 섭취하다   proportion 비율, 균형
gender 성별   function 기능

1 Do you agree or disagree with the following statement? People today spend too much time on personal enjoyment and not enough time on more serious duties and obligations. Use specific reasons and examples to support your answer.

다음 명제에 찬성하는가 반대하는가? 오늘날 사람들은 더 많은 시간을 좀 더 진지한 의무나 책임에 사용하기 보다는 개인적인 쾌락에 보낸다. 이유와 예를 들어 자신의 입장을 뒷받침하시오.

AGREE	DISAGREE
- leisure: many kinds of activities are available 여가: 많은 활동이 가능해짐 - value of life has changed 삶의 가치가 변했음	- most people are devoted to their jobs / work 대부분의 사람들은 그들의 직업 / 일에 헌신적임 - more people are volunteering in their communities / society 더 많은 사람들이 단체 / 사회를 위해 봉사활동을 함

2 Do you agree or disagree with the following statement? When people succeed, it is entirely because of hard work. Luck has nothing to do with their success. Use specific reasons and examples to support your answer.

다음 명제에 찬성하는가 반대하는가? 사람들이 성공을 할 때, 그것은 순전히 열심히 일한 덕분이다. 행운은 성공과는 아무 관련이 없다. 이유와 예를 들어 자신의 입장을 뒷받침하시오.

AGREE	DISAGREE
- luck only helps when person has strong foundation and abilities 행운은 탄탄한 기초와 실력을 가진 사람에게만 도움이 됨 - other factors: many other factors needed besides luck 많은 요소들: 행운 이외에 필요한 요소들이 많이 있음	- timing (luck) is very important 시간 (운)은 중요함 - many people put in a lot of effort with similar ideas: few succeed 비슷한 아이디어를 가진 수많은 사람들이 노력함: 오직 몇 명만 성공

3 Do you agree or disagree with the following statement? In my country, young people have better lives than their parents enjoyed when they were young. Use specific reasons and examples to support your answer.

다음 명제에 찬성하는가 반대하는가? 우리 나라에서 젊은이들은 그들의 부모가 어렸을 때 즐겼던 것보다 더 나은 삶을 살고 있다. 이유와 예를 들어 자신의 입장을 뒷받침하시오.

AGREE	DISAGREE
- convenient 편리함 - vast amount of information available 굉장히 많은 정보가 이용 가능함	- too busy: no time to enjoy 너무 바쁨: 즐길 시간이 없음 - too competitive: stressful 과도한 경쟁: 스트레스

TOEFL® MAP
ACTUAL TEST Writing 1

12

ACTUAL TEST **12**

The Earth is going through the most dramatic climate change ever: Some people are dying from floods in some parts of the world while other people have to evacuate their homes due to wildfires in different parts of this world. Not many people are aware that cows, chickens, and pigs are some of the primary culprits of this climate crisis. Numerous scientists and environmentalists are warning of the necessity of reducing the number of cattle before the Earth reaches a worst-case scenario.

According to numerous studies, cows are the main source of greenhouse gases at 14%, causing a global problem. They produce methane through a process called enteric fermentation. This involves microbes decomposing and fermenting the plant materials eaten by the animals, which produces methane as a byproduct. Plant fibers are found in all plants, so the more plants cattle eat, the more methane they produce, contributing greatly to the environmental issue.

Overgrazing is another factor that contributes to climate change. Nearly a third of the land in the United States is used for grazing. Overgrazing enables the compaction and erosion of the land by rain and wind. Compaction hampers plants from growing and water from penetrating the soil, eventually leading to desertification. Another issue with overgrazing is that invasive species will spread instead of native plants and will cause a loss of biodiversity.

There is a solution to this problem. Cultured meat can be an alternative to beef thanks to the development of food technology. It is lab-grown meat which looks and tastes like conventional meat. Cultured meat is grown in culture flasks specifically designed for the propagation and growth of microbial cells instead of inside of a cow. Changing to cultured meat can reduce greenhouse gas emissions produced by cows by up to 90%. Other advantages include less use of water and land and reduced amounts of raw waste.

🎧 12-01

Directions You have 20 minutes to plan and write your response. Your response will be judged on the basis of the quality of your writing and on how well your response presents the points in the lecture and their relationship to the passage. Typically, an effective response will be 150-225 words.

Question Summarize the points made in the lecture, being sure to explain how they challenge specific claims made in the reading passage.

CUT | PASTE | UNDO | REDO   Hide Word Count : 0

The Earth is going through the most dramatic climate change ever: Some people are dying from floods in some parts of the world while other people have to evacuate their homes due to wildfires in different parts of this world. Not many people are aware that cows, chickens, and pigs are some of the primary culprits of this climate crisis. Numerous scientists and environmentalists are warning of the necessity of reducing the number of cattle before the Earth reaches a worst-case scenario.

According to numerous studies, cows are the main source of greenhouse gases at 14%, causing a global problem. They produce methane through a process called enteric fermentation. This involves microbes decomposing and fermenting the plant materials eaten by the animals, which produces methane as a byproduct. Plant fibers are found in all plants, so the more plants cattle eat, the more methane they produce, contributing greatly to the environmental issue.

Overgrazing is another factor that contributes to climate change. Nearly a third of the land in the United States is used for grazing. Overgrazing enables the compaction and erosion of the land by rain and wind. Compaction hampers plants from growing and water from penetrating the soil, eventually leading to desertification. Another issue with overgrazing is that invasive species will spread instead of native plants and will cause a loss of biodiversity.

There is a solution to this problem. Cultured meat can be an alternative to beef thanks to the development of food technology. It is lab-grown meat which looks and tastes like conventional meat. Cultured meat is grown in culture flasks specifically designed for the propagation and growth of microbial cells instead of inside of a cow. Changing to cultured meat can reduce greenhouse gas emissions produced by cows by up to 90%. Other advantages include less use of water and land and reduced amounts of raw waste.

READING

dramatic climate change ← cows, chicken, pigs 급격한 기후 변화 ← 소, 닭, 돼지

❶ *cows: 14% of greenhouse gases / produce methane through enteric fermentation*
소: 온실가스의 14% / 장의 발효를 통해 메탄가스 생산

- eating more plant fibers → more methane 더 많은 식물 섬유 섭취 → 더 많은 메탄가스

> Cows create a global problem by eating plants and by producing a lot of methane.

❷ *overgrazing → erosion + compaction (hampers plant growth + water to penetrate) → desertification* 과도한 방목 → 침식 + 압밀 (식물의 성장 + 물의 침투를 막음) → 사막화

- invasive species over native plants → biodiversity ✕ 외래종의 증가 → 생물의 다양성 ✕

> Overgrazing can cause desertification as well as a loss of biodiversity.

❸ *cultured meat: solution / alternative to beef* 배양육: 해결책 / 소고기 대용

- reduce greenhouse gases, less use of water + land, reduced amount of raw waste
온실가스 감소, 물과 땅의 사용 감소, 배설물 양 감소

> Cultured meat, which not only tastes like beef but also uses less water and land, can be a great alternative to beef.

ACTUAL TEST 12

WORD REMINDER

dramatic 급격한 evacuate 대피시키다 aware 알고 있는 primary 주된 culprit 원인 crisis 위기 cattle 소 (무리)
greenhouse gas 온실가스 methane 메탄가스 enteric (신체) 장의 fermentation 발효 microbe 미생물 decompose ~을 분해하다
byproduct 부산물 fiber 섬유 contribute to 원인이 되다 overgraze ~에 지나치게 많이 방목하다 factor 요인 compaction 압축, 압밀
erosion 침식, 부식 hamper 방해 penetrate 침투하다 desertification 사막화 biodiversity 생물의 다양성 cultured meat 배양육
alternative 대안 thanks so ~ 덕분에 conventional 전통적인 flask 병 propagation 보급 microbial 미생물의 emission 배출
raw 날것의

LISTENING

cannot make cows go extinct → find other solutions 소를 멸종시킬 수 없음 → 다른 해결책을 찾음

❶ *reducing methane: changing diet → seaweed* 메탄가스의 감소: 식단 변경 → 해초

- methane emissions: ↓ up to 60% with 1% of seaweed → inexpensive + easy way
메탄가스 방출: 1%의 해초로 최대 60% ↓ → 저렴하고 쉬운 방법

> Reducing the amount of methane from cows can easily be solved by changing their diets.

❷ *desertification → solution: good herd management* 사막화 → 해결책: 올바른 방목축 관리

- proper grazing management → even alleviate climate change 올바른 방목 관리 → 기후 변화를 완화시킬 수도 있음

> Proper herd management such as rotational grazing will not only allow plants to recover and maintain a diversity of native grasses but will also slow down climate change.

❸ *cultured meat: more CO₂ than methane → takes longer to dissipate*
배양육: 메탄가스보다 더 많은 CO₂ 생산 → 분산시키는데 더 많은 시간이 걸림

- too expensive for the average consumer 일반 소비자에게는 너무 비쌈

> Cultured meat is more costly; thus, only a certain number of people will be able to afford it.

WORD REMINDER

hide 가죽 extinct 멸종한 rational 합리적인 sustainable 지속 가능한 diet 식단 seaweed 해초 promising 유망한
readily 쉽게, 기꺼이 herd management 방목축 관리 rotate 회전하다 pasture 목초지 restore 되찾다, 회복하다 enhance 향상하다, 강화하다
ecological 생태학적 alleviate 완화하다 attempt 시도 downside 불리한 면 dissipate 분산시키다

The lecturer contends that eco-friendly ways should be considered in the domestication of cows. This directly contradicts the reading passage's claim that the number of cattle must be reduced due to their severe effects on the environment.

First, reducing the amount of methane from cows can easily be solved by changing their diets. In addition, milk from a changed diet does not taste bad, making the whole process easy to pursue. This refutes the reading passage's claim that cows are causing global problems by eating plant fibers and by producing a lot of methane.

On top of that, the lecturer says that proper herd management, such as rotational grazing, will not only allow plants to recover and maintain a diversity of native grasses but will also slow down climate change. This contradicts the idea mentioned in the reading passage that overgrazing can cause desertification as well as a loss of biodiversity.

Finally, cultured meat cannot be a substitute for beef; in fact, it can have a worse effect on the environment by producing more CO_2. Moreover, it is more costly than beef; thus, only a certain number of people will be able to afford it. This rebuts the reading passage's claim that cultured meat, which not only tastes like beef but also uses less water and land, can be a great alternative to beef.

WORD REMINDER

domesticate 길들이다   severe 심각한   consequence 결과, 영향   pursue 추진하다   substitute 대안   afford 할 수 있다

Hide Word Count : 0

Directions Read the question below. You have 30 minutes to plan, write, and revise your essay. Typically, an effective response will contain a minimum of 300 words.

Question

Do you agree or disagree with the following statement?

People in the past ate healthier food than people today.

Use specific reasons and examples to support your answer.

ACTUAL TEST **12**

 **NOTE-TAKING**

AGREE

- ***transgenic food & irradiation process*** 유전자 변형 식품 및 방사선 처리
  - − transgenic food 유전자 변형 식품
    → hasten growth of crops + slow the food-deterioration process 농작물의 성장 촉진 + 음식의 부패 지연
  - − irradiation process 방사선 처리
    → slow ripening → nutritional value ↓ 익는 속도를 늦춤 → 영양 가치 ↓

- ***environment: unpolluted in the past*** 환경: 과거에 오염되지 않았음
  - ∴ food was safer for people to ingest 음식은 섭취하기에 안전했음
    Ex oil spill: fish ate pollutants 기름 유출: 물고기들이 오염 물질 섭취
    → toxic + harmful as a food source 음식 자원으로 유독 + 해로움

> ### INTRODUCTION
>
> **generalization**: improvements in agriculture + culinary art
> 일반화: 농업과 요리법의 발달
> ⬇
> **well-being trend**: influence in food industry
> 웰빙 유행: 음식 산업에 영향을 끼침
> ⬇
> **thesis**: agree (many changes in food, unpolluted environment in the past)
> 논제: 찬성 (음식의 많은 변화, 과거의 오염되지 않았던 환경)

DISAGREE

- ***preservation methods in the past: inferior*** 과거의 보존법: 열악했음
  - − food: unavailable/ often spoiled 음식: 구할 수 없었음 / 종종 상해 있었음
    Ex blueberries: not available due to storage problem despite effectiveness
    블루베리: 효과에도 불구하고 보관 문제로 구할 수 없었음
    → today: easy access 오늘날: 쉽게 구할 수 있음

- ***many people in the past: unaware of healthy food*** 과거의 많은 사람들: 건강식에 대해 알지 못했음
  - − satisfied just to be able to eat 먹을 수 있다는 점에 만족했음
    Ex grandmother: lived through a war 할머니: 전쟁을 겪으셨음
    → a healthy diet: extravagance 건강식: 사치
    mother: more concerned about nutritional values 어머니: 영양에 대해 신경을 더 많이 쓰심

> ### INTRODUCTION
>
> **generalization**: improvements in agriculture + culinary art
> 일반화: 농업과 요리법의 발달
> ⬇
> **well-being trend**: influence in food industry
> 웰빙 유행: 음식 산업에 영향을 끼침
> ⬇
> **thesis**: disagree (preservation method / rising concern toward nutrition)
> 논제: 반대 (보관법 / 영양 섭취에 대해 높아진 관심)

CUT   PASTE   UNDO   REDO

Thanks to improvements in agricultural technology and the culinary arts, food has changed a lot over the years. In addition, the recent well-being trend has affected the food industry. Some contend that people eat healthier food today. However, I strongly believe the food that people had in the past was much healthier than the food eaten today. The reason is that we now have transgenic foods, which can be extremely harmful to humans. Furthermore, the unpolluted environment of the past yielded healthier crops.

Agricultural technology has brought about a number of changes in the crops we eat. For one thing, today, many people are likely to ingest transgenic foods. Two reasons for the use of transgenic crops are to hasten growth of crops and to slow the food-deterioration process. Second, in order to slow ripening, some foods such as apples go through an irradiation process, which may reduce their nutritional value. The long-term effects of these technologies are not yet certain.

Moreover, in the past, the environment was unpolluted. Thus, the environment in which crops, cattle, and other animals were raised was not harmful compared to that of today, making food in the past safer for people to ingest. To illustrate, tremendous oil spills in the sea have caused a lot of fish to eat pollutants. As a result, many have died, and those that have managed to survive have become toxic and are harmful as food sources. Though there are a lot of efforts to remedy the damage, there is no guarantee that people in the future will be able to eat fish as fresh as they were in the past.

It is true that improved technology has broadened the availability of food and that people are able to enjoy a variety of foods regardless of the weather conditions that specific foods require. However, technology has also produced transgenic and irradiated foods. In addition, the environment today is too polluted to yield fresh crops and other products as well as it did in the past. For the above reasons, I firmly agree that people in the past ate healthier food than people do today.

WORD REMINDER

culinary arts 요리   trend 유행   industry 산업   transgenic 이식 유전자의   yield (농작물을) 산출하다   bring about 야기하다   ingest 섭취하다
hasten 서두르다   deterioration 악화   ripen 익다   irradiation 방사   nutritional 영양분의   cattle 가축   raise 기르다   tremendous 거대한
spill 유출   toxic 유독한   source 자원   remedy 복구하다   broaden 넓히다

■ TIPS for SUCCESS

독립형 에세이: 서론

서론은 역삼각형을 떠올리며 쓰는 것이 좋다. 일단 주제의 키워드를 생각해 보자.
food

세계의 상황이나 일반적인 삶의 방식, 과거의 삶 등의 큰 단위를 생각해 보자.
improvements in agriculture + culinary arts

농업과 요리에서 조금 더 좁혀갈 수 있는 단어를 떠올려보자. 일단, 어떤 의견에 대해 설득력을 펼칠 것인지를 나타내 주는 thesis statement 를 써 보자.
well-being trends: influence on food

정확히 어떤 의견에 대해 설득력을 펼칠 것인지를 thesis statement를 통해서 써 보자.
I agree with the idea that people in the past ate healthier food than people do today.

Thanks to improvements in agricultural technology and the culinary arts, food has changed a lot over the years. In addition, the recent well-being trend has affected the food industry. Some contend that people ate healthier food in the past. However, I strongly believe that the food that people ingest today is much healthier than the food eaten in the past. The reason is that preservation methods for keeping food fresh have improved a great deal. Furthermore, people are more exposed to information regarding healthy diets.

First of all, the preservation methods of the past were comparatively inferior to those of today; thus, even if the food itself was fresh when cultivated, it was often spoiled by the time it was delivered to a kitchen. Therefore, food was either unavailable or not fresh. For instance, people in Korea have long been aware of the effectiveness of blueberries on brain functions. However, importing them fresh was infeasible in the past due to the lack of technology back then. Today, thanks to improvements in the means of preservation, people have easy access to blueberries.

Moreover, a few decades ago, not many people were cautious in terms of eating healthy diets, especially in countries experiencing wars or economic difficulties. Rather, most people were satisfied just to be able to eat. To illustrate, my grandmother, who lived through a war, said she had no choice but to eat whatever she could obtain. Apparently, a healthy diet was an extravagance. Conversely, my mother is concerned with the nutritional value of the food that my family eats since the media as well as books provide us with endless information on how food has a direct influence on health.

It is true that environmental damage has caused food deterioration, and one consequence is the advent of new diseases. However, improvements in medical technology have aided researchers in finding countermeasures. In addition, preservation methods and concerns regarding diets have exposed people to healthy food. For the above reasons, I firmly disagree that people in the past ate healthier food than those today.

WORD REMINDER

preservation 보존　expose 노출시키다　comparatively 비교적　inferior 열등한　cultivate 경작하다　spoil 상하다　import 수입하다
lack 결핍　cautious 조심성 있는　in terms of ~에 관하여　obtain 얻다　apparently 분명히　extravagance 사치　consequence 결과
advent 출현　aid 돕다　countermeasure 대응책

TIPS for SUCCESS

능동태 vs. 수동태 Active vs. Passive

능동태의 문장에서 목적어가 주어보다 중요해질 때 수동태를 쓴다. 따라서 문장의 〈주어 + 동사 + 목적어〉에서 주어와 목적어의 위치가 바뀌며 동사는 〈be동사 + 과거분사〉의 형식을 취하게 된다. 두 번째 단락의 문장의 일부를 살펴보자.

People **delivered** the food to a kitchen. (사람들이 음식을 주방까지 배달했다.)

위의 문장에서 '사람들'이라는 주어는 '음식'에 비해 중요성이 떨어진다. 따라서, 수동태로 고쳐보면 다음과 같다.

The food **was delivered** to a kitchen by people. (음식은 사람들에 의해 주방까지 배달되었다.)

위의 문장에서 가장 중요한 '음식'은 주어가 되었고 by people은 목적어가 되었으며 이때 목적어는 생략 가능하다.
※단지 문장을 화려하게 만들기 위해, 혹은 글자수를 늘리기 위해 수동태를 사용하는 것은 피하도록 하자.

RELATED TOPICS

1 People were more polite and friendlier in the past than they are nowadays.

오늘날보다 과거의 사람들이 더욱 예의 바르고 친절했다.

AGREE	DISAGREE
- fewer people → less crowded → many people knew each other 인구가 적었음 → 덜 복잡 → 많은 사람들이 서로 알았음 - today: individualized → no care for others 오늘날: 개인주의화 → 타인에 대한 배려 X	- interpersonal relationships → important 인간 관계 → 중요 - education on manners at school 학교에서의 예절 교육

2 It was much easier to succeed in the past than it is now. 오늘날보다 과거에 성공하기가 훨씬 쉬웠다.

AGREE	DISAGREE
- less competitive 경쟁이 덜했음 - fewer inventions + discoveries: people had a lot to discover 적은 양의 발명품 + 발견: 사람들은 발견할 것이 많았음	- more jobs 더 많은 직업 - easy access to various sources + opportunities 다양한 자료와 기회에 대한 접근이 용이

3 Literacy has become more important now than it was in the past. 오늘날 읽고 쓰는 능력은 과거보다 중요해졌다.

AGREE	DISAGREE
- most contracts: documented 대부분의 계약: 문서화되어 있음 - average education level ↑ 평균 교육 수준 ↑	- voice recognition system 음성 인식 시스템 - more modes and methods of communication 더 많은 의사소통 방식 + 방법 ex) video clips, interactive interfaces 동영상, 인터렉티브 인터페이스

TOEFL® MAP
ACTUAL TEST Writing 1

13

Marsupials are a group of animals that are considered mammals. The kangaroo is the best-known marsupial. It mainly lives in Australia; however, some species are found in New Guinea, South America, and North America. Fossil evidence, however, shows that marsupials once lived virtually everywhere on the planet. Yet because marsupials had trouble adapting to their environments, they died out in most of those places.

Marsupials differ from other mammals in that they do not have placentas, and thus mothers do not carry their babies to term. Instead, baby marsupials are born before they are fully developed. Upon being born, a baby marsupial crawls inside a pouch in its mother's body, where it remains until it matures. Unfortunately, being born prematurely means that most marsupials have undeveloped immune systems. This makes them more susceptible to infections and premature death, which happens with great frequency.

Marsupials have a low metabolic rate in comparison with other mammals. To control their body temperatures, mammals must eat food to give them energy. But the low metabolic rate of marsupials means that they have trouble maintaining warmth in their bodies when the temperature becomes cold. As a result, they mostly died out in colder lands and are now primarily found in places with warmer environments such as Australia and South America.

In addition, marsupials are absent from many lands nowadays because they were simply outcompeted by mammals. Animals in the same ecosystems typically vie with one another for their food and habitats. Marsupials, weakened by their immune systems and inability to cope with cold weather, were pushed out of many places by mammals, which proved to be far stronger. As a result, marsupials today only live in a few areas around the world.

🎧 13-01

ACTUAL TEST **13**

137

Directions You have 20 minutes to plan and write your response. Your response will be judged on the basis of the quality of your writing and on how well your response presents the points in the lecture and their relationship to the passage. Typically, an effective response will be 150-225 words.

Question Summarize the points made in the lecture, being sure to explain how they challenge specific claims made in the reading passage.

CUT   PASTE   UNDO   REDO   Hide Word Count : 0

Marsupials are a group of animals that are considered mammals. The kangaroo is the best-known marsupial. It mainly lives in Australia; however, some species are found in New Guinea, South America, and North America. Fossil evidence, however, shows that marsupials once lived virtually everywhere on the planet. Yet because marsupials had trouble adapting to their environments, they died out in most of those places.

Marsupials differ from other mammals in that they do not have placentas, and thus mothers do not carry their babies to term. Instead, baby marsupials are born before they are fully developed. Upon being born, a baby marsupial crawls inside a pouch in its mother's body, where it remains until it matures. Unfortunately, being born prematurely means that most marsupials have undeveloped immune systems. This makes them more susceptible to infections and premature death, which happens with great frequency.

Marsupials have a low metabolic rate in comparison with other mammals. To control their body temperatures, mammals must eat food to give them energy. But the low metabolic rate of marsupials means that they have trouble maintaining warmth in their bodies when the temperature becomes cold. As a result, they mostly died out in colder lands and are now primarily found in places with warmer environments such as Australia and South America.

In addition, marsupials are absent from many lands nowadays because they were simply outcompeted by mammals. Animals in the same ecosystems typically vie with one another for their food and habitats. Marsupials, weakened by their immune systems and inability to cope with cold weather, were pushed out of many places by mammals, which proved to be far stronger. As a result, marsupials today only live in a few areas around the world.

READING

marsupials died out in most places due to their inability to adapt to their environments 유대 동물들은 환경 적응의 어려움 때문에 대부분의 지역에서 사라졌음

❶ *m: born before fully developed* 유대 동물들: 완전히 성숙되지 않은 상태에서 태어남

∴ undeveloped immune system 덜 발달된 면역 체계

→ susceptible to infections + premature death 감염 + 초기 사망에 취약함

> **Paraphrasing Example** A marsupial's premature birth often results in infection and death.

❷ *low metabolic rate* 낮은 신진대사율

– trouble maintaining warmth in body 몸의 온기를 유지하는데 문제가 있음

→ die out in colder lands (≠ Australia, S. America) 추운 지역에서 사라졌음 (≠ 호주, 남미)

> **Paraphrasing Example** Their low metabolic rate can account for their disappearance in most places.

❸ *outcompeted by mammals* 포유 동물들에 의해 압도당했음

– animals: vie for food + habitats 동물: 식량 + 서식지를 위한 경쟁

– m: weaker immune system + inability to cope w/coldness 유대류: 약한 면역 체계 + 추위를 견딜 수 있는 능력 ×

> **Paraphrasing Example** The rule of the survival of the fittest eliminated marsupials from where mammals now live.

WORD REMINDER

marsupial 유대류의 포유 동물 species 종(種) virtually 사실상 die out 차차 소멸하다 placenta 태반 term 출산 예정일 crawl 기어가다 pouch 작은 주머니 immune system 면역 체계 infection 감염 metabolic rate 신진대사율 outcompete ~보다 경쟁에서 우월하다 ecosystem 생태계 vie 경쟁하다 cope with ~에 대처하다

LISTENING

each species has its optimal habitat 각각의 종에게는 자신만의 최적의 서식지가 있음

❶ *no placentas* 태반 ×

– placental mammals: carry babies until they are mature enough → mothers: vulnerable
태반을 가진 포유 동물: 충분히 성숙할 때까지 새끼를 지니고 다님 → 어미: 취약

– marsupials: develop in pouch 유대 동물: 주머니에서 성장

→ protected by mothers + strengthen immune systems 어미로부터 보호를 받음 + 면역 체계 강화

→ strong + healthy 강하고 건강해짐

> **Paraphrasing Example** Marsupials have the advantage of not having placentas.

❷ *create energy from food they eat slowly* 천천히 섭취하는 음식으로부터 에너지를 얻음

– adapt to harsh environment 혹독한 환경에 적응함

Ex Australia: dry → hard to find food 호주: 건조함 → 먹이를 찾기 어려움

– marsupials: endure for long periods w/out food 유대 동물: 식량 없이 장기간 견딤

– regulate temperatures better than mammals 포유 동물들보다 체온 조절을 잘함

> **Paraphrasing Example** Their habit of slowly ingesting food and converting it to energy afterward has enabled marsupials to withstand severe conditions.

❸ *fossil evidence* 화석 증거

– mammals lived in Australia→ couldn't handle harsh environment 호주에 살았던 포유 동물 → 혹독한 환경을 견딜 수 없었음

→ marsupials: outcompeted mammals 유대 동물들: 포유 동물들을 압도

> **Paraphrasing Example** By examining fossils, it has been proven that a huge number of mammals lived in Australia in the past.

WORD REMINDER

zoologist 동물학자 notion 개념 thrive 번성하다 vulnerable 취약한 opossum 주머니쥐 harsh 혹독한 regulate 조절하다 overheat 과열시키다 vanish 사라지다 suited for ~에 적당한

The lecturer argues that each species has its most optimal place for a habitat. Thus, marsupials are not weaker than mammals. This directly refutes the reading passage's claim that marsupials vanished in most places due to their inability to adjust to their harsh surroundings.

First, marsupials have the advantage of not having placentas. Conversely, marsupials carry their young in a pouch immediately after birth so that their security and health from breastfeeding are guaranteed. This fact contradicts the reading passage's claim that the premature births of marsupials often results in infection and death.

On top of that, the lecturer contends marsupials' habit of slowly ingesting food and converting it to energy afterward has enabled marsupials to withstand severe conditions. This helps them endure long periods of time without food. Moreover, they can control their body temperatures better than others. This fact casts doubt on the reading passage's claim that their low metabolic rate can account for their disappearance in most places.

Finally, by examining fossils, it has been proven that a huge number of mammals lived in Australia in the past. However, they could not overcome the severe environment and had to move out of the land. This refutes the reading passage's claim that the rule of the survival of the fittest eliminated marsupials from where mammals now live.

WORD REMINDER

optimal 최적의   habitat 서식지   adjust to ~에 맞추다   surrounding 환경   breastfeeding 모유 수유   ingest 섭취하다
withstand 견디어 내다   severe 가혹한   endure 견디다   account for 설명하다   overcome 극복하다   the survival of the fittest 적자 생존
eliminate 제거하다

TIPS for SUCCESS

the reading passage's claim that ~과 바꿔 쓸 수 있는 표현들

the reading passage's assertion/contention/argument that ~

the points made in the reading passage that ~

the ideas presented in the reading passage that ~

CUT PASTE UNDO REDO

Hide Word Count : 0

Directions Read the question below. You have 30 minutes to plan, write, and revise your essay. Typically, an effective response will contain a minimum of 300 words.

Question

A company wants to train its employees to use new techniques. Which is the better way to train the workers?

- Have all of them attend a training program together
- Have some of the employees attend a training program and later tell their coworkers what they learned

Use specific reasons and examples to support your answer.

📝 NOTE-TAKING

Everyone Together

- *learn to cooperate + share ideas* 협동 + 아이디어 공유를 배움
  - sense of unity 일체감
    Ex new tech challenging → support one another 새로운 기술이 어려울 때 → 서로 도움
  - when dividing work → overall knowledge of tech 일을 분담 할 때 → 기술에 대한 전반적인 지식

- *miscommunication* ✕ 잘못된 전달 ✕
  - how worker conveys information → can have diff results 직원이 어떻게 정보를 전달하느냐 → 다른 결론 가능성
    Ex telephone game 전화기 게임 (귀에 대고 한 사람에게만 전달하는 게임)
    → how the person perceives knowledge might affect the other worker who learns from him
    그 사람이 어떻게 지식을 인지하는지가 그에게 배우는 다른 직원에 영향을 끼칠 수 있음

INTRODUCTION

generalization: companies: train when using new techniques
일반화: 기업: 새로운 기술을 사용할 때에는 훈련을 시킴

⬇

chance to learn up-to-date methods, share ideas, and give feedback
최신 기술 습득의 기회, 아이디어 공유, 의견 전달

⬇

thesis: every employee attending together (cooperation + effective communication)
논제: 모든 직원이 함께 참여 (협동심 + 효율적인 의사소통)

Only Some

- *best way to learn: teach others* 배움의 가장 좋은 방법: 다른 이들을 가르치는 것
  - explaining → fully understand 설명 → 완전히 이해
    Ex feel as if grasped 이해한 듯한 느낌
  - showing / answering Q's → might realize he hasn't fully understood + chance to review
    보여 주기 / 질문에 대답하기 → 완전히 이해한 것은 아니라는 걸 깨달을 수 있음 + 복습 기회

- *theory: not always work in actual practice* 이론: 항상 실제 업무에서 작동하는 것은 아님
  - might detect errors / necessary modification 오류 검출 가능 / 필요한 수정 감지 가능
    Ex new tech at assembly procedure → takes longer than expected
    조립 과정에서의 새로운 기술 → 예상보다 오래 걸릴 수 있음
    → adjustment → reduce possible errors 수정 → 가능한 오류 감소

INTRODUCTION

generalization: companies: train when using new techniques
일반화: 기업: 새로운 기술을 사용할 때에는 훈련을 시킴

⬇

chance to learn up-to-date methods, share ideas, and give feedback
최신 기술 습득의 기회, 아이디어 공유, 의견 전달

⬇

thesis: some attending and showing coworkers what they've learned (review + adjustment)
논제: 일부 직원 참여 후 다른 직원들에게 그들이 배운 지식 전달 (복습 + 조정)

No matter how competent or skillful a worker is, companies train employees when implementing new techniques. Workers can learn up-to-date methods, share ideas, and receive feedback during training sessions. Some companies have all their employees attend a training program together whereas others have some attend the program and later tell their coworkers what they have learned. Though both have advantages as well as disadvantages, I prefer the former one. I feel this way because of cooperation and effective communication.

First of all, employees learn to cooperate and share ideas with one another by attending training sessions together. Having everyone at a training session also provides a sense of unity. For instance, if the new technology a company is implementing is challenging, workers can support one another by helping others on a particular part they are stronger at while receiving aid on a different part. Thus, even when employees work in different departments, they still have an overall understanding of how to do various tasks.

In addition, there is no possibility of miscommunication when employees are trained by the same instructors. To be specific, if employees were to train one another, how an employee conveys the information can yield different results. For example, each person may perceive the knowledge or instructions in his own way, just like what normally happens in the telephone game. Thus, if a person learns a new technique and puts it in his own words, another employee might understand it in a very different way.

It is true that an employee can review the material learned by conveying the knowledge to a coworker. However, it is each employee's responsibility to comprehend what he has learned during a training session. By attending training sessions together, employees can learn to cooperate with one another. Moreover, there is a very low chance of misunderstandings happening between workers. Therefore, when training employees to use a new technique, I prefer companies having every worker attend a training session together.

▼**WORD REMINDER**

competent 유능한   implement 실행하다   feedback 의견   former 전자   miscommunication 잘못된 전달   convey 전달하다
yield (결과, 대답 등을) 가져오다   perceive 인지하다   the telephone game 귀에 대고 한 사람에게만 전달하는 게임

No matter how competent or skillful a worker is, companies train employees when implementing new techniques. Workers can learn up-to-date methods, share ideas, and receive feedback during training sessions. Some companies have all their employees attend a training program together whereas others have some attend the program and later tell their coworkers what they have learned. Though both have advantages as well as disadvantages, I prefer the latter one. I feel this way because workers can review through practice and adjustments can be made.

First of all, the best way to learn is to apply the knowledge gained by teaching others. By explaining what the person has learned, he can fully understand the concept. For instance, a worker might feel he has grasped the information on a new technique. Nevertheless, by showing a coworker the new technique or by answering questions, he may realize there are some parts he, in fact, does not completely comprehend.

On top of that, a theory does not always work in practice. When explaining to a coworker, an employee might detect points that need to be modified or should be further explained. For example, while showing a skill to a coworker, an employee could discover that the new technique takes longer to put parts together. Then, adjustments can be made to help the company reduce possible errors.

It is true that training employees together would minimize miscommunication; however, it is the responsibility of employees to study and review the information they learn. While showing other workers what they have learned, employees can review and thoroughly grasp new techniques. Moreover, companies can get feedback on the new techniques as employees demonstrate skills to their coworkers. Therefore, when training employees to use new techniques, I prefer that companies have some workers attend a training session and later show their coworkers what they have learned.

► **WORD REMINDER**

latter 후자의   practice 업무   adjustment 조정   grasp 이해하다   comprehend 이해하다   detect 감지하다   modify 변경하다
demonstrate 설명하다

RELATED TOPICS

1   Do you agree or disagree with the following statement? It is better to read books on an electronic device than to read traditional books on paper. Use specific reasons and examples to support your answer.

다음 명제에 찬성하는가 반대하는가? 종이로 된 전통적인 책을 읽는 것 보다 전자 기기에서 책을 읽는 것이 낫다. 구체적인 이유와 예를 들어 자신의 입장을 뒷받침하시오.

AGREE	DISAGREE
- eyesight could get bad 시력이 나빠질 수 있음 - cannot mark with notes 노트를 표시해 둘 수 없음	- convenient: able to carry many books on one device 편리: 많은 책을 한 장치에 가지고 다닐 수 있음 - able to turn on audio books when driving 운전하는 동안 오디오 책을 켤 수 있음

2   Which one would you prefer as a final project, giving a class presentation or writing an essay? Use specific reasons and examples to support your answer.

다음 중 어떤 것을 기말 프로젝트로 선호하는가, 수업 시간에 발표 혹은 에세이를 쓰는 것? 구체적인 이유와 예를 들어 자신의 입장을 뒷받침하시오.

GIVING A CLASS PRESENTATION	WRITE AN ESSAY
- interaction with classmates + teacher → able to get feedback / reactions simultaneously 학우들 + 교사와 교류 → 의견 / 반응을 동시에 받을 수 있음 - able to use many resources (visual aids) 많은 자료 사용 가능 (시각 자료)	- no need to get nervous / anxious 떨거나 불안해 할 필요 없음 - able to edit while writing 쓰면서 수정 가능

3   The administration at a university is revising the budget and has decided to change its funding priorities. As a result, the university will now spend more money on sports and athletic facilities than it does on the campus libraries. Do you think this is a good idea? Why or why not? Use specific reasons and examples to support your answer.

대학 관계자가 학교의 예산을 변경하며, 지원금의 우선 순위를 바꾸기로 결정했다. 결과적으로, 학교는 이제 교내 도서관에 쓰는 것보다 스포츠와 체육 시설에 돈을 더 쓰려고 한다. 이것이 좋은 생각인가? 왜 혹은 왜 아닌가? 구체적인 이유와 예를 들어 자신의 입장을 뒷받침하시오.

TEAM	LIBRARY
- school spirit 애교심 - keep healthy by doing exercise 운동을 함으로써 건강을 지킴	- purpose of learning 배우는 목적 - resourceful: reputation ↑ 풍부한 자료: 명성 ↑

TOEFL® MAP
ACTUAL TEST Writing 1

14

Oil sands are a mixture of sand, clay, water, and oil called bitumen and are the largest deposits of crude oil on the Earth. They have been found in Alberta, Canada, and have made Canada the top foreign supplier of oil to the United States. Though it has brought many economic benefits to Canada, the amount of damage caused by oil sands is tremendous. A number of experts predict that Canada's oil sands development will continue to accelerate and insist that proper sanctions must be imposed.

First of all, water is necessary in oil sands extraction. Bitumen, which is heavy crude oil, needs to be separated from sand, clay, and water. In this recovery process, a significant amount of water and chemicals are required. Up to 4.5 gallons of fresh water are needed for each barrel of oil produced. Many people question if it is worth using water to produce oil than to grow crops, especially during a drought.

Another serious problem with oil sands is leaks from the tailing ponds and the dam and dike facilities used to capture tailing materials. These leaks have killed many aquatic organisms. For example, numerous ducks have been exposed to toxic substances such as mercury and ammonia, and most of them have been killed. The contaminated tailing ponds have also killed a lot of migrating birds.

On top of that, industrial development, including logging, hydroelectric dams, and mining within boreal forests, puts boreal ecosystems in danger, and oil sands development is no exception. Extracting bitumen is disruptive to boreal forests. Some of the negative factors are pipelines, open-pit mines, and roads, which displace wildlife species. Canada's boreal forests are unbelievably diverse and are very important not only to Canada but also to the world, and they are under threat.

ACTUAL TEST **14**

🎧 14-01

Directions You have 20 minutes to plan and write your response. Your response will be judged on the basis of the quality of your writing and on how well your response presents the points in the lecture and their relationship to the passage. Typically, an effective response will be 150-225 words.

Question Summarize the points made in the lecture, being sure to explain how they challenge specific claims made in the reading passage.

CUT PASTE UNDO REDO   Hide Word Count : 0

Oil sands are a mixture of sand, clay, water, and oil called bitumen and are the largest deposits of crude oil on the Earth. They have been found in Alberta, Canada, and have made Canada the top foreign supplier of oil to the United States. Though it has brought many economic benefits to Canada, the amount of damage caused by oil sands is tremendous. A number of experts predict that Canada's oil sands development will continue to accelerate and insist that proper sanctions must be imposed.

First of all, water is necessary in oil sands extraction. Bitumen, which is heavy crude oil, needs to be separated from sand, clay, and water. In this recovery process, a significant amount of water and chemicals are required. Up to 4.5 gallons of fresh water are needed for each barrel of oil produced. Many people question if it is worth using water to produce oil than to grow crops, especially during a drought.

Another serious problem with oil sands is leaks from the tailing ponds and the dam and dike facilities used to capture tailing materials. These leaks have killed many aquatic organisms. For example, numerous ducks have been exposed to toxic substances such as mercury and ammonia, and most of them have been killed. The contaminated tailing ponds have also killed a lot of migrating birds.

On top of that, industrial development, including logging, hydroelectric dams, and mining within boreal forests, puts boreal ecosystems in danger, and oil sands development is no exception. Extracting bitumen is disruptive to boreal forests. Some of the negative factors are pipelines, open-pit mines, and roads, which displace wildlife species. Canada's boreal forests are unbelievably diverse and are very important not only to Canada but also to the world, and they are under threat.

✍ NOTE-TAKING

OS: putting the world at risk by causing tremendous amount of environmental damage 오일 샌드: 어마어마한 환경 손상을 하여 세계를 위험에 빠뜨림

❶ *water: necessary* 물: 필수

- recovery process → 4.5G of water for barrel of oil 분리 과정 → 기름 1 배럴당 4.5갤론의 물이 필요함

> **Paraphrasing Example** A tremendous amount of water is used in the recovery process.

❷ *leaks from tailing ponds* 잔해물을 담고 있는 호수에서의 유출

- harmful to many aquatic organisms + migrating birds 많은 수생동물 + 철새들에게 위험

> **Paraphrasing Example** The leaks from tailing materials have killed a lot of aquatic creatures as well as migrating birds.

❸ *industrial development in boreal forest → ecosystems in danger*
북부 수림대의 산업 발전 → 생태계가 위험에 빠짐

- –ve factors: pipelines, open-pit mines, roads → displace wildlife species
부정적인 요소: 수송관, 노천광, 길 → 야생동물들을 쫓아냄

> **Paraphrasing Example** Industrial development puts boreal forests, which are very important to the world, in danger.

WORD REMINDER

mixture 혼합 bitumen 역청 deposit 침전물 crude oil 원유 supplier 원료 공급국 accelerate 가속하다 sanction 제재 impose 시행하다 extraction 추출 recovery process 분리 과정 significant 상당한 crop 농작물 leak 유출 tailing 잔해물 dike 제방 capture 잡다 aquatic 수생의 mercury 수은 contaminated 오염된 migrating 이동하는 industrial 산업의, 공업의 logging 벌목 hydroelectric 수력 발전의 boreal forest 북부 수림대 disruptive 지장을 주는 open-pit mine 노천굴 광산 displace 바꾸어 놓다, 추방하다

OS: the damage is barely noticeable and the government has established stringent rules 오일 샌드: 손상은 눈에 거의 띄지 않고 정부에서 엄격한 규정을 세움

❶ *water: recycled* 물: 재활용

- new water: from various sources (precipitation, rivers, and onsite drainage)
새로운 물: 여러 원천에서 옴 (강수, 강, 현장 배수)

> **Paraphrasing Example** Most of the water used in oil sands is recycled.

❷ *tailings: majority remains as mud almost permanently*
잔해물: 대부분 거의 영구적으로 진흙으로 남아 있음

- oil sands mining companies + government → close monitoring 오일 샌드 채광 기업들 + 정부 → 근접 관찰

> **Paraphrasing Example** Tailings remain as mud indefinitely, and water is recycled.

❸ *boreal forest in Alberta → only 0.2% destroyed over the past forty years*
알버타의 북부 수림대 → 지난 40년간 0.2%만 파손됨

- remaining materials: put back in the reserve for restoration 남은 물질: 복구를 위해 다시 보호 구역에 넣어둠

> **Paraphrasing Example** Just 0.2% of boreal forests in Alberta have been destroyed by oil sands mining.

WORD REMINDER

environmentalist 환경 보호론자 barely 거의 ~하지 않다 vast 광대한 stringent 엄격한 adhere 고수하다 misconception 잘못된 생각 in-situ 원 위치에 establish 세우다 operation 사업, 공사 precipitation 강우 onsite 현장의 drainage 배수, 방수 regulation 규정 accumulation 축적 residual 잔여의 compound 혼합물 permanently 영구적으로 conduct 시행하다 commit 약속하다 potential 잠재적인 misinformation 오보 reserve 보호 지역 restoration 복구, 회복

The lecturer argues that the damage caused by oil sands is hardly recognizable and that companies follow strict rules established by the government of Canada. These assertions directly contradict the claim made in the reading passage that Canada's oil sands are the main contributor to environmental destruction.

First, she emphasizes that most of the water used in oil sands is recycled. In addition, new water comes from other sources like rain and rivers. This challenges the reading passage's argument that a tremendous amount of water is used in the recovery process.

Then, the professor asserts that tailings, which are waste materials from oil sands extraction, contain toxic materials. However, they remain as mud indefinitely, and water is recycled. In addition, the government is watching closely to decrease the possible harm to the environment. This casts doubt on the assertion shown in the reading passage that the leaks from tailing materials have killed a lot of aquatic creatures as well as migrating birds.

Lastly, over the course of forty years, just 0.2% of boreal forests in Alberta have been destroyed by oil sands mining. According to the professor, after bitumen is extracted, the remaining material is put back in the reserve. This rebuts the idea presented in the reading passage that industrial development puts boreal forests, which are very important to the world, in danger.

WORD REMINDER
contributor 원인 제공자   emphasize 강조하다   source 원천   indefinitely 무기한으로

CUT PASTE UNDO REDO Hide Word Count : 0

Directions Read the question below. You have 30 minutes to plan, write, and revise your essay. Typically, an effective response will contain a minimum of 300 words.

Question

Do you agree or disagree with the following statement?

Most of our problems will be solved by this generation.

Use specific reasons and examples to support your answer.

ACTUAL TEST **14**

 **NOTE-TAKING**

- *development of tech: resolution of problems* 과학 기술의 발달: 문제의 해결
  - new finding + solutions 새로운 연구 + 해결 방안
    Ex medical tech → cure for cancer 의학 기술 → 암의 치료법
    architectural + eco-friendly approaches in construction → pollutants ✗
    건설 분야의 건축 + 친환경적 접근 방법 → 오염 물질 ✗

- *many organizations, corporations, individuals → more conscious of issues*
  많은 단체, 기업, 개인 → 문제에 대해 더욱 자각함
  - effort to heal destruction 파괴를 회복시키기 위한 노력
    Ex recycle + use paper bags instead of plastic bags 재활용 + 비닐 가방 대신 종이 가방 사용
    → nature will recover soon 자연이 빠른 시간 안에 회복할 것임

INTRODUCTION

generalization: each generation suffers from problems
일반화: 각 세대는 문제로부터 고통을 겪음

⬇

deal w/problems → influence on the future 문제의 대처 → 미래에 영향을 끼침
∴ try to achieve +ve outcomes for the following generations 후대를 위해 좋은 결과를 이루기 위해 노력함

⬇

thesis: agree (improving tech, effort)
논제: 찬성 (발전하는 과학 기술, 노력)

- *tech: cannot solve every problem* 과학 기술: 모든 문제를 해결할 수는 없음
  - certain problems need more time 특정 문제는 더 많은 시간을 필요로 함
    Ex global warming during the Eocene Epoch 시신세 동안의 온난화
    → took more than 2,000 years to recover 회복하는데 2천년 이상이 걸렸음

- *some social issues remain as long as society is based on materialism*
  일부 사회 문제는 사회가 물질주의에 바탕을 두는 한 지속될 것임
  - gap btwn the rich + poor: crime 빈부 격차: 범죄
    Ex theft: since humans began possessing + storing 절도: 인간이 소유 + 저장하기 시작한 이래로 시작
    → crime will never be solved 범죄는 결코 해결될 수 없음

INTRODUCTION

generalization: each generation suffers from problems
일반화: 각 세대는 문제로부터 고통을 겪음

⬇

deal w/problems → influence on the future 문제의 대처 → 미래에 영향을 끼침
∴ try to achieve +ve outcomes for the following generations 후대를 위해 좋은 결과를 이루기 위해 노력함

⬇

thesis: disagree (required time, impossibility of resolution)
논제: 반대 (필요한 시간, 해결 불가능)

Each generation suffers from various problems, including environmental and social matters. How the people of a particular generation deal with the issues will have a great influence on the future, and people strive hard to achieve positive outcomes for the following generations. Some contend that our problems cannot be solved by our generation. However, I strongly believe these predicaments can be resolved soon. For one, rapidly improving technology will aid us in finding solutions. In addition, many organizations as well as individuals are trying their best to deal with the issues.

First of all, the development of technology always accelerates the resolution of issues in diverse fields, including medicine and environmental science. Thus, new findings and studies have solved a number of problems. For instance, medical technology has found cures for patients in even the final stages of cancer. Moreover, architectural improvements and eco-friendly approaches to construction have resolved problems that used to cause pollution. Consequently, the means to improve different issues will clear up the trouble within our generation.

On top of that, compared to the past, many organizations, corporations, and individuals are more conscious of various environmental and social issues. As a result, they are putting a lot of effort into healing the destruction. To illustrate, environmental organizations promote participation in green campaigns, and most people in Korea are actively involved in such exercises as recycling and using paper bags instead of plastic bags. This will eventually help nature recover to the level in the past when there was less environmental damage.

It is true that results may not become apparent until later generations. However, the problems will be solved and will not continue in the following generations. The rapid progress of technology in various fields fosters the resolution of problems. Furthermore, a majority of people and groups have taken a step forward in working out the difficulties that we are going through. For the above reasons, I firmly agree with the statement that most of our problems will be solved in our generation.

WORD REMINDER

predicament 곤경   accelerate 촉진하다   architectural 건축의   approach 접근   construction 건설   clear up (문제를) 풀다
conscious 의식하고 있는   promote 장려하다   foster 촉진하다   take a step forward 일보 전진하다   work out (문제를) 풀다

▌ TIPS for SUCCESS

명사절Noun Clause**의 세 가지 사용법**

1. 주어: 문장의 가장 앞에 나옴으로써, 절 자체가 주어 역할을 할 수 있다. 첫 단락의 문장을 살펴보자.

   How the people of a particular generation deal with the issues will have a great influence on the future.

   위의 문장에서 명사절은 How the people of a particular generation deal with the issues이며 문장에서 주어 역할을 한다.

2. 전치사의 목적어: 명사절은 전치사의 뒤에 쓰여서 목적어 역할을 할 수도 있다.

   The issue concerning **how the people of a particular generation treat nature** will have a great influence on the future.

   전치사인 concerning뒤에 명사절이 와서 '~에 관한 이슈'의 뜻으로 쓰였다.

3. 동사의 목적어: 2번과 마찬가지로 동사의 뒤에 와서 동사의 목적어 역할을 할 수도 있다.

   Our environment will be destroyed **if people keep urbanizing land**.

   destructed에서 문장을 끝낼 수 있지만, if를 동반한 명사절을 써서 내용을 보다 더 자세히 말해줄 수 있다.

ACTUAL TEST **14**

CUT PASTE UNDO REDO

Each generation suffers from various problems, including environmental and social matters. How the people of a particular generation deal with the issues will have a great influence on the future, and people strive hard to achieve positive outcomes for the following generations. Some contend that our problems can be solved by our generation. However, I strongly believe some of our predicaments will take a lot more time. For one, some environmental damage will require a tremendous amount of time to recover. In addition, some social issues can never be solved.

First of all, though technology is improving rapidly, it cannot solve every problem within a relatively short period of time. For instance, global warming occurred during the Eocene Epoch, and it took more than two thousand years for the heat to diffuse and for the atmosphere to return to normal temperatures. Likewise, certain matters, environmental concerns in particular, require a lot of time and effort that cannot be accomplished within a single generation.

On top of that, some social issues will remain as long as society is based on materialism. Because a gap between the rich and the poor exists, crime will never vanish. For example, crimes involving theft have been around since humans began possessing and storing belongings. Whether it is due to hunger or greed, stealing will always remain a problem to be solved.

It is true that people nowadays are more aware of our serious problems and are trying to find solutions to resolve them. However, some matters require long-term effort. Furthermore, in spite of a mature sense of citizenship and the existence of strict laws, certain crimes will last as long as society is based on capitalism. For the above reasons, I firmly disagree with the statement that most of our problems will be solved in our generation.

WORD REMINDER

relatively 비교적   diffuse 발산하다   atmosphere 대기   likewise 마찬가지로   concern 걱정, 근심   in particular 특히   accomplish 성취하다
materialism 물질주의   vanish 사라지다   theft 절도   possess 소유하다   store 저장하다   belonging 소유물   greed 탐욕
in spite of ~에도 불구하고   mature 성숙한   citizenship 시민의 신분   strict 엄격한   capitalism 자본주의

TIPS for SUCCESS

명사절 접속사
whether/if('~ 인지 아닌지'의 뜻을 가지고 있으므로 가정법으로 쓰이지 않음, 뒤에 전치사가 올 수 없음), who/whose, what, which, when, where, why, how, whoever, whatever, whomever, whichever, that(전치사와 함께 쓰일 수 없음) 등이 있다.

RELATED TOPICS

1 Having a dress code at one's workplace is important. 직장에는 복장 규정이 있는 것이 중요하다.

AGREE	DISAGREE
- unity of employees 직원들의 통일성	- practicality > unity 실용성 > 통일성
- reminder of one's occupation: appropriate speech + behavior 자신의 직업을 상기시켜 줌: 적절한 발언 + 행동	ex) some females feel more comfortable in pants than in a skirt 일부 여성들은 치마보다 바지를 입을 때 더 편안함을 느낌
	- freedom of expression 표현의 자유

2 It is better to say nothing than to say negative things. 부정적인 것을 말할 바에는 아무것도 말하지 않는 것이 낫다.

AGREE	DISAGREE
- may hurt another's feelings 상대방의 기분을 상하게 할 수 있음	- criticism: helps others improve more → stimulus 비평: 상대방이 더욱 발전하도록 도움이 됨 → 자극
- possibility of an argument 다툼의 가능성	- the person may not realize his / her drawbacks 그 사람은 자신의 단점에 대해 모르고 있을 수도 있음

3 It is difficult to become friends with people with different interests or personalities.
다른 관심사나 성격을 가진 사람과 친구가 되는 것은 힘들다.

AGREE	DISAGREE
- may create discomfort / stress btwn the two 둘 사이에 불쾌감 / 스트레스를 일으킬 수 있음	- experience new activities + share different thoughts 새로운 활동을 경험 + 다른 생각을 공유
ex) introvert vs. extrovert 내성적인 사람 대 외향적인 사람	- supplement others' shortcomings 다른 이의 부족한 점을 보완함
- hard to find a common topic: may result in arguments 공통 주제를 찾기 힘듦: 논쟁을 일으킬 수 있음	

4 It is important to give the same grade to every member of a group. 팀의 모든 구성원에게 같은 점수를 주는 것은 중요하다.

AGREE	DISAGREE
- building a strong sense of cooperation 강한 협동심을 키워 줌	- unfair for those who tried harder than the rest 더 열심히 노력한 구성원들에게 불공평함
- responsibility: one's idleness may affect every member's grade 책임감: 자신의 게으름이 모든 구성원의 점수에 영향을 줄 수 있음	- may cause excessive reliance on other members 다른 구성원들에게 지나치게 의존할 수 있음

5 Sports helps people learn about life. 스포츠는 삶에 대해 배우도록 도와 준다.

AGREE	DISAGREE
- accomplishment 성취감	- life: many variables 삶: 많은 변수가 있음
- endurance 인내심	- people w/no talent in sports: may only feel frustrated 스포츠에 소질이 없는 사람들: 좌절감만 안겨 줄 수 있음

TOEFL® MAP

ACTUAL TEST Writing 1

15

Dogs have lived and worked alongside men for thousands of years. In fact, it is believed that dogs were the first animals humans ever domesticated. Since then, the two have been inseparable from each other.

It is clear that dogs are descended from wolves. Somehow, wolves started living with humans. After numerous generations, they evolved into domestic dogs. The evidence defends this theory. Both animals are four-legged mammals with fur, long tails, long pointed snouts, large teeth, and binocular vision. They breed litters of pups, mark their territory, and have other similar aspects in their behavior. Wolves and dogs can also interbreed, and studies of their DNA reveal that they are closely related.

How exactly wolves and humans first came into close contact is a matter of conjecture. Perhaps some wolves were raised as pups, or maybe a human simply fed a hungry wolf. Whatever the case, wolves somehow came to trust humans more. These wolves likely visited the campfires of prehistoric humans and were fed leftover scraps of meat. Gradually, the wolves became part of some human groups. They probably helped humans hunt large game and protected them from predators and enemy tribes. In the process, they became domesticated.

Through selective breeding, wolves became more like modern dogs. This breeding accounts for the enormous variety of dog species that exist today. Anthropologists estimate that this process began around 14,000 years ago. Some ancient tombs dating to that time have been unearthed. In them, dogs were found buried with their human masters, which clearly showed the close companionship that already existed between the two. By the time that Egyptian and other ancient cultures arose thousands of years later, dogs were considered pets, not wild animals.

🎧 15-01

ACTUAL TEST **15**

157

Directions You have 20 minutes to plan and write your response. Your response will be judged on the basis of the quality of your writing and on how well your response presents the points in the lecture and their relationship to the passage. Typically, an effective response will be 150-225 words.

Question Summarize the points made in the lecture, being sure to explain how they challenge specific claims made in the reading passage.

CUT   PASTE   UNDO   REDO   Hide Word Count : 0

Dogs have lived and worked alongside men for thousands of years. In fact, it is believed that dogs were the first animals humans ever domesticated. Since then, the two have been inseparable from each other.

It is clear that dogs are descended from wolves. Somehow, wolves started living with humans. After numerous generations, they evolved into domestic dogs. The evidence defends this theory. Both animals are four-legged mammals with fur, long tails, long pointed snouts, large teeth, and binocular vision. They breed litters of pups, mark their territory, and have other similar aspects in their behavior. Wolves and dogs can also interbreed, and studies of their DNA reveal that they are closely related.

How exactly wolves and humans first came into close contact is a matter of conjecture. Perhaps some wolves were raised as pups, or maybe a human simply fed a hungry wolf. Whatever the case, wolves somehow came to trust humans more. These wolves likely visited the campfires of prehistoric humans and were fed leftover scraps of meat. Gradually, the wolves became part of some human groups. They probably helped humans hunt large game and protected them from predators and enemy tribes. In the process, they became domesticated.

Through selective breeding, wolves became more like modern dogs. This breeding accounts for the enormous variety of dog species that exist today. Anthropologists estimate that this process began around 14,000 years ago. Some ancient tombs dating to that time have been unearthed. In them, dogs were found buried with their human masters, which clearly showed the close companionship that already existed between the two. By the time that Egyptian and other ancient cultures arose thousands of years later, dogs were considered pets, not wild animals.

📝 NOTE-TAKING

dogs were the first domesticated animals in human history
개들은 인류 역사상 최초로 사육된 동물임

❶ *dogs: descended from wolves* 개: 늑대의 자손

- similarities in physical appearance, behavior, DNA 외모, 행동, DNA의 유사점

 Based upon similarities in physical appearance, behavior, and DNA, dogs are descendants of wolves.

❷ *reciprocal relationship btwn wolves + humans* 늑대 + 인간 간의 상호 관계

- humans: food 인간: 음식
- wolves: help in hunting large game + protecting humans 늑대: 큰 사냥감을 사냥할 때 도움 + 인간 보호

 There was a reciprocal relationship between humans and wolves.

❸ *tombs: dogs were buried w/human masters* 무덤: 개는 인간 주인과 함께 매장되었음

→ companionship 우정

Paraphrasing Example The tombs represent friendship between the two.

WORD REMINDER

domesticate 길들이다   descend 자손이다   evolve 진화하다   defend 지지하다   pointed 뾰족한   snout 주둥이
binocular vision 쌍안시   breed 낳다, 양육하다   litter 한배 새끼   territory 영역   aspect 관점   interbreed 이종 교배시키다   reveal 나타내다
conjecture 추측   prehistoric 선사의   leftover 나머지, 찌꺼기   scrap 한 조각   gradually 차츰   game 사냥감   date 어느 시대를 나타내다
bury 매장하다   companionship 우정

the origins of dogs: difficult to determine 개의 기원: 결정하기 어려움

❶ *difference btwn wolves + dogs* 늑대 + 개 사이의 차이점

- wolves: larger + more aggressive than the biggest species of dogs 늑대: 개들 중 가장 큰 종 보다 더 크고 공격적임
- domesticating wolves: mostly failed 늑대 사육: 대부분 실패
- dogs in the wild: can be tamed 야생에 있던 개: 길들여질 수 있음
- same mammal family → diverged 같은 포유류 → 갈라졌음
  ∴ ancestor: similar to wolves that were smaller + less aggressive 조상: 더 작고 덜 공격적인 늑대와 유사

Paraphrasing Example Dogs are distinguishable from wolves.

❷ *how dogs were domesticated* 개가 어떻게 길들여졌는지

- more friendly + nonaggressive dogs 더 친근 + 호의적인 개들
  → more food + permission to sleep w/humans 더 많은 음식 + 인간과 같이 잘 수 있게 허락
  ∴ friendly dogs → outcompeted aggressive ones 친근한 개들 → 공격적인 개들을 압도

Paraphrasing Example It is also uncertain how dogs were tamed.

❸ *remains from 14,000 years ago → dogs + humans buried together* 14,000년 전의 유골 → 개 + 인간 함께 매장

- until 8,000-10,000 years: burial → not common 8,000~10,000년 전까지: 매장 → 흔하지 ✗

Paraphrasing Example Unearthed remains from 14,000 years ago show that dogs and humans were buried together.

WORD REMINDER

origin 근원   share 공유하다   aggressive 공격적인   the wild 야생   tame 길들이다   diverge 갈라지다   ancestor 조상   approach 접근하다
pose 자세를 취하다   threat 위협   outcompete 이기다, 제치다   dominate 지배하다   remain 유골   abandon 버리다
hunter-gatherer 수렵 채집민   settle 정주하다

ACTUAL TEST 15

The lecturer asserts that it is impossible to determine the origins of dogs. This argument contradicts the idea presented in the reading passage that dogs were the first animals domesticated in human history.

First off, dogs are distinguishable from wolves because wolves are larger and much more hostile compared to the largest species of dogs. Moreover, even dogs found in the wild can be tamed, leading to the conclusion that dogs are probably descended from wolf-like animals with smaller sizes and less aggressiveness. This refutes the reading passage's claim that based upon similarities in physical appearance, behavior, and DNA, dogs are descendants of wolves.

Next, it is also uncertain how dogs were tamed. As more sociable dogs had an advantage over those more belligerent, their population most likely overtook that of the aggressive dogs. This rebuts the reading passage's argument that there was a reciprocal relationship between humans and wolves.

The last point the lecturer makes is that unearthed remains from 14,000 years ago show that dogs and humans were buried together. However, only 8,000 to 10,000 years ago did burial become a typical practice. This directly contradicts the reading passage's contention that the tombs represent friendship between the two.

WORD REMINDER

distinguishable 구별할 수 있는   hostile 적대하는   sociable 사교적인   have an advantages over ~보다 유리하다   belligerent 적대적인
overtake 압도하다   reciprocal 상호적인   unearth 발굴하다   typical 전형적인   practice 관습   contention 주장   represent 나타내다

TIPS for SUCCESS

only의 도치

'~가 되어서야'라는 뜻을 가진 표현들 뒤의 절은 의문문 형태로 고쳐 주어야 한다.

Not until ~ / Only after ~ / Only when ~

마지막 단락의 문장을 살펴보자.

However, **only** 8,000 to 10,000 years ago did burial become a typical practice.

only라는 표현이 나왔으므로 burial became이 아닌 did burial become으로 쓴다. (2권 TEST 01 참조)

위의 문장에서 only를 포함한 구가 문장의 뒤에 왔다면 도치시킬 필요가 없어진다. 즉, However, burial became a typical practice only 8,000 to 10,000 years ago.로 쓸 수 있다.

또한 〈it is/was ~ that . . . 〉 문장(it is ~ that…은 강조를 할 때 쓰임)에서도 도치시킬 필요가 없다. 즉, It was **only** 8,000 to 10,000 years ago that burial became a typical practice.가 된다.

CUT　PASTE　UNDO　REDO　　　Hide Word Count : 0

Directions Read the question below. You have 30 minutes to plan, write, and revise your essay. Typically, an effective response will contain a minimum of 300 words.

Question

Do you agree or disagree with the following statement?

Parents should make decisions for their children's future.

Use specific reasons and examples to support your answer.

📝 NOTE-TAKING

AGREE

- *parents: more experienced* 부모: 더 많은 경험이 있음
    - easier paths → making mistakes / being frustrated / wasting time ✕ 쉬운 길 → 실수 / 좌질 / 시간 낭비 ✕
    - **Ex** studies: set a goal with parents → tend to adhere to it
        연구: 부모님과 같이 목표를 세우기 → 고수하는 경향이 있음
        → parents' involvement: important role 모의 참여도는 아주 중요한 역할을 함

- *more objective + rational* 좀더 객관적 + 논리적
    - children: own perspective → logical + insightful ✕ 아이들: 자기만의 관점 → 논리적 + 통찰력 ✕
    - **Ex** many want to become singers: competitive + difficult to get attention
        많은 이들이 가수가 되고 싶어함: 경쟁 + 주목 받기 어려움
        → if not talented → waste of effort + time 만약 소질이 없다면 → 노력 + 시간 낭비

INTRODUCTION

generalization: parents: guide children
일반화: 부모: 아이들을 지도

⬇

whether to stop making decisions for children's future or not
아이들을 위해 미래에 대한 결정을 해야 하는가 중단해야 하는가

⬇

thesis: agree (more experienced, objective)
논제: 찬성 (경험,객관적)

DISAGREE

- *choose own life* 스스로의 삶을 선택
    - own interests + potential 자신만의 관심사 + 잠재력
        Ex prospective job → guarantee happiness ✕ 전망이 밝은 직업 →행복을 보장 ✕
        → different standard + value of life 삶에 대한 다른 기준 + 가치

- *mistake → tolerable + acceptable* 실수 → 허용 + 받아들여짐
    - trial + error: critical + logical 시행착오: 비판적 + 논리적
        Ex parents → research, predict consequences, think of alternatives ✕ 부모 → 연구, 결과 예측, 대안 제시 ✕
        → responsibility + independent skills 책임감 + 독립심

INTRODUCTION

generalization: parents: guide children
일반화: 부모: 아이들을 지도

⬇

whether to stop making decisions for children's future or not
아이들을 위해 미래에 대한 결정을 해야 하는가 아닌가

⬇

thesis: disagree (own life, trial and error)
논제: 반대 (자신의 삶, 시행착오)

On top of providing endless love, motivation, and faith, parents are the ones who guide their children on the correct path. However, once their children reach a certain age, it is hard to say whether parents should let their children set their own goals. Though some people contend that parents should let children decide their own future, I strongly believe parents should help them make decisions. The reasons are that experiences are important to a person's life and that parents know their children well.

First of all, parents have lived longer than their children; oftentimes, they know easier and smoother paths that would save their children from making mistakes, becoming frustrated, or wasting time. Numerous studies have shown that children who set a goal with their parents tend to adhere to it compared to others who keep changing decisions which they make on their own. This clearly displays that parents' involvement in decision making plays a very important role.

Moreover, parents can be more objective and rational. Children tend to see the world from their own perspectives, making it hard to be logical or insightful. For instance, many children nowadays want to become singers as they do not know how competitive and difficult it is to get the attention of an entertainment company. If a child is not talented at singing, the time and the effort the child puts into it might be done in vain.

Trying many activities is a good way for children to find their real strengths and interests. However, not being able to succeed in a field can create a tremendous amount of frustration and stress. By identifying their children's strengths and weaknesses, parents can work together with their children and guide them. Children are also still too young to determine their future. Therefore, I strongly agree with the statement that parents should decide their children's future.

WORD REMINDER

motivation 동기 부여   path 길, 방향   reach 도달하다   oftentimes 종종   frustrated 낙담한   tend to ~하는 경향이 있다
adhere to ~을 고수하다   involvement 개입   objective 객관적인   rational 합리적인, 이성적인   perspective 관점   insightful 통찰력 있는
in vain 헛된

On top of provining endless love, motivation, and faith, parents are the ones who guide their children on the correct path. However, once their children reach a certain age, it is hard to say whether parents should let their children set their own goals. Though some people contend that parents should take part in making decision, I strongly believe children should decide their own future. One reason is that people have different interests and goals in their lives. Moreover, children learn from their mistakes.

First of all, no one can live a life on behalf of another. In other words, children should decide what they want to do in the future according to their own interests and potential. For instance, many parents want their children to have jobs that are secure and stable instead of jobs which are more challenging. However, having a prospective job does not guarantee that one will be content. Since each person has different standards and values on certain factors in life, it is up to children to make their decisions for themselves.

Moreover, it is tolerable and acceptable for children to make mistakes since there is enough time to make changes. For instance, through trial and error, children learn how to think critically and logically before coming up with a final decision. On the other hand, if parents intervene and make decisions for their children, their children will never learn to research, to predict consequences, or to bring forward alternatives.

Though some parents think they know their children better than anyone else, children should do what they truly wish to do based on their interests and talent. Even if what children have decided to do will lead to failure, they will still learn from their mistakes and will become more disciplined and self-supporting. Therefore, I strongly disagree with the statement that parents should decide the future for their children.

WORD REMINDER

take part in 참여하다   on behalf of 대신하여   potential 가능성, 잠재성   secure 안전한   stable 안정적인   prospective 기대되는
guarantee 보장하다   content 만족하다   tolerable 허용할 수 있는   trial and error 시행착오   critically 비평적으로   logically 논리적으로
intervene 개입하다   consequence 결과   bring forward 제시하다   failure 실패   disciplined 올바른   self-supporting 자립하는

1 Do you agree or disagree with the following statement? Video games provide benefits to children. Use specific reasons and examples to support your position.

다음 명제에 찬성하는가 반대하는가? 오락은 아이들에게 이득을 안겨준다. 구체적인 이유와 예를 들어 자신의 입장을 뒷받침하시오.

AGREE	DISAGREE
- learn strategy 전략을 배움	- can be addictive 중독될 수 있음
- way to socialize with peers today 오늘날 친구들과 어울리는 방법	- children need to spend more time on physical activities such as sports 아이들은 스포츠 같은 신체 운동에 더 많은 시간을 보내야 할 필요가 있음

2 Some people think parents should plan their children's leisure time carefully while others believe children should decide how to spend their own free time. Which do you prefer and why? Use specific reasons and examples to support your position.

어떤 이들은 아이들이 자신의 여기 시간을 어떻게 보낼 것인지 결정해야 한다고 믿는 반면 어떤 이들은 아이들의 여가 시간은 부모들이 계획해줘야 한다고 생각한다. 당신은 어떤 것을 선호하고 그 이유는 무엇인가? 구체적인 이유와 예를 들어 자신의 입장을 뒷받침하시오.

PARENTS	CHILDREN
- introduce how to plan spare time: children can learn to do the same in the future 여가 시간을 어떻게 계획하는지 보여줌: 아이들이 나중에 똑같이 하는 것을 배울 수 있음	- learn to make decisions on their own 스스로 결정을 내리는 것을 배움
- children have chances to experience various hobbies 아이들은 여러 가지 취미를 경험할 수 있는 기회가 있음	- discover and explore hobbies and interests 취미나 흥밋거리를 발견하고 개발할 수 있음

3 Which do you prefer, growing up in a large family with several brothers and sisters or being the only child in a small family? Use specific reasons and examples to support your position.

다음 중 어떤 것을 선호하는가, 많은 형제, 자매와 함께 대가족에서 자라는 것 혹은 작은 가족에서 외동으로 자라는 것? 구체적인 이유와 예를 들어 자신의 입장을 뒷받침하시오.

A LARGE FAMILY	THE ONLY CHILD
- learn to cooperate + harmonize 협동 + 화합을 배움	- can get more attention from parents 부모들로부터 더 많은 관심을 받음
- do not feel lonely 외롭지 않음	- no competition / conflicts with siblings 형제들과 경쟁 / 마찰 ✗

TOEFL® MAP
ACTUAL TEST — Writing 1

16

Accuracy is of the utmost importance in pharmacies. Getting the right medication to patients at the right time can greatly affect a patient's health. The development of pharmacy automation has had a significant impact on the pharmacy industry. Some newly automated processes include medication dispensing, the retrieval of medication, and storage. This new mechanization has advantages for both patients and pharmacies.

First off, since humans make mistakes, it is sometimes inevitable that a pharmacist will miscalculate and give the wrong medication or dosage. This can cause very serious problems and put patients at risk. In fact, in the United States, about 7,000 people die as a result of medication errors each year. The automated solution provides machines that are programmed with specific information on medications and guarantees accuracy and safety.

Pharmacy automation has not only changed the process of filling prescriptions but has also changed the role of pharmacists. Many people have experienced standing in a long line waiting for their turn because the pharmacist was busy filling prescriptions. Thanks to robots, pharmacists now have more time for direct patient care and can even provide clinical services such as immunizations, resulting in higher satisfaction among patients.

Managing and storing medication inventory is another crucial aspect in the pharmacy industry which benefits from advanced pharmacy technology. Robots can easily detect expired medicine and identify shortages. This helps pharmacists reorder medications on time. Checking on inventory has saved a tremendous amount of medicine from being disposed of every month. The system allows more effective staffing and inventory, which eventually leads to decreased waste and lower costs.

🎧 16-01

Directions You have 20 minutes to plan and write your response. Your response will be judged on the basis of the quality of your writing and on how well your response presents the points in the lecture and their relationship to the passage. Typically, an effective response will be 150-225 words.

Question Summarize the points made in the lecture, being sure to explain how they challenge specific claims made in the reading passage.

CUT   PASTE   UNDO   REDO   Hide Word Count : 0

Accuracy is of the utmost importance in pharmacies. Getting the right medication to patients at the right time can greatly affect a patient's health. The development of pharmacy automation has had a significant impact on the pharmacy industry. Some newly automated processes include medication dispensing, the retrieval of medication, and storage. This new mechanization has advantages for both patients and pharmacies.

First off, since humans make mistakes, it is sometimes inevitable that a pharmacist will miscalculate and give the wrong medication or dosage. This can cause very serious problems and put patients at risk. In fact, in the United States, about 7,000 people die as a result of medication errors each year. The automated solution provides machines that are programmed with specific information on medications and guarantees accuracy and safety.

Pharmacy automation has not only changed the process of filling prescriptions but has also changed the role of pharmacists. Many people have experienced standing in a long line waiting for their turn because the pharmacist was busy filling prescriptions. Thanks to robots, pharmacists now have more time for direct patient care and can even provide clinical services such as immunizations, resulting in higher satisfaction among patients.

Managing and storing medication inventory is another crucial aspect in the pharmacy industry which benefits from advanced pharmacy technology. Robots can easily detect expired medicine and identify shortages. This helps pharmacists reorder medications on time. Checking on inventory has saved a tremendous amount of medicine from being disposed of every month. The system allows more effective staffing and inventory, which eventually leads to decreased waste and lower costs.

READING

PA → advantageous to patients and pharmacies 약품의 자동화: 환자와 약국 모두에게 이익

❶ computerization processes (medication dispensing, retrieval of medication, storage) → accuracy + safety 과정의 전산화 (약 조제, 회수, 보관) → 정확성 + 안전성

- pharmacist: possible to miscalculate + give wrong medication → patient at risk
  약사: 잘못된 계산 + 약을 잘못 제조 → 환자가 위험에 빠질 수 있음

 The accuracy and the safety that the system provides will reduce deaths caused by medication errors.

❷ role of pharmacist: direct patient care + clinical services (immunization)
약사의 역할: 환자의 전속 케어 + 병원 업무 (예방 접종)

- PA saves time → satisfaction 약품의 자동화는 시간을 절약해 줌 → 만족

 Robots will make it feasible for pharmacists to provide patients with direct patient care and even clinical services.

❸ managing + storing 관리 + 보관

- robots: detect expired medicine / identify shortages → reorder medication on time
  로봇: 유효기간이 지난 약을 감지 / 부족한 물품 구분 → 제시간에 재주문 가능

- effective management in staffing + inventory → waste ↓ + costs ↓ 효율적인 인력 + 재고 관리 → 쓰레기 ↓ + 가격 ↓

 Effective management by an automation will result in less waste and lower costs.

WORD REMINDER

accuracy 정확   utmost 최대한   pharmacy 약국, 약학, 약품   medication 약물   automation 자동화   impact 영향   dispense 조제하다
retrieval 회수   mechanization 기계화   inevitable 불가피   dosage 복용량   guarantee 보장하다   fill a prescription 처방약을 조제하다
thanks to 덕분에   immunization 예방 접종   inventory 재고   crucial 중요한   detect 찾아내다   expire 만료되다   shortage 부족
tremendous 엄청난   dispose 폐기하다

LISTENING

PA: developed in the 1960s 약품의 자동화는 1960년대에 발달됨

❶ machine → operated by humans 기계 ← 사람에 의해 움직임

∴ error with input / malfunction → serious consequences 잘못된 입력 / 고장 → 심각한 문제

 If a pharmacist makes a mistake, it can bring about serious consequences.

❷ pharmacy needs backup plan 약국은 백업 계획이 필요함

- more time + staffing 더 많은 시간 + 인력 필요

 To avoid any disorganized situations, pharmacies should spend a lot of time and staffing making arrangements for alternatives.

❸ person needs to refill robots 사람이 로봇을 (기계를) 다시 채워야 함

- robots: expensive ($8,000-$50,000) → not worth investing so much money in
  로봇: 비쌈 ($8,000-$50,000) → 그렇게 많은 돈을 투자할 가치가 없음

Inventory management is still needed since an authorized person or pharmacist should check for refilling or maintenance.

WORD REMINDER

implement 실행하다   growing 증가하는   trend 현상   efficiency 효율, 효과   operation 운영   downside 불리한 면
take into consideration 고려하다   reliable 신뢰할 만한   in the first place 우선   input 입력   malfunction 오작동   consequence 결과
overall 종합적으로   break down 고장나다   adequate 적당한   chaotic 혼돈 상태인   alternative 대안   skeptical 회의적인   refill 다시 채우다
authorized 권한이 부여된   present (서술적) 있는   maintenance (유지) 보수   stock 재고

The lecturer argues that the advantages of pharmacy automation are questionable. This directly challenges the reading passage's claim that pharmacy automation is innovative and improves the pharmaceutical industry.

First of all, if a pharmacist makes a mistake, it can bring about serious consequences. According to the professor, the number of deaths mentioned in the reading passage includes both errors made by pharmacists and robots. This contradicts the reading passage's claim that the accuracy and the safety that the system provides will reduce deaths caused by medication errors.

Furthermore, the lecturer contends that there is a possibility of machines going out of order. To avoid any disorganized situations, pharmacies should spend a lot of time and staffing making arrangements for alternatives. Thus, the preparations will take up very much time, leaving less time available for pharmacists with patients. This casts doubt on the reading passage's claim that robots will make it feasible for pharmacists to provide patients with direct patient care and even clinical services.

Finally, inventory management is still needed since an authorized person or pharmacist should check for refilling or maintenance. Furthermore, robots are costly to purchase. This goes against the reading passage's claim that effective management through automation will result in less waste and lower costs.

WORD REMINDER

innovative 혁신적인   bring about 일으키다   arrangement 계획   feasible 실현 가능한   costly 값이 비싼

CUT   PASTE   UNDO   REDO   Hide Word Count : 0

Directions Read the question below. You have 30 minutes to plan, write, and revise your essay. Typically, an effective response will contain a minimum of 300 words.

Question

Do you agree or disagree with the following statement?

Technology has made people happier than before.

Use specific reasons and examples to support your answer.

📝 NOTE-TAKING

- *many electronic devices* 많은 전자 기기
  - convenience + vast amount of info 편리함 + 많은 양의 정보
    Ex smartphones 스마트폰
      → useful data + applications 유용한 자료 + 애플리케이션

- *active interactions between people* 사람들 사이의 활발한 교류
  - able to socialize w/others around the world 세계의 다른 이들과 사귈 수 있음
    Ex emails 이메일
      → access to communicate w/those far away 멀리 있는 이들과 의사소통 가능

INTRODUCTION

generalization: development of tech
일반화: 과학 기술의 발달

⬇

life ➡ more convenient
삶 → 더욱 편리해짐

⬇

thesis: agree (more facilitated, globalized)
논제: 동의 (더욱 용이해짐, 세계화)

- *feeling emotionally close*✕ 친밀감 ×
  - people: more cautious about privacy 사람들: 사생활에 대해 더욱 경계함
    Ex CCTV: guarantees safety CCTV: 안전을 보장
      → taken away freedom 자유를 빼앗음

- *environmental problems* 환경 문제
  - electromagnetic waves + noxious materials 전자파 + 해로운 물질
    Ex greenhouse gases: global warming 이산화탄소: 지구 온난화
      → natural disasters 자연 재해

INTRODUCTION

generalization: development of tech
일반화: 과학 기술의 발달

⬇

life ➡ more convenient
삶 → 더욱 편리해짐

⬇

thesis: disagree (invasion of privacy, environmental damage)
논제: 반대 (사생활 침해, 환경 파괴)

With the development of technology, life has become more convenient than ever before. Accordingly, people have learned to adapt themselves to this fast-paced world. Some people contend that technology has made people's lives more difficult; however, for two reasons, I strongly believe that it has made people much happier. First, technology has made life much more facilitated. Secondly, the world has become globalized thanks to technological improvements.

First of all, technology has produced numerous electronic devices such as TVs and computers. This situation has exposed many people to a vast quantity of information as well as made their lives more convenient. For example, a number of people possess smartphones nowadays. With their phones, people have easy access to useful data such as directions and information regarding specific products. Many applications are being developed in order to satisfy the needs of consumers. For example, students use apps to get help with studying. Hence, it would be difficult to imagine life without electronic devices.

In addition, interactions between people of different backgrounds have become commonplace. Since the advent of electronic communication devices, people have been able to socialize with others around the world. For instance, most people have email accounts which many of them check a few times a day. Emails has made it feasible for people to communicate with one another even when they are far apart. People can also keep in touch with one another by uploading photos and videos on social media.

It is true that technology has also caused some problems, including the invasion of people's privacy. However, experts are in the process of searching for corresponding solutions, and governments are passing new laws to protect citizens. Many electronic devices have assisted people in enjoying more convenient lifestyles. Furthermore, technological improvements allow people to socialize with others even in remote areas. For the above reasons, I agree with the statement that technology has made people happier than before.

WORD REMINDER

adapt 적응시키다　fast-paced 빠른 속도의　facilitate 용이하게 하다　numerous 많은　device 기계　expose 노출시키다　vast 막대한
quantity 양　possess 소유하다　interaction 상호 작용　commonplace 흔한 일　advent 출현　socialize 사회화하다　account 계정
feasible 가능한　invasion 침해　corresponding 상응하는　assist 돕다

ACTUAL TEST 16

TIPS for SUCCESS

현재완료 Present Perfect
현재완료의 용법 중 하나는 과거의 어느 시점부터 현재까지 이어 온 것에 대해 쓰는 것이다. 마지막 단락의 문장을 살펴보자.
Many electronic devices **have assisted** people in enjoying more convenient lifestyles.
전자 기기가 이전의 어느 시점부터 오늘날까지 사람들을 도와주고 있다는 의미를 담고 있다. 자세한 정보 제공을 위해 since yesterday 등
의 일이 발발했던 특정 시간 또는 for two years라는 기간을 쓸 수도 있다.

With the development of technology, life has become more convenient than ever before. Accordingly, people have learned to adapt themselves to this fast-paced world. Some people contend that technology has made people happier; however, for two reasons, I strongly believe it has made life more difficult. Firstly, the invasion of privacy caused by some technology has led to negative consequences. In addition, it causes a lot of environmental damage.

First of all, many people do not feel emotionally close to one another. Although it may appear that the Internet has made people closer, the reality is that it has caused many people to become more cautious with their privacy. For instance, surveillance cameras have improved safety for many people. However, the cameras have also taken freedom away from people by monitoring what they do in public places. Thus, people continuously feel that they are being watched by others and get stressed out.

In addition, technology has created numerous environmental concerns. Many electronic devices themselves emit harmful electromagnetic waves, and many noxious materials are produced during the manufacturing process. Moreover, companies constantly produce new devices, encouraging consumers to keep purchasing updated versions of the products. To illustrate, the electricity required to power electronic devices, including cell phones and televisions, is drawn from power plants, which create the greenhouse gases that have increased the average temperature on the Earth, resulting in global warming. The consequences are natural disasters such as violent storms and rising sea levels.

It is true that life has become very convenient and comfortable thanks to constantly developing technology. Conversely, there are far more problems than there are advantages regarding the matter. Technology has made people feel uneasy that someone may be watching them. It has also brought about tremendous environmental damage. For the above reasons, I firmly disagree with the statement that technology has made people happier than before.

> **WORD REMINDER**

cautious 조심성 있는   take away from ~에게서 빼앗다   electromagnetic wave 전자파   power 동력을 공급하다   draw 끌어당기다
power plant 발전소   disaster 재앙   regarding ~에 관해서   uneasy 불안한   bring about 야기하다

▌ TIPS for SUCCESS

강조 Emphasis

말하고자 하는 단어를 다시 한 번 강조하고 싶을 때는 재귀대명사를 쓰는 경우가 많다. 세 번째 단락의 문장을 살펴보자.

Many electronic devices **themselves** emit harmful electromagnetic waves, ~

Many electronic devices emit harmful electromagnetic waves라고 표현해도 문장에 전혀 이상이 없지만, 다른 것도 아닌 전자 기기가 방출했다는 점을 강조하고 싶을 경우 themselves를 쓸 수 있다. 만약 An electronic device라는 단수명사가 쓰였다면 이에 상응하는 itself를 쓰면 된다.

강조하고자 하는 것이 동사일 때에는, 복수명사, 단수명사에 따라 조동사 do 또는 does를 쓴 후 동사 원형을 쓰면 된다.

Many electronic devices emit harmful electromagnetic waves라는 부분에서 '정말 방출한다'라는 뜻을 부여하여 강조하려면 Many electronic devices **do** emit harmful electromagnetic waves라고 쓸 수 있다. An electronic device라는 단수명사가 쓰였다면 이에 상응하는 does emit을 쓰면 된다.

1 Technology has made children less creative today compared to children in the past.
과학 기술은 아이들의 창의력을 과거에 비해 떨어뜨린다.

AGREE	DISAGREE
- automated: no need to experiment / manipulate around 자동화: 이리저리 실험하며 바꿀 필요가 없음 - electronic devices outcompete books: imagination skill ↓ 전자 기기가 책을 능가: 상상력 ↓	- complexity: leads to further development 복잡성: 더 나은 발전으로 인도 - many tools to use from 사용할 수 있는 많은 도구

2 Technology developed to make our lives easier has actually made our lives more complicated.
우리의 삶을 보다 용이하게 만들기 위해 개발된 과학 기술은 우리의 삶을 오히려 복잡하게 만들었다.

AGREE	DISAGREE
- too many options to choose from 선택의 폭이 너무 많아짐 - need to update new products + instructions 새로운 제품 + 사용법을 업데이트해야 함 ex) smartphones 스마트폰	- more convenient w/automated machines 자동화된 기계로 더욱 편리해짐 ex) cars 자동차 - the Internet: easier to get info needed 인터넷: 필요한 정보를 보다 쉽게 얻을 수 있음

3 Scientists are responsible for their inventions that have negative effects.
과학자들은 부정적인 영향을 끼친 그들의 발명품에 대한 책임이 있다.

AGREE	DISAGREE
- environmental destruction 환경 파괴 ex) pollutants from factories 공장에서 나오는 오염 물질 - crime ↑ 범죄 ↑ ex) arms 무기	- more positive influences: inventions to make life more convenient 더 많은 긍정적인 영향: 우리의 삶을 더 편리하게 해 준 발명품 - intention: to bring benefits to the world 의도: 세계에 이득을 가져오기 위함

TOEFL® MAP

ACTUAL TEST Writing 1

17

From approximately 1300 to 1850, much of the planet, especially the Northern Hemisphere, endured extremely cold temperatures. This period is called the Little Ice Age.

No one knows what caused the Little Ice Age. There is some speculation that the cooling of the Gulf Stream caused temperatures to drop. The Gulf Stream is a warm-water current that runs up the eastern coast of North America and then crosses the Atlantic Ocean and goes by Northern Europe. Everywhere the Gulf Stream flows, the nearby lands experience warmer-than-normal temperatures. Prior to the Little Ice Age was a time called the Medieval Warming Period. Warm temperatures during it may have caused glaciers to melt and to release ice-cold water into the Gulf Stream. Because of that, the Gulf Stream could no longer keep the temperatures of the areas it passed by warm.

Occasionally, volcanic eruptions have caused temperatures to drop on a global scale. For instance, the 1883 eruption of Krakatoa and the 1815 eruption of Tambora both made temperatures around the world decrease. It is possible that a volcanic eruption—or multiple eruptions—on a gargantuan scale sent dark clouds of ash into the atmosphere, which blocked the sun's light and started the Little Ice Age.

One notable feature of the 1300s was a decrease in the population in Asia and Europe. This is mostly attributable to the Black Death, a plague that killed at least one third of Europe's population and countless millions elsewhere. As the global population decreased, some areas became empty of people, so forests begin growing back. Trees use carbon dioxide to undergo photosynthesis, their food-making process. So many new trees might have rapidly depleted the amount of carbon dioxide in the atmosphere. This could have led to global cooling and brought about the mini-ice age.

🎧 17-01

Directions You have 20 minutes to plan and write your response. Your response will be judged on the basis of the quality of your writing and on how well your response presents the points in the lecture and their relationship to the passage. Typically, an effective response will be 150-225 words.

Question Summarize the points made in the lecture, being sure to explain how they cast doubt on specific points made in the reading passage.

CUT   PASTE   UNDO   REDO   Hide Word Count : 0

From approximately 1300 to 1850, much of the planet, especially the Northern Hemisphere, endured extremely cold temperatures. This period is called the Little Ice Age.

No one knows what caused the Little Ice Age. There is some speculation that the cooling of the Gulf Stream caused temperatures to drop. The Gulf Stream is a warm-water current that runs up the eastern coast of North America and then crosses the Atlantic Ocean and goes by Northern Europe. Everywhere the Gulf Stream flows, the nearby lands experience warmer-than-normal temperatures. Prior to the Little Ice Age was a time called the Medieval Warming Period. Warm temperatures during it may have caused glaciers to melt and to release ice-cold water into the Gulf Stream. Because of that, the Gulf Stream could no longer keep the temperatures of the areas it passed by warm.

Occasionally, volcanic eruptions have caused temperatures to drop on a global scale. For instance, the 1883 eruption of Krakatoa and the 1815 eruption of Tambora both made temperatures around the world decrease. It is possible that a volcanic eruption—or multiple eruptions—on a gargantuan scale sent dark clouds of ash into the atmosphere, which blocked the sun's light and started the Little Ice Age.

One notable feature of the 1300s was a decrease in the population in Asia and Europe. This is mostly attributable to the Black Death, a plague that killed at least one third of Europe's population and countless millions elsewhere. As the global population decreased, some areas became empty of people, so forests begin growing back. Trees use carbon dioxide to undergo photosynthesis, their food-making process. So many new trees might have rapidly depleted the amount of carbon dioxide in the atmosphere. This could have led to global cooling and brought about the mini-ice age.

 **NOTE-TAKING**

three causes of the extreme cold during the Little Ice Age
소빙하기 동안의 극한에 대한 세 가지 이유

❶ *cooling of the Gulf Stream* 멕시코 만류의 냉각
- Medieval Warming Period: warm temperature → glacier melt → cold water into the Gulf Stream
  중세 온난기: 따뜻한 기후 → 녹은 빙하 → 멕시코 만류로의 차가운 물

  Paraphrasing Example Glaciers which melted during the Medieval Warming Period sent cold water into the Gulf Stream, decreasing the overall temperature of the Earth.

❷ *volcanic eruptions* 화산 폭발
- dark clouds + ash into atmosphere → blocked sun's light 먹구름 + 재를 대기로 보냄 → 태양 빛을 막음

  Paraphrasing Example The scarcity of sunlight caused by the dark clouds and the ash from the volcanic eruptions caused a significant temperature drop.

❸ *the Black Death → human population* ↓ 흑사병 → 인구 ↓
- reforestation: deplete CO_2 → global cooling 재조림: 이산화탄소를 고갈시킴 → 세계적인 냉각

  Paraphrasing Example Depleted carbon dioxide from reduced logging caused the Little Ice Age.

WORD REMINDER

hemisphere 반구   endure 견디다   speculation 추측   current 해류   prior to ~에 앞서   glacier 빙하   release 방출하다   eruption 폭발
scale 규모   gargantuan 거대한   notable 주목할 만한   feature 특성   attributable ~의 탓으로 돌릴 수 있는   plague 전염병
countless 셀 수 없는   undergo 겪다   photosynthesis 광합성   deplete 고갈시키다   bring about 야기하다

the cause of the Little Ice Age: unknown 소빙하기의 원인: 알 수 없음

❶ *many parts of Europe go through unreasonably warm weather*
유럽의 많은 부분은 이상할 정도로 따뜻한 기후를 겪음
∴ theory → applicable 이론 → 적용 가능
- S. Hem (New Zealand + S. Africa): no Gulf Stream → experienced the Little Ice Age
  남반구 (뉴질랜드 + 남아프리카): 멕시코 만류 ✕ → 소빙하기를 겪었음
  ∴ theory → inapplicable 이론 → 적용 가능 ✕

  Paraphrasing Example The theory would have applied only in certain regions of the Earth.

❷ *Tambora: "the year w/out summer"* 탐보라: '여름이 없었던 해'
- low temp: lasted for a year or two 낮은 온도: 1~2년 동안 지속
- the Little Ice Age: lasted for centuries 소빙하기: 수세기 동안 지속
  → only supervolcano: possible / but didn't occur 오직 대화산 폭발 때만 가능함 / 그러나 일어나지 않았음

  Paraphrasing Example Only supervolcanoes could cause a temperature drop lasting for centuries.

❸ *forest didn't grow back so fast* 그렇게 빨리 재조림화되지 않았음
- the Little Ice Age should've ended soon 소빙하기가 빨리 끝났어야 함
  → population: back to pre-Black Death lev → deforestation 인구: 흑사병 전 수치로 돌아갔음 → 삼림 벌채

  Paraphrasing Example The speed of the regrowth of the forest could not have affected the temperature.

WORD REMINDER

harsh 가혹한   bleak 처절한   considerably 상당히   unseasonably 때 아닌   account for ~을 설명하다   strictly 엄밀히   last 지속하다
geologist 지질학자   positive 확신하고 있는   reforestation 재조림   deforest 살림을 벌채하다   subsequently 그 후에   rule out 제외하다

The lecturer argues that the cause of the Little Ice Age is unknown and rebuts the reading passage's claim that there are three causes of the extreme cold during the period in question.

First, the theory would have applied only in certain regions of the Earth. Many parts of Europe by the Gulf Stream had unusually warm weather; nevertheless, the Southern Hemisphere also experienced the Little Ice Age. This contradicts the reading passage's claim that glaciers which melted during the Medieval Warming Period sent cold water into the Gulf Stream, decreasing the overall temperature of the Earth.

On top of that, the lecturer contends that only supervolcanoes could cause a temperature drop lasting for centuries. However, there is no evidence that a supervolcano erupted during the period. This refutes the reading passage's claim that the scarcity of sunlight caused by the dark clouds and the ash from the volcanic eruptions caused a significant temperature drop.

Finally, the speed of the regrowth of the forest could not have affected the temperature, and the Little Ice Age should have ended as soon as the population rebounded to the level it had reached before the Black Death. This contradicts the reading passage's idea that depleted carbon dioxide from reduced logging caused the Little Ice Age.

WORD REMINDER

apply 적용하다   unusually 이상하게   overall 전체에 걸친   scarcity 부족   rebound 돌이키다   reach 도달하다   logging 재목 벌채

TIPS for SUCCESS

돌발 상황

통합형 에세이를 쓸 때, 긴 시험의 마지막 부분에서 오는 피곤함 또는 정말 내용이 어려워서 못 듣는 경우가 생길 수 있다. 내용을 듣고 세부적인 설명이나 예를 적으면 좋겠지만 그러지 못했다면 읽기 지문의 내용을 반대로 생각해 보는 것이 하나의 방법이 될 수 있다. 아무것도 쓰여 있지 않은 화면을 전송하는 것은 결코 해서는 안 되는 일임을 명심하자.

CUT PASTE UNDO REDO   Hide Word Count : 0

Directions Read the question below. You have 30 minutes to plan, write, and revise your essay. Typically, an effective response will contain a minimum of 300 words.

Question

Do you agree or disagree with the following statement?

The best way to learn about a foreign country is to read newspapers and magazines.

Use specific reasons and examples to support your answer.

 **NOTE-TAKING**

- *present situations* 현재 상황

  Ex newspapers + magazines about the Winter Olympics in Vancouver 밴쿠버의 동계 올림픽에 관한 신문 + 잡지
    - → historical + geographical reasons for superiority in winter sports
      겨울 스포츠의 우수함에 대한 역사적 + 지리적 이유
    - → political issues + opinions of local people 정치적 사안 + 현지인들의 의견

- *important source* 중요한 출처

  - mirror local lifestyles 현지 생활 방식을 반영

    Ex Yosemite: snow gear + concerns about preservation of environment
    요세미티: 눈 장비 + 환경 보호에 관한 관심
      - → exact reflection 정확한 반영

INTRODUCTION

generalization: many ways to learn about a foreign country
일반화: 외국에 대해 배우는 많은 방법

⬇

visiting a museum, reading books, watching TV programs
박물관 방문, 독서, TV 프로그램 시청

⬇

thesis: agree (current issues, most up-to-date sources)
논제: 동의 (현재 이슈, 가장 최신 자료)

- *freedom of journalism: not always* 언론의 자유: 항상 그렇지는 않음

  - controlled by government 정부에 의해 통제됨

    Ex communist country: reviews before releasing 공산 국가: 공개하기 전 검토
      - → a way of indoctrinating citizens 국민들을 세뇌하는 방법

- *biased / subjective* 편향 / 주관적

  - can only be used as a supplementary source 보충 자료로만 사용될 수 있음

    Ex newspapers + magazines didn't reflect actual lifestyles + opinions of people
    신문 + 잡지: 실제 생활 방식이나 사람들의 의견을 반영 x
      - → subjectivity of a writer / editor: limitation 작가 / 편집자의 주관성: 한계

INTRODUCTION

generalization: many ways to learn about a foreign country
일반화: 외국에 대해 배우는 많은 방법

⬇

visiting a museum, reading books, watching TV programs
박물관 방문, 독서, TV 프로그램 시청

⬇

thesis: disagree (intervention of government, bias)
논제: 반대 (정부의 개입, 편견)

CUT PASTE UNDO REDO

Hide Word Count : 384

There are many ways to learn about a foreign country. People may visit museums, read related books, or watch TV programs on the country they would like to know about. While some people contend that visiting a country is the most effective means to learn about it, I strongly believe reading newspapers and magazines helps one gain a full understanding of a country. For one thing, press coverage reflects the current issues in a nation. In addition, newspapers and magazines are the most up-to-date sources available.

Firstly, readers can learn about the present situation in a nation by reading newspapers and magazines. For instance, I learned about important local events, including the Winter Olympics, before traveling to Vancouver. Since the newspapers and the magazines dealt with the historical and geographical reasons why Canadians are skilled at winter sports, I was able to understand the culture of the country. The newspapers covered political issues as well as the opinions of the people residing in Vancouver. Had I only read books about the place, I would not have had a chance to find out about the ongoing stories of the time.

On top of that, magazine ads serve as an important source of knowledge about a country. This is true because they directly mirror local lifestyles. To illustrate, when I was preparing for a trip to Yosemite, I saw a lot of ads about snow gear, including snow tires, in magazines and newspapers. Moreover, there were numerous articles concerning the preservation of the natural environment. When I actually got there, the place had a tremendous amount of snow at that time, and I was surprised to see the local people taking great care to protect the natural resources.

It is true that direct experience provides people with specific information about a country. However, it may be infeasible to visit every region of a nation, and since each region has its own culture, one cannot always get a complete picture of the various regional cultures. Conversely, newspapers and magazines reflect the most up-to-date situations in a nation. Furthermore, many ads in newspapers and magazines display the culture of a particular place. For the above reasons, I firmly agree with the idea that the best way to learn about a foreign country is to read newspapers and magazines.

▶ **WORD REMINDER**

means 방법 press coverage 언론 보도 reflect 반영하다 current 현재의 up-to-date 최신의 source 정보원 present 현재의 local 한 지방 특유의 geographical 지리적인 be skilled in ~에 능숙하다 political 정치적인 reside 거주하다 ongoing 진행 중인 mirror 반영하다 gear 장비 article 기사 preservation 보존 get 도달하다 tremendous 대단한 resource 자원 infeasible 실행 불가능한 particular 특정한

ACTUAL TEST **17**

TIPS for SUCCESS

시제 일치

특히 예를 쓸 경우, 시제 일치에 신경 쓰도록 하자. 위의 글에서 두 번째와 세 번째 단락의 예는 모두 과거로 쓰이고 있다. 시제 일치를 시키는 데 자신이 없다면, note-taking의 목적으로 받는 종이에 크게 '과거' 혹은 '현재완료' 등을 써놓으면 도움이 될 수 있다.

There are many ways to learn about a foreign country. People may visit museums, read related books, or watch TV programs on the country they would like to know about. Though some people contend that reading publications such as newspapers and magazines helps them understand a country better than direct experience, I strongly refute this argument. For one thing, governments often intervene before publications are released. In addition, newspapers and magazines can be biased or subjective depending on the writers or editors.

Firstly, newspapers and magazines do not always take advantage of the freedom of journalism. Often, they are controlled by political as well as local situations in a nation. For instance, every communist country controls the press, and the government deliberately reviews press releases before they are printed. Thus, rather than representing the truth, newspapers and magazines can be used as ways to indoctrinate citizens.

On top of that, newspapers and magazines are often biased and reflect only certain sides of an issue, suggesting that they can only serve as supplementary sources in understanding a foreign country. In fact, there is nothing better than getting direct experience. To illustrate, I read local newspapers and magazines from Canada before visiting for a holiday. However, I was very surprised to realize the differences in terms of the actual lifestyles and opinions of local people. Therefore, the subjectivity of writers and editors poses limitations on the press.

It is true that newspapers and magazines exist for the local people of a country; hence, they can display particular ideas or tastes of a region. However, as some articles and advertisements are written or reviewed by private companies or individuals, they can be rather exaggerated or neglect the actual truth. Furthermore, the intervention of the government and the subjectivity of the press can make it even harder to grasp the actual situation in a nation. For the above reasons, I firmly disagree with the statement that the best way to learn about a foreign country is to read newspapers and magazines.

WORD REMINDER

publication 출판물 intervene 개입하다 release 발매하다 biased 편견을 지닌 subjective 주관적인 editor 편집자 journalism 언론계
communist 공산주의 control 통제하다 deliberately 신중히 press release 보도 자료 represent 나타내다 indoctrinate 주입하다
supplementary 보충하는 limitation 한계 display 나타내다 exaggerate 과장하다 neglect 무시하다

TIPS for SUCCESS

'~에 관해서'라는 표현은 에세이에서 많이 쓰이는데, 많은 학생들이 about을 가장 먼저 떠올린다. 같은 뜻을 가진 다른 표현들을 살펴보자.

Moreover, there were numerous articles **concerning** the preservation of the natural environment. (Agree: P3)

However, I was very surprised to realize the differences **in terms of** the actual lifestyles and opinions of local people. (Disagree: P3)

People may visit museums, read related books, or watch TV programs **on** the country they would like to know about. (Agree: P1)

그 외에도, regarding, in regard to, as to, as for 등이 있으며, 이 표현들은 모두 명사, 동명사, 명사절, 대명사를 동반할 수 있다. in regard to 또는 as to 다음에는 동사원형이 올 수 없다는 것을 기억하자.

1 Taking prompt action is better than planning carefully to solve a problem.

문제를 해결하는데 있어 신속한 조치를 취하는 것이 신중한 계획을 세우는 것보다 낫다.

AGREE	DISAGREE
- taking time might worsen the problem 시간을 끌면 문제를 악화시킬 수 있음 - saving time 시간 절약	- a possibility of making mistakes 실수를 할 가능성 ex) Haste makes waste. 서두르면 일을 그르친다. - more organized → time saving 더욱 체계적 → 시간 절약

2 It is more important to give rewards to students according to their effort, not their results.

결과보다는 노력에 따라 학생들에게 상을 주는 것이 더 중요하다.

AGREE	DISAGREE
- sometimes a result doesn't reflect one's effort / result: sometimes depends on one's luck 가끔 결과가 노력을 반영하지는 않음 / 결과: 가끔 개인의 운에 좌우됨 - a way to motivate a student to try harder 더욱 열심히 노력하도록 학생을 격려하는 방법	- student might be putting effort in a wrong way → may need to change his or her way of studying 학생들이 잘못된 방법으로 노력하는 것일 수 있음 → 그들의 공부 방법을 바꾸어 야 할 수도 있음 - society: recognition → based on results 사회: 인정 → 결과에 토대

3 Giving grades promotes learning for students. 성적을 주는 것은 학생들의 학습을 증진시킨다.

AGREE	DISAGREE
- grades: recognition for performance + effort 점수: 결과 + 노력에 대한 인정 - motivation 동기 부여	- may discourage students 학생들을 좌절시킬 수 있음 - getting a good grade may be the only goal for a student 좋은 점수를 얻는 것이 학생의 유일한 목표가 될 수 있음

4 People should read newspapers in order to understand the world's circumstances since the news on TV does not provide viewers with enough information.

TV는 충분한 정보를 제공하지 않으므로 사람들이 세계 정세를 이해하기 위해서는 신문을 읽어야 한다.

AGREE	DISAGREE
- news on TV: limited amount of time → only major issues TV 뉴스: 정해진 시간 → 주요 뉴스만 다룸 - more specific descriptions on each article 각 기사에 대한 자세한 묘사	- TV: summarizes important points TV: 중요한 요점을 요약 - visual image: helps viewers understand other cultures more easily 영상: 시청자들이 다른 문화를 좀 더 쉽게 이해하도록 도와 줌

ACTUAL TEST **17**

TOEFL® MAP
ACTUAL
TEST Writing 1

18

There are more than eight million living species on the Earth, but only 1.2 million species have been identified. Each year, about 18,000 new species are discovered and named. In taxonomy, this naming system is called nomenclature, the choosing or devising names for newly found species. There are some rules to this procedure: The name must be unique, the name cannot be rude, and the species cannot be named after the scientist who discovered it.

Perhaps, the most common way to name a species is to choose a name based on its special characteristics. This can tell people about the creature itself. There are a variety of combinations and possibilities as the features include the species' shapes, colors, sizes, or anything that is noteworthy.

Another popular method of choosing a name for a species is to use the name of a famous person. For example, it could be someone who has contributed a lot in a field, a celebrity, or a notable figure whom the creature has some resemblance to. Some creatures are even named after mythological figures.

Some names also make it feasible to guess where the species are from or discovered. Some are easy to recognize—some of which are africanus, americanus, or madagascariensis—while others require a little more insight. For example, chinensis would refer to species from China, and indicus would refer to species from India. The names can refer to more specific areas such as a river, town, or cave as well.

🎧 18-01

Directions You have 20 minutes to plan and write your response. Your response will be judged on the basis of the quality of your writing and on how well your response presents the points in the lecture and their relationship to the passage. Typically, an effective response will be 150-225 words.

Question Summarize the points made in the lecture, being sure to specifically explain how they support the explanations in the reading passage.

| CUT | PASTE | UNDO | REDO | Hide Word Count : 0 |

There are more than eight million living species on the Earth, but only 1.2 million species have been identified. Each year, about 18,000 new species are discovered and named. In taxonomy, this naming system is called nomenclature, the choosing or devising names for newly found species. There are some rules to this procedure: The name must be unique, the name cannot be rude, and the species cannot be named after the scientist who discovered it.

Perhaps, the most common way to name a species is to choose a name based on its special characteristics. This can tell people about the creature itself. There are a variety of combinations and possibilities as the features include the species' shapes, colors, sizes, or anything that is noteworthy.

Another popular method of choosing a name for a species is to use the name of a famous person. For example, it could be someone who has contributed a lot in a field, a celebrity, or a notable figure whom the creature has some resemblance to. Some creatures are even named after mythological figures.

Some names also make it feasible to guess where the species are from or discovered. Some are easy to recognize—some of which are africanus, americanus, or madagascariensis—while others require a little more insight. For example, chinensis would refer to species from China, and indicus would refer to species from India. The names can refer to more specific areas such as a river, town, or cave as well.

 **NOTE-TAKING**

READING

nomenclature: choosing a name for a newly discovered species
명명법: 새로 발견된 종의 이름을 고름

❶ *special traits: species' shapes, colors, sizes* 특별한 특징: 종의 모양, 색깔, 사이즈

   – many combinations + possibilities 다수의 조합 + 가능

   Paraphrasing Example   Special physical traits can contribute to giving the new species the new name.

❷ *famous person: contributed to a field, celebrity, notable figure, mythological figure*
유명인: 그 분야의 공헌한 사람, 유명 인사, 주목할 만한 인물, 신화적 인물

   Paraphrasing Example   A new species can be named after a famous or notable figure.

❸ *place: where the species is discovered or lives* 장소: 어디서 그 종이 발견되었는지 혹은 사는지

   Ex chinensis: from China, indicus: from India chinensis: 중국에서 발견, indicus: 인도에서 발견

   – specific place: river, town, cave 세부적인 장소: 강, 마을, 동굴

   Paraphrasing Example   One can make a hypothesis in terms of habitats or origins of species.

WORD REMINDER

taxonomy 분류법 system 체계, 제도 nomenclature 명명법 devise 고안하다 procedure 절차, 과정 combination 조합
noteworthy 주목할 만한 contribute 기여하다 celebrity 유명인 notable 주목할 만한 figure 인물 resemblance 유사
mythological 신화적인 실행할 수 있는 insight 통찰력 refer 가리키다

LISTENING

3 ways to name a new species and examples 새로운 종에 이름을 붙이는 3가지 방법 + 예들

❶ *external feature* 외관의 특징

   Ex gelae (fungus beetle): gelae rol, gelae fish, gelae balae → look like jelly beans
   예) 젤리 (곰팡이 딱정벌레): 젤리 롤, 젤리 피쉬, 젤리 벨리 → 젤리 빈처럼 생겼음

   Paraphrasing Example   Example of amusing names that are related to the species' appearance.

❷ *famous person* 유명인

   Ex dermophis donaldtrumpi: moth / former U.S. president 더모피스 도널드트럼피: 나방 / 미국 전 대통령

   – head: covered with yellowish white scales 머리: 누르스름한 하얀 비늘로 덮여있음

   Paraphrasing Example   A moth named after a former U.S. president is another example that shows how a species can get a name from a notable figure.

❸ *place: ex) anemone hertensis: garden → can be spotted in gardens*
장소: 아네모네 허텐시스: 정원 → 정원에서 찾아질 수 있음

   Ex erinaceus europaeus: hedgehog living in Europe 이리나수스 유로피어스: 유럽에 사는 고슴도치

   Paraphrasing Example   As the meaning of hortensis is "garden," it is possible to assume where the anemone hortensis lives: in gardens.

WORD REMINDER

fascinating 멋진 take place 일어나다, 발생하다 particular 특정한 playful 쾌활한 external 외관의 genus 종류 fungus 곰팡이
beetle 딱정벌레 oval 타원형의 familiar 익숙한, 친숙한 perhaps 아마도 relatively 비교적 moth 나방 scale 비늘 habitat 서식지
hedgehog 고슴도치

The reading passage explains how a new species gets its name and what procedures are required for the process. Then, in the lecture, the professor explains three kinds of methods by providing examples.

First, the professor provides an example of an amusing name that is related to a species' appearance: Gelae genus, which is used for fungus beetles. The beetles' names include Gelae balae, Gelae donut, and Gelae rol. These are some examples showing that special physical traits can contribute to giving a new species a new name.

On top of that, a moth which has recently been found has finally gotten a proper name: Dermophis donaldtrumpi. Its head is covered with yellowish white scales. This is a great example in support of the idea presented in the reading passage that a new species can be named after a famous or notable figure.

Lastly, the professor provides an example of a plant called the anemone hortensis. As the meaning of hortensis is "garden," it is possible to guess where the anemone hortensis lives: in gardens. Another example is Erinaceus europaeus, a hedgehog. As its name suggests, the hedgehog is from Europe. These examples support the reading passage's claim that people can guess where a species lives and comes from based upon its name.

WORD REMINDER

procedure 절차, 과정   require 필요하다   amusing 재미있는   related 연관된   genus 종류   belong to ~에 속하다   proper 정식의   assume 가정하다   inhabit 서식하다   hypothesis 가정   in terms of ~면에서

CUT   PASTE   UNDO   REDO   Hide Word Count : 0

Directions Read the question below. You have 30 minutes to plan, write, and revise your essay. Typically, an effective response will contain a minimum of 300 words.

Question

Do you agree or disagree with the following statement?

Since society has become busy and crowded, people should not expect politeness from one another.

Use specific reasons and examples to support your answer.

NOTE-TAKING

- *society: demanding* 사회: 많은 것을 요구함
  - ∴ individualized: can't afford to pay attention to others 개인화: 다른 이들에게 신경을 쓸 여유가 없음
    - Ex people in the past: eye contact → greeting 과거의 사람들: 시선을 마주침 → 인사
      - → now: no salutations w/strangers 오늘날: 낯선 사람들과의 인사 ✕

- *tolerance to rudeness* 무례함에 대한 관용
  - − not reacting to situations that have only a minor impact on ourselves
    우리 자신에게 큰 영향이 없는 상황에는 대응 ✕
    - Ex workers exhausted from work: unwilling to give their seats to others
      회사에서 지친 직장인들: 다른 이들에게 자리 양보하기를 꺼림
      - → people understand fatigue → rarely criticize them
        사람들은 피곤함을 이해함 → 그들을 비난하는 경우는 거의 없음

INTRODUCTION

generalization: enormous # of people residing in metropolitan areas
일반화: 많은 사람들이 대도시에 거주

most have experienced to physically bothering / being bothered by others
대부분의 사람들은 피해를 주거나 다른 이들로 인해 피해를 입은 경험이 있음

thesis: agree (individualism, change of the threshold)
논제: 찬성 (개인주의, 역치의 변화)

- *knowing many people → important in today's society* 많은 이들을 아는 것 → 오늘날의 사회에서 중요함
  - ∴ good manners → crucial when socializing w/others 훌륭한 매너 → 다른 이들과 어울리는데 중요함
    - Ex 90% of workers: can't tolerate a coworker w/inappropriate way of speaking / behaving
      90%의 직장인: 부적절한 발언 / 태도를 가진 동료를 참을 수 없음
      - → unwilling to work w/the person in a group task 단체 업무를 함께 하는 것을 꺼림

- *courtesy: saves time* 예의: 시간 절약
  - − being rude: wastes time + creates discomfort 무례함: 시간 낭비 + 불편함 초래
    - Ex the Japanese standing in long lines 길게 줄을 서 있었던 일본인들
      - → respect toward others 타인에 대한 존중

INTRODUCTION

generalization: enormous # of people residing in metropolitan areas
일반화: 많은 사람들이 대도시에 거주

most have experienced to physically bothering / being bothered by others
대부분의 사람들은 피해를 주거나 다른 이들로 인해 피해를 입은 경험이 있음

thesis: disagree (interpersonal relationships, negative consequences)
논제: 반대 (대인 관계, 부정적인 결과)

There are an enormous number of people residing in metropolitan areas, and most people there have experienced at least a few times when they were hit on the arm by others or when they hit others with no intention of offending them. Some contend that people should expect to be polite to one another even though society has become busy and crowded. However, I firmly disagree with this idea for the following reasons: Individualism makes people less sensitive to a lack of politeness, and the threshold for reacting to rudeness has changed.

First, today's society is very demanding; thus, people have become individualized and cannot afford to pay much attention to others. In fact, though it seems that we live in such a compact world, everyone is isolated from one another. For example, people in the past used to greet each other when they made eye contact on the street. On the other hand, not many people these days exchange salutations with strangers.

Secondly, as people are exposed to others who unintentionally cause inconveniences repeatedly, they have built up tolerance toward disrespect, resulting in people not reacting to situations that have only a minor impact on them. For example, it is common to see workers nowadays not yielding seats to the elderly on public transportation. This consequence has arisen because workers are exhausted from work and are unwilling to give their seats to others; rarely do people criticize them since they understand the fatigue that working people feel.

It is true that having courtesy and manners toward others creates harmony among people. Conversely, certain circumstances make it inevitable for people to tolerate impudence from others. Individuals tend to be selfish and do not care about others in a busy society. Furthermore, people have developed a tolerance for insolence. For these reasons, I agree with the statement that since the world has become busy and crowded, people should not expect politeness from one another.

WORD REMINDER

individualism 개인주의   threshold 한계점, 역(자극에 대해 반응하기 시작하는 분계점)   demanding 큰 노력을 요하는   can afford to ~할 여유가 있다
compact 조밀한   greet ~에게 인사하다   salutation 인사   expose 노출시키다   repeatedly 되풀이하여   disrespect 무례   impact 영향
yield 양보하다   the elderly 중장년층   public transportation 대중교통   consequence 결과   arise 일어나다   exhausted 지칠 대로 지친
unwilling 마음 내키지 않는   criticize 비난하다   fatigue 피로   courtesy 예의   impudence 경솔, 경망   selfish 이기적인

■ TIPS for SUCCESS

문제에 주의하자.

People should not expect to be polite ~에서 이미 부정문이 쓰였기 때문에 그에 대한 찬성인지 혹은 예의를 갖추어야 한다는 긍정을 하기 위해 전체 진술을 반대해야 하는지 잘 판단하자. 즉, 이 글에서는 찬성을 할 경우 서로에게서 예의를 기대하면 안 된다는 내용의 글이 나와야 하고, 반대를 할 경우 서로가 예의를 지켜야 한다는 내용이 글이 나와야 한다.

There are an enormous number of people residing in metropolitan areas, and most people there have probably experienced at least a few times when they were hit on the arm by others or when they hit others with no intention of offending them. Some contend that people should not expect to be courteous to one another since society has become busy and crowded. However, I firmly disagree with this idea for the following reasons: Interpersonal relationships have become extremely important nowadays, and rudeness toward others may delay certain types of work.

First, knowing many people in different fields is a major factor in today's society. As our lifestyles have improved over the years, having good manners has become crucial when socializing with others. To illustrate, studies have shown that ninety percent of workers cannot tolerate a coworker with an inappropriate way of speaking or behaving and are reluctant to work with that person on a group task, suggesting that people who are insolent will experience difficulty forming close relationships with others.

Secondly, showing courtesy to others in crowded circumstances saves time. Being rude to others not only wastes time but also creates discomfort among people. For instance, the actions of the Japanese, who stood in long lines to obtain water after the March 2011 earthquake, came from respect toward others, and those actions startled people around the world. It is obvious that had people tried to cut in line, it would have taken longer for them to get water, and it could have even caused violence.

It is true that there are inevitable situations in which people cause inconvenience to others. Nevertheless, people try to avoid these circumstances because etiquette is essential when socializing with other people. Furthermore, showing respect to others will help people solve problems more effectively. For these reasons, I disagree with the statement that since the world has become busy and crowded, people should not expect politeness from one another.

▶ **WORD REMINDER**
enormous 엄청난   reside 거주하다   metropolitan 대도시의   intention 의도   offend ~의 감정을 상하게 하다   courteous 예의 바른
interpersonal relationship 대인 관계   delay 늦추다   factor 요소   crucial 중요한   socialize 어울리다   tolerate 참다
inappropriate 부적당한   reluctant 마음 내키지 않는   insolent 무례함   circumstance 상황   discomfort 불쾌   respect 존중
startle 깜짝 놀라게 하다   inevitable 피할 수 없는   inconvenience 불편   avoid 피하다

■ **TIPS for SUCCESS**
에세이를 쓸 때는 같은 표현이나 단어를 계속 쓰는 것보다는 동의어를 적절히 사용하여 단어의 다양성을 보여주는 것이 중요하다. 위의 에세이에서 '무례함'의 뜻을 가진 rudeness, impudence, insolence, ill-mannered behavior, disrespect, impertinence 등의 단어를 서로 바꾸어서 쓸 수 있다.

1 It is important to know about events around the world even if they have only minor effects on one's routine life. 자신의 일상 생활에 영향을 거의 끼치지 않는다고 할지라도 국제 정세를 아는 것은 중요하다.

AGREE	DISAGREE

- may affect future life 미래의 삶에 영향을 줄 수 있음
  ex) environmental issues around the world 세계의 환경 문제
- interrelated 서로 연관되어 있음
  ex) the world's economy is rarely independent
  세계의 경제는 독립적이지 않음
	- too much stress: enough w/the ones directly affecting our daily lives
	  과다한 스트레스: 이미 우리의 삶에 직접적인 영향을 미치는 것들이 충분함
	- more efficient to spend time and effort on domestic issues that one can have impact on
	  직접 영향을 줄 수 있는 사안에 대해 시간과 노력을 기울이는 것이 더 효과적임

2 Society should impose a toll on busy streets during rush hour. 사회는 러시아워 동안 혼잡한 도로에 통행료를 징수해야 한다.

AGREE	DISAGREE
- promotes public transportation 대중교통 장려 - decongest traffic jams 교통 체증을 분산	- unfair for workers 직장인들에게 불공평 - financial burden for many 다수에게 재정적 부담

3 Land should be used for farms, housing, or other developments that would help humans rather than as places for endangered animals.
토지는 멸종 위기의 동물들을 위한 공간이 아닌, 농장, 주택, 또는 사람을 도울 개발 부지로 사용되어야 한다.

AGREE	DISAGREE
- many people w/out homes 집이 없는 많은 사람들 - supply of food: important 식량 공급: 중요함	- preservation of species → educational 종의 보존 → 교육적 - extinction of species → destruction of ecosystem in the future 멸종 → 미래의 생태계 파괴

MEMO

MEMO

TOEFL MAP
ACTUAL TEST

New TOEFL® Edition

Susan Kim
Michael A. Putlack

Writing **1**

Scripts and Translations

TOEFL MAP ACTUAL TEST

New TOEFL Edition

Writing 1

Scripts and Translations

Actual Test 01

TASK 1 · INTEGRATED TASK
Education: Online Degree Programs

`READING`   p.015

현대의 과학 기술 덕분에, 학생은 실제 캠퍼스에 발을 디디지 않고서도 대학을 다닐 수 있다. 교실에서 강의를 듣는 대신, 온라인 강의를 들을 수가 있는 것이다. 온라인 학위 프로그램은 기존의 대학과 사이버 대학 모두에서 제공되고 있다. 하지만, 온라인 프로그램으로 학위를 받은 학생들은 구직에 있어서 전통적인 학교에서 학위를 받은 학생들에 비해 불이익을 받고 있다.

첫째, 대부분의 매니저들은 온라인 교육에 친숙하지 못하다. 이러한 사람들은 오늘날에 비해 컴퓨터가 널리 보급되지 않았던 시절에 성장한 경우가 많다. 이들 역시 전통적인 학교를 다녔는데, 이는 그들로 하여금 온라인 프로그램에 대한 다소의 의구심과 편견을 가지도록 만들었다. 그들은 종종 실제 학교에서 달성할 수 있는 교육에 비해 온라인 프로그램이 열등한 교육을 제공한다고 믿는다. 온라인 프로그램이 비교적 새로운 것이고 아직 좋은 평판을 얻지 못했기 때문에 이러한 감정은 악화되고 있다.

게다가, 많은 매니저들은 온라인 프로그램의 졸업생들이 다른 이들과 어울려 일을 하는데 필요한 사회적 능력 및 대인 관계 능력이 부족하다는 점을 우려한다. 어쨌거나, 온라인 강의만 수강하는 학생들은 혼자서 공부를 하며, 교수나 급우들과 교류를 하는 것은 아니다. 그러므로 이와 같은 학생들은 다른 이들과 함께 일하는 방법을 배우지 않았으며 따라서 좋은 팀의 구성원이 되지 못할 것이라는 염려는 타당한 것이다.

또 다른 염려는 온라인 프로그램에 등록한 학생들이 손쉽게 부정 행위를 할 수 있다는 점에 있다. 예를 들어, 시험을 볼 때 교수들이 시험 감독을 할 수 없기 때문에 학생들은 시험에서 부정 행위를 할 수가 있다. 마찬가지로, 온라인으로 교육을 받는 많은 학생들은 인터넷을 이용하여 표절한 것을 자신의 과제로 제출할 수도 있다. 온라인 프로그램에서의 학위 소지가 한 사람의 능력을 평가하는데 충분하지 않다고 일부 관리자들이 염려하는 것은 정당하다. 그 결과, 많은 이들이 온라인 프로그램으로 학위를 취득한 사람을 고용하려는 위험은 피하고 있다.

`LISTENING`   🎧 01-01

M Professor: While we're in a physical classroom, many students these days are, for various reasons, shunning the classroom experience and doing their studying online. So unfortunately for these individuals, some companies are refusing to hire them since the people doing the actual hiring are, um, skeptical of online education programs. Well, they shouldn't be. Let me tell you why.

First, many hiring managers erroneously believe that, uh, cyber universities are all new and thus have no educational traditions. That's simply not true. Our school, for one, has an online degree program. Many of the world's best universities, including Ivy League schools such as Harvard and Yale, offer online classes as well. The administrators and professors in these programs make sure that the education their students receive is just as good as what students taking in-person classes get.

Now, I can understand how some people might be worried that online education students don't interact with their professors and classmates. That happened in the past. But it doesn't happen anymore. Virtually all online classes require web conferencing, during which students speak with their professors and classmates. So the students must communicate with others, share information, and even do group projects despite the fact that they almost never meet in person. So . . . to me, it seems like doing these activities requires a great amount of teamwork.

Nowadays, um, it's difficult for students in online programs to cheat, too. First, all exams must be proctored by someone who's preapproved by the professor. Additionally, while it's possible to use the Internet to plagiarize work such as term papers, there are websites on the Internet that professors can use to detect copied assignments. So students in online programs definitely have to do the work they're assigned in their classes. As a result, when they graduate, they've legitimately earned their degrees due to their hard work.

교수: 우리는 물리적인 교실에 있지만, 요즘 많은 학생들은, 여러 가지 이유로, 교실에서의 수업을 피하고 온라인으로 공부를 하고 있습니다. 이러한 개인들에게는 안타까운 일이지만, 그들을 실제로 고용하는 사람들이 온라인 교육 프로그램에 대해 부정적이기 때문에 일부 회사들은 이들을 고용하는 것을 거부하고 있습니다. 음, 그래서는 안 되는데 말이죠. 왜 그런지에 대해서 설명해 드리겠습니다.

첫째, 많은 채용 담당자들이 사이버 대학교가 모두 새로운 것이며 따라서 교육 전통이 없다는 잘못된 믿음을 갖고 있습니다. 그건 그렇지 않습니다. 일례로, 우리 학교에는 온라인 학위 프로그램이 있습니다. Harvard나 Yale 등의 아이비리그 학교들을 포함한 세계 최고의 대학들도 온라인 강의를 제공하고 있습니다. 이러한 프로그램의 운영자들과 교수들은 온라인상의 학생들이 받는 교육이 학생들이 대면으로 듣는 수업만큼 좋다는 것을 확실히 하고 있습니다.

자, 저는 온라인 교육을 받는 학생들이 교수나 급우들과 교류를 하지 않는다는 일부 사람들의 우려를 이해할 수 있습니다. 그런 일은 과거에 발생했습니다. 하지만 더 이상은 일어나지 않고 있죠. 사실상 모든 온라인 강의는 강의가 진행되는 동안 학생들이 교수와 급우들과 함께 말을 하는 화상 회의를 요구하고 있습니다. 그래서 학생들은 다른 이들과 반드시 의사소통을 해야 하고, 정보를 공유하며, 거의 직접 만나는 일이 없다는 사실에도 불구하고, 그룹 과제까지도 해야 합니다. 저에게는, 이러한 활동을 하는 것이 상당한 팀워크를 필요로 하는 것처럼 보이는군요.

근래에는, 온라인 프로그램을 수강하는 학생들이 부정 행위를 하는 것도 어렵습니다. 첫째, 모든 시험은 교수에게 사전 허락을 받은 사람에 의해서 감독되어야 합니다. 게다가, 학기말 리포트 같은 과제를 표절하기 위해 인터넷을 사용하는 것이 가능하긴 하지만, 베낀 과제를 찾아내기 위해 교수들이 사용할 수 있는 인터넷 웹사이트들도 있습니다. 그래서 온라인 프로그램 수강생들은 강의에서 주어진 과제를 확실히 해야 합니다. 결과적으로, 그들이 졸업을 하면, 수강생들은 열심히 노력한 대가로 정당하게 학위를 받는 것이죠.

교수는 매니저들이 온라인 대학 졸업생들의 고용에 대해 부정적이어서는 안 된다고 주장한다. 이는 온라인 대학 학위를 받은 졸업생들의 고용에 있어서 몇몇 매니저들이 주저한다는 지문의 주장을 직접적으로 반박한다.

첫째, 교수에 따르면, 매니저들은 온라인 학위 프로그램에 대해 잘못된 생각을 가지고 있다. 그는 유명한 대학 중 다수가 학생들이 수강할 수 있는 온라인 프로그램을 갖추고 있다고 말한다. 이는 온라인 학위 프로그램이 비교적 새로운 것이며 아직 자리를 잡지 못하고 있다는 지문의 주장과 대조를 이룬다.

뿐만 아니라, 교수는 학생들과 교수와 급우들 사이의 교류에 대한 문제는 걱정하지 않아도 된다고 주장한다. 온라인 회의가 이러한 프로그램의 일부이기 때문에, 교수 그리고 급우들과 함께 의사소통을 하며 정보를 공유하는 것은 의무적이다. 게다가, 심지어 학생들은 그룹 과제도 함께 한다. 이는 온라인 프로그램의 학생들이 사회적 능력 및 대인 관계 능력이 능숙하지 않다는 지문의 주장에 의문을 제기한다.

마지막으로, 부정 행위는 일어나기가 힘들어지고 있다. 학생이 시험을 볼 때 마다 감독관이 있어야 하기 때문에, 시험을 보는 동안 부정 행위를 하는 것은 거의 불가능하다. 게다가, 표절된 과제가 있는지를 신중하게 살피는 교수들이 있다. 이는 온라인 프로그램에서 학생들이 쉽게 부정 행위를 할 수 있는 환경이 만들어진다는 지문의 주장과 반대된다.

TASK 2 · INDEPENDENT TASK
Grading Systems

학교는 학생들이 지식을 쌓는 곳이다. 학생들의 노력과 결과에 따라, 성적이 주어진다. 일부 사람들은 성적이 학생들로 하여금 더욱 열심히 공부하도록 격려한다고 말하는 반면 다른 이들은 성적 제도가 폐지되어야 한다고 주장한다. 성적 없이 배우는 것에 몇 가지의 이점이 있지만, 나는 성적이 학생들로 하여금 학교에서 더 열심히 공부하도록 장려한다는 논제에 강력히 찬성한다. 이는 채점은 학생들에게 동기와 목표를 제공하기 때문이다.

첫째, 성적 제도는 학생의 노력과 성취를 인정하는 도구이다. 예를 들면, 한 연구가 학교에서 이루어졌는데, 한 그룹의 학생들은 성적을 받았던 반면 다른 그룹의 학생들은 성적을 받지 않았다. 후자 그룹의 대부분의 학생들은 평가를 받지 않았기 때문에 열심히 하도록 동기가 부여되지 않았다. 반면, 전자 그룹에서는 학생들이 특정 과목에 흥미가 없었을지라도, 성적을 잘 받기 위해 많은 노력을 했고, 그 과목에서 영감을 얻었다.

뿐만 아니라, 개인은 목표를 정하는 것이 중요하다. 특히나 어린 나이에, 학생들은 장기 목표를 세워 꿈을 추구하기 위해 열심히 노력하는 것이 어렵다. 예를 들어, 학생들이 에세이 쓰기에 대한 평가를 받지 않고, 단지 작문 실력을 쌓는 것에 만족해야 한다면, 열심히 한 학생은 결국 동기를 잃어버릴 것이고, 다음 과제들에 많은 노력을 하지 않을 것이다.

배움의 궁극적인 목표가 좋은 성적을 받는다기 보다는 지식을 쌓는 것이어야 하는 것은 사실이다. 하지만, 성적은 학생이 수업에 투입한 노력과 시간을 인정하기 위한 도구의 역할을 한다. 덧붙여, 성취하고자 하는 학구적 목표에 도달하고자 하는 열망은 학생들이 공부에 더 노력을 쏟도록 장려한다. 그러므로 나는 학생이 최선을 다하도록 격려하기 위해 성적 제도가 필요하다고 굳게 믿는다.

학교는 학생들이 지식을 쌓는 곳이다. 학생들의 노력과 결과에 따라, 성적이 주어진다. 일부 사람들은 성적 제도가 폐지되어야 한다고 주장하는 반면 다른 이들은 성적이 학생들로 하여금 더욱 열심히 공부하도록 격려한다고 주장한다. 학생들의 과제에 성적을 매기는 것에는 몇 가지 이점이 있지만, 나는 성적이 학생들로 하여금 학교에서 더 열심히 공부하도록 장려한다는 논제에 강력히 반대한다. 이는 학생들이 스트레스를 경험할 것이고 동기 부여를 잃을 수 있기 때문이다.

첫째, 성적을 잘 받아야 하는 것은 굉장히 스트레스일 수 있다. 채점을 하고 점수를 주는 것은 종종 학생들을 좌절시키고 그들이 낙담하도록 만들며, 결국 특정 과목에 대해 흥미를 잃도록 이끈다. 예를 들어, 학생이 수학 시험을 못 봐서 성적이 나쁘면, 학생은 점수를 회복해서 A를 받는 것은 불가능하다고 생각할 수 있다. 이는 그가 동기 부여를 잃고 포기하게 만들지도 모른다.

뿐만 아니라, 성적을 주는 것은 학생들이 더 많은 지식을 얻는 것을 방해한다. 학생들이 배워야 하는 개념에 대한 깊이 있는 지식을 얻는 대신, 그들의 관심은 시험에 나올 법한 부분에만 집중될 것이다. 시험에 준비가 다 되면, 그들은 해당 주제에 대해 더 많은 지식을 얻고자 하는 의욕이 없을 것이다. 따라서, 그 과목에 대한 배움에서 즐거움을 찾기 보다는, 학생들이 가지는 유일한 목표는 성적을 잘 받는 일일 것이다.

성적을 잘 받기 위해 목표를 세우는 것이 학생으로 하여금 더 열심히 공부하게 할 것이라는 점은 사실이다. 하지만, 그것은 특정 기간에만 유효할 것이며, 많은 학생들은 결국 동기 부여를 잃을 것이다. 이는 학생들이 좋은 성적을 유지하지 않는 이상, 그들은 스트레스를 받고 심지어는 포기할 수도 있기 때문이다. 또한, 성적에 중점을 두는 것은 학생들이 다양한 과목을 배우는 것을 저해할 것이다. 그러므로, 나는 성적은 학생들이 더 열심히 공부하게 만든다기 보다는 학생들을 좌절시키기만 할 것이라고 굳게 믿는다.

Actual Test 02

TASK 1 · INTEGRATED TASK
Ecology: Alternative Energy

언젠가, 석탄, 석유, 그리고 천연 가스와 같은 지구의 화석 연료는 고갈될 것이다. 그러면, 필요한 전력을 공급하기 위해서는 대체 에너지원에 의존해야 할 것이다. 가장 유망한 에너지원 중 하나가 태양 에너지이다.

첫째, 태양 에너지는 석탄이나 석유를 사용하는 방식과 달리 환경에 해가 되지 않는다. 다양한 화석 연료들을 연소시키면 대기에 오염 물질이 방출되며, 이는 또한 환경 및 살아있는 유기체에 피해를 줄 수 있는 대기 오염을 초래하게 된다. 태양 에너지는, 반면, 친환경적이다. 오염 물질이나 유해한 물질을 방출하지 않기 때문에 태양 에너지는 환경이나 살아있는 유기체에게 피해를 주지 않는다.

태양 에너지는 무궁무진한 에너지원이다. 태양이 빛나는 한, 태양 에너지는 활용될 수 있다. 당연히, 태양 에너지는 밤이나 기후 조건이 최적이 아닌 이상 이용될 수 없으나, 하루 중 태양의 힘을 사용할 수 있는 여러 차례의 시간대가 있다. 과학 기술이 끊임없이 발전함에 따라, 태양 에너지를 저장하는 방법들이 발견될 것이며, 이로써 사람들은 하루 24시간 동안 태양 에너지를 이용할 수 있게 될 것이다.

마지막으로, 태양 에너지는 사실상 지구의 어느 곳에서도 사용될 수 있다. 대부분의 사람들은 태양 에너지가 뜨거운 사막이나 구름이 거의 없는 지역에서만 사용될 수 있다는 잘못된 생각을 가지고 있다. 하지만, 이는 사실이 아니다. 사람들은 산이나 울창한 숲 같은 외진 지역에서도 태양 에너지에 의지할 수 있다. 태양 광선이 태양 전지판에 닿을 수 있으면, 그것으로부터 전기를 만들어 낼 수 있다. 이러한 점 때문에 태양 에너지는 풍력, 수력, 그리고 지열을 포함한 모든 종류의 대체 에너지원 중에서 가장 편리하다.

LISTENING 🎧 02-01

W Professor: Wouldn't it be nice if we could wean ourselves off fossil fuels? Well, we're trying, but the technology isn't good enough at present. Take solar energy as an example.

Solar energy isn't perfect. After all, it's not true that it doesn't pollute the environment. All right, um, the energy itself is clean. But how about the solar panels? They're made of various types of materials, including, uh, silicon, cadmium, and nickel. We get most of these materials from mining the land, which harms the environment. And the process of manufacturing the panels releases numerous harmful chemicals into the atmosphere. So solar energy isn't quite free of pollutants.

Solar energy is also useful but limited. For instance, my home has solar panels, but they're only good for heating the water. That's it. Why's that? Well, solar panels are fairly inefficient at capturing the sun's rays and converting them to electricity. How inefficient . . . ? Hmm . . . Let's say we want to power the entire United States with solar energy. We'd need an area about, uh, 160 kilometers long by 210 kilometers wide filled entirely with solar panels. That's an enormous area. It's bigger than some states. And remember that the area would require constant sunshine. I'm talking about twenty-four hours a day. That's impossible.

Finally, we have to deal with solar panels malfunctioning or not working at all. Breakdowns are rather common since the panels are complex. Imagine you've got a remote cabin in the woods that you power with solar energy. Suddenly, your solar panels stop working. You can't fix the panels by yourself. And how are you going to find a repairman? After all, you're far away from society. In that case, it would be more convenient to use traditional energy sources to get electricity, wouldn't it?

교수: 화석 연료의 사용을 중단할 수만 있다면 얼마나 좋을까요? 글쎄요, 노력을 하고 있지만 현재로써는 과학 기술이 그 정도로 뛰어나지는 않습니다. 한 예로 태양 에너지를 들어 봅시다.

태양 에너지는 완벽하지 않습니다. 어쨌든, 태양 에너지가 환경을 오염시키지 않는다는 것은 사실이 아닙니다. 좋아요, 음, 그 에너지 자체는 깨끗합니다. 하지만, 태양 전지판은 어떨까요? 태양 전지판은 실리콘, 카드뮴, 그리고 니켈 등을 포함한 다양한 종류의 물질로 만들어져 있습니다. 우리는 이 물질들의 대부분을 채굴해서 얻고 있는데, 이는 환경을 해치는 일입니다. 그리고 전지판을 제작하는 과정에서도 많은 해로운 화학 물질들이 대기로 방출되고 있습니다. 그러니까, 태양 에너지에 오염 물질이 없는 것은 아닙니다.

태양 에너지는 또한 유용하지만 한정되어 있습니다. 예를 들면, 저희 집에 태양 전지판이 있지만, 고작 물을 데우는 데만 쓸모가 있죠. 그것뿐입니다. 왜 그럴까요? 자, 태양 전지판은 태양 광선을 저장해서 전기로 변환시키는데 있어서 꽤 비효율적입니다. 얼만큼 비효율적이냐고요...? 흠... 미국 전체에 태양 에너지를 공급한다고 해봅시다. 우리에게는 태양 전지판들로 약 160킬로미터 길이에 210킬로미터의 폭을 완전히 꽉 채운 지역이 필요할 것입니다. 엄청난 크기의 지역인 것이죠. 일부 주 보다 더 큽니다. 그리고 그 지역은 끊임없는 햇빛을 필요로 할 것이라는 점을 기억해 두십시오. 하루 24시간을 말하고 있는 것입니다. 불가능한 일이죠.

마지막으로, 우리는 고장이 나거나 아예 작동을 하지 않는 태양 전지판들을 처리해야 합니다. 전지판이 복잡하기 때문에 고장은 다소 흔한 일입니다. 숲 속 멀리 떨어져 있는, 태양 에너지로 전력이 공급되는 오두막집을 구입했다고 상상해 보십시오. 갑자기, 태양 전지판이 작동을 하지 않습니다. 스스로 고칠 수도 없고요. 그러면 어떻게 수리 기사를 찾으시겠습니까? 어쨌든 사회로부터 멀리 떨어져 있습니다. 그런 경우, 전기를 얻기 위해 기존의 에너지원을 사용하는 것이 훨씬 더 편리할 것입니다, 그렇지 않나요?

Sample Essay p.028

교수는 태양 에너지가 보여지는 것처럼 전망이 좋은 것은 아니라고 논하면서, 왜 그 에너지원이 비효율적인지에 대해 세 가지 의견을 제시하고 있다. 이는 태양 에너지가 쉽게 활용될 수 있는 가장 이로운 대체 에너지 중 하나라는 지문의 주장에 직접적으로 반대된다.

태양 에너지는 태양 전지판에 환경에 해로운 많은 종류의 물질들이 포함되어 있기 때문에 실제로 환경에 해롭다. 게다가, 전지판을 제작하는 과정에서 유해한 화학 물질이 방출된다. 이는 태양 에너지가 친환경적이며, 오염 물질을 전혀 방출하지 않는다는 지문의 주장과 모순된다.

뿐만 아니라, 태양 에너지는 특정한 양만 이용이 가능하다. 예를 들어, 미국에 전기를 공급하기 위해서는 태양 전지판이 광범위하게 배치되어 있어야 하고 끊임없는 태양 광선의 공급이 필요하다. 이는 태양 광선이 있는 한 태양 에너지의 양은 무궁무진하다는 지문의 주장에 의문을 제기한다.

마지막으로, 태양 전지판의 고장은 심각한 문제가 될 수 있다. 전지판은 구조가 복잡하기 때문에 종종 고장이 날 수 있고, 전지판이 고장나면 외딴 지역 사람들은 이를 고치기가 어렵다는 난점에 직면할 것이다. 이러한 점은 태양 에너지가 어디서든 이용될 수 있다는 지문의 의견을 반박한다.

TASK 2 · INDEPENDENT TASK
The Future World

Sample Essay 1 | AGREE p.031

개인의 취향에 맞추려는 목적으로, 자동차 회사들은 소비자들에게 자동차의 매우 다양한 디자인, 옵션, 그리고 가격 범위를 제공한다. 길에서 자동차 수가 매일 증가함에 따라 새로운 도로, 주차 건물, 그리고 주유소가 생긴다. 많은 이들이 사람들은 자동차가 만드는 환경 문제에 대해 더 의식한다고 주장하지만, 대부분의 사람들은 자동차에 지나치게 의존하게 되었다. 이는 워라벨이 더욱 의미 있게 되었고 자동차가 편리함을 주기 때문이다.

첫째, 워라벨이 중요해지면서, 많은 사람들은 해마다 적어도 한 번의 휴가를 다녀오는 것을 선택한다. 그리고 많은 사람들은 국립 공원이나 해변 같은 지역을 차로 다녀온다. 더 자세히 말하자면, 한 연구는 미국에서 여행자들이 가는 휴가의 40% 이상이 장거리 자동차 여행에 해당한다는 것을 보여준다. 그러므로, 사람들은 더욱 차에 의존하게 되고, 이런 급상승하는 수요는 시장에서 자동차 부족난까지 야기하고 있다.

뿐만 아니라, 사람들은 차가 주는 편리함에 익숙해져 있다. 그래서, 많은 사람들은 걸어 다닐 수 있는 거리에 있는 장소에도 차를 운전하고 가는 경향이 있다. 연구에 따르면, 85% 이상의 사람들은 동네에 있는 슈퍼마켓에도 그들의 차를 타고 가는 것을 선택했다. 그들의 차를 운전하며, 사람들은 걷는데 시간을 쓰거나 손으로 무거운 장바구니를 들고 다니지 않아도 된다.

많은 사람들이 차를 소유함으로써 오는 환경 결과에 대해 걱정을 하는 것은 사실이다. 하지만, 자동차 회사들은 천천히 화석 원료 자동차에서 친환경적인 전기차로 바꾸고 있다. 워라벨 때문에, 더 많은 사람들은 장거리 자동차 여행을 선택한다. 덧붙여, 많은 사람들은 편리함 때문에 차를 운전하고 다닌다. 그러므로, 나는 오늘날 사람들은 자동차에 굉장히 의존적으로 되었다는 주장에 강력히 찬성한다.

Sample Essay 2 | DISAGREE
p.032

개인의 취향에 맞추려는 목적으로, 자동차 회사들은 소비자들에게 자동차의 매우 다양한 디자인, 옵션, 그리고 가격 범위를 제공한다. 길에서 자동차 수가 매일 증가함에 따라 새로운 도로, 주차 건물, 그리고 주유소가 생긴다. 많은 이들이 자동차는 편리함을 제공한다고 주장하지만, 대부분의 사람들이 자동차에 덜 의존하는 건 명백하다. 이는 사람들이 가지는 환경 경각심과 온라인 쇼핑 때문이다.

기후 변화가 과거 그 여느 때보다도 심각해졌고, 자동차는 지구 온난화의 원인이 되는 엄청난 양의 온실가스를 생산한다. 따라서, 많은 자동차 회사들은 비극적인 재난으로부터 세계를 보호하기 위해 노력하고 있고, 전기 자동차를 생산하기 시작했다. 하지만, 그들이 환경을 파괴한다는 비난으로부터 자유로울 수 없는데, 이유는 전기 자체가 화석 원료를 필요로 하기 때문이다. 따라서, 환경 경각심은 사람들로 하여금 자전거를 비롯한 대중교통을 이용하도록 했으며 이는 사람들이 자동차에 덜 의존적으로 되도록 이끌었다.

뿐만 아니라, 대부분의 사람들은 적어도 일주일에 한 번은 쇼핑 센터나 슈퍼마켓으로 운전을 한다. 하지만, 온라인 쇼핑 덕분에, 더 많은 사람들이 가게에서보다 집에서 쇼핑을 하는 것으로 바뀌고 있다. 예를 들면, 아마존은 미국에서 가장 큰 전자 상거래 기업들 중 하나인데 사람들은 대부분의 물건들을 거기서 찾을 수 있다. 그러므로 이러한 비교적 새로운 온라인 쇼핑 유행은 사람들이 가게까지 가는 것을 피하게 만들었다.

많은 소비자들이 자동차가 제공하는 편리함에 익숙해진 것은 사실이다. 하지만, 온라인 쇼핑은 사람들이 가게에 오고 가는 번거로움을 덜해주는 등 더 많은 이점을 가져다 준다. 게다가, 더 많은 사람들이 환경 문제를 자각하고 대중교통을 이용하거나 자전거를 타기로 결정한다. 그러므로, 나는 오늘날 사람들은 자동차에 더 의존적이라는 주장에 강력히 반대한다.

Actual Test 03

TASK 1 · INTEGRATED TASK

Archaeology: Mima Mounds

READING
p.035

미국의 여러 서부 지역에는, 낮은 원형의 흙더미가 있다. 미마 둔덕이라 불리는 이것은 지름이 3에서 50미터 사이 정도이며, 높이는 30센티미터에서 2미터 사이이다. 미국 내 세 곳의 주요 지역과 몇몇 작은 지역에서 미마 둔덕이 발견된다. 여러 지역에서 미마 둔덕이 존재하고 있음에도 불구하고,

전문가들은 미마 둔덕이 정확히 어떻게 형성되었는지 확신하지 못하고 있다. 그렇지만, 그것들의 형성에 관한 세 개의 주요한 이론들이 있다.

몇몇 전문가들은 미마 둔덕이 과거 다양한 미국 원주민 부족들에 의해서 만들어졌다고 믿는다. 미국의 크고 작은 미마 둔덕 지역은 모두 한때 원주민 부족들이 번성했던 장소에 위치해 있다. 이러한 전문가들은 둔덕이 의식의 목적으로 만들어 졌다고 추측한다. 부족의 구성원들은 둔덕을 다양한 종교적 의식에 사용했을 수도 있고, 죽은 부족 구성원의 매장을 위한 무덤으로 이용했을 수도 있다.

둔덕의 형성에 관한 두 번째 주요 이론은 지진 활동에 중점을 두고 있다. 미국에 있는 세 곳의 주요 미마 둔덕의 장소 중 두 곳은 지질학적인 활동이 활발한 장소이다. 이는 많은 작은 장소에 있어서도 사실이다. 일부 지질학자들은 지진이 바람이나 물과 같은 다른 자연적인 힘과 결합하여 어떻게든 땅의 표면을 변화시켜서 미마 둔덕이 형성되었을 것이라고 주장한다.

뿐만 아니라, 동물들이 미마 둔덕을 만들었다고 추측하는 전문가들도 몇몇 있다. 그들은 굴을 파는 동물인 땅다람쥐들이 미마 둔덕을 형성시킨 원인이 되었을 것이라고 주장한다. 간단히 말하면, 땅다람쥐들이 그 안에 살기 위해 둔덕을 만든 것이다. 이들 전문가들은 많은 미마 둔덕이 땅다람쥐 무리에게 서식지를 제공해 주고 있다고 지적함으로써 자신들의 주장을 뒷받침하고 있다. 그들의 의견에 따르면, 지하에 터널을 파는 땅다람쥐들이 아래에 있는 흙을 위로 밀어 올리기 때문에, 이러한 불가사의한 둔덕이 만들어졌을 가능성이 높다.

LISTENING
🎧 03-01

M Professor: Mima mounds are the next geological feature we need to cover. These mounds are found in many places, uh, but they're especially prevalent in the northwestern part of the United States. Um . . . Let's take a look at them here on the screen . . . Now, mima mounds are rather mysterious because no one's exactly sure how they were formed. And the three major theories all have serious problems.

For instance, some experts have concluded that Native American tribes built mima mounds to conduct religious ceremonies or to bury their dead in. However, a close examination of these tribes' histories shows that there's, um, no evidence of them ever making any mounds. None at all. In addition, when archaeologists excavated some mounds, they failed to find any Native American artifacts or human remains. It therefore seems unlikely that mima mounds are manmade.

Some have theorized that earthquakes caused mima mounds to form. Now, it's true that a lot of places in the Northwest are geologically active and get earthquakes. But you ought to know that mima mounds are found in other places throughout the country. And in those areas, the ground is quite stable, so they almost never get any earthquakes. I think we can state with authority that mima mounds aren't the result of earthquakes as well.

Here's another one . . . Some scholars actually believe that, uh, gophers made mima mounds. There are many gophers that live in them, but no one knows if the gophers made the mounds or if they simply moved into them since they seemed like, well, like nice places to live. And nobody has witnessed gophers building homes that look anything like mima mounds either. As you can see, we just don't have enough evidence to know who or what caused mima mounds to form.

교수: 미마 둔덕은 우리가 다음으로 다뤄야 할 지질학적 특성입니다. 이러한 둔덕은 많은 지역에서 발견되고 있지만 특히 미국의 북서쪽에 널리 퍼져 있습니다. 음... 여기 화면을 봅시다... 자, 그 어느 누구도 미마 둔덕이 어떻게 형성되었는지 정확히 알고 있지 못하기 때문에 미마 둔덕은 상당히 불가사의합니다. 그리고 세 가지 주요 이론들 모두 심각한 문제점을 가지고 있습니다.

예를 들어, 일부 전문가들은 미 원주민 부족들이 종교적 의식을 거행하거나 죽은 이들을 묻기 위해 미마 둔덕을 만들었을 것이라고 결론을 지었습니다. 하지만, 이러한 부족들의 역사를 자세히 살펴보면, 그 부족들이 어떠한 둔덕을 만들었다는 증거는 하나도 찾아볼 수 없습니다. 전혀요. 게다가, 고고학자들이 일부 둔덕을 발굴했을 때, 그들은 그 어떤 북미 원주민의 유물이나 사람의 유해도 찾지 못했습니다. 따라서 미마 둔덕을 사람이 만들었다고 하는 것은 가능성이 희박해 보입니다.

몇몇은 지진이 미마 둔덕 형성의 원인이 되었다는 이론을 제시하고 있습니다. 자, 북서쪽의 많은 지역에서 지질학적인 활동이 활발하며 지진이 발생하고 있다는 점은 사실입니다. 하지만, 여러분은 미마 둔덕이 미 전역에 걸쳐 다른 지역에서도 발견된다는 것을 알아야 합니다. 그리고, 그러한 지역에서는 지면이 꽤 안정적이라, 거의 전혀 지진이 발생하지 않습니다. 제 생각에는 미마 둔덕이 지진에 의한 결과 역시 아니라고 엄연히 말할 수 있을 것 같습니다.

또 하나가 있습니다... 일부 학자들은 땅다람쥐들이 실제 미마 둔덕을 만들었다고 믿습니다. 미마 둔덕에서 사는 땅다람쥐들은 많습니다. 하지만 누구도 그 땅다람쥐들이 둔덕을 만든 것인지, 혹은 단순히 땅다람쥐들이 음... 살기 좋은 곳이라고 보여서 거기로 이동한 것인지는 알 수 없습니다. 그리고 땅다람쥐들이 미마 둔덕처럼 보이는 집을 짓고 있는 것 역시 누구도 본 적이 없습니다. 여기서 알 수 있듯이, 우리는 누가 또는 무엇이 미마 둔덕을 만들었는지 알기에는, 정말이지 충분한 근거를 가지고 있지 않습니다.

Sample Essay   p.038

교수는 미국의 미마 둔덕의 형성 원인에 대해 여전히 알려진 바가 없다고 주장한다. 이는 미마 둔덕의 형성 원인이 세 개의 주요 이론 중 하나에 꼭 들어맞는다는 지문의 주장과 직접적으로 반대된다.

첫째, 교수는 미마 둔덕이 인위적으로 만들어졌다고 말한다. 교수에 따르면, 발굴 작업 중에 어떤 유물이나 인간의 유골이 발견되지 않았다고 한다. 이는 의식을 목적으로 북미 원주민들이 미마 둔덕을 만들었을 것이라는 지문의 내용에 의문을 제기한다.

그리고, 교수는 미마 둔덕이 미국 여러 지역에서 발견되었다고 주장한다. 하지만, 그러한 지역들은 지질학적으로 안정적이다. 사실, 그 지역들은 지진이 거의 일어나지 않는다. 그런 의미에서, 미마 둔덕이 지진과 같은 지질학적 활동에 의한 결과물이라고 말하는 것은 불합리해 보인다.

마지막으로, 땅다람쥐들도 미마 둔덕의 생성과는 무관하다고 판명된다. 땅다람쥐들이 실제로 둔덕을 만들었는지 혹은 거주를 하기 위해 둔덕으로 이동했는지는 누구도 확신하지 못한다. 게다가, 아무도 땅다람쥐들이 둔덕을 짓는 것을 보지 못했기 때문에, 땅다람쥐들이 둔덕을 만들었다고 말하는 이론은 입증될 수 없다. 이는 땅다람쥐들이 둔덕을 만들었다는 공로를 인정받아야 한다는 지문에 언급된 견해에 반대된다.

TASK 2 · INDEPENDENT TASK
Traveling

Sample Essay 1 | TRAVELING ALONE   p.041

수년간 우리의 생활 방식이 향상됨에 따라, 오늘날 사람들이 해외로 널리 여행하는 것을 보는 것은 드문 일이 아니다. 가장 인기 있는 두 가지 여행 방법은 여행 가이드와 함께 하는 것과, 그리고 책과 대중매체로 인해 가능해진 혼자서 하는 여행이다. 비록 몇몇 사람들은 가이드와 함께 여행하는 것을 선호하지만, 나는 홀로 여행을 함으로써 더 많은 자유를 누릴 수 있기 때문에 혼자서 여행하는 것을 강하게 선호한다. 게다가, 사람들은 문화를 보다 가까이에서 직접 체험할 수 있다.

첫째, 홀로 여행할 때는 자유가 많다. 다시 말해서, 나는 다른 사람들의 일정에 대한 걱정을 하지 않고서 스스로의 속도에 맞추어 여행을 할 수가 있다. 예를 들면, 프랑스로 여행을 갔을 때, 나는 오르세 박물관의 미술 작품에 많은 흥미를 느꼈다. 따라서, 본래는 오후에 베르사유를 방문할 계획이었지만, 계획을 바꾸었다. 대신, 나는 박물관에서 하루 종일 머물며 위대한 예술가들의 작품을 감상하였다.

게다가, 홀로 여행할 때, 문화를 보다 더 가까이에서 경험해 볼 수 있다. 현지인들과 교류하고 대중교통을 이용함으로써, 여행객은 그 문화에 대해 직접적인 경험을 할 수 있다. 예를 들어, 내 친구는 홍콩을 여행했을 때, 딤섬으로 유명한 곳을 추천해 달라고 현지인에게 부탁을 했다. 그 식당은 여행객들 사이에서 유명한 호화로운 곳은 아니었지만, 현지인들로 붐비고 있었다. 게다가, 그녀도 또한 딤섬의 진정한 맛을 즐길 수가 있었다. 그녀가 가이드와 여행을 했다면, 그렇게 훌륭한 식당에서 식사를 하지 못했을 것이다.

몇몇 사람들은 가이드와 다니는 것이 보다 더 안전하고 체계적인 여행이 된다고 말한다. 하지만, 여행하면서 실수를 하는 것은 여행에 재미를 더해 준다. 홀로 여행하는 것은 내 일상으로부터 물러나 쉴 수 있는 시간을 나에게 준다. 따라서 휴식을 취하며 나의 자유를 즐길 수 있다. 덧붙여, 문화를 직접적으로 체험할 수 있는 기회를 보다 많이 갖게 된다. 이러한 이유로, 나는 가이드와 함께 여행을 하기 보다는 혼자서 해외 여행을 하는 것을 선호한다.

Sample Essay 2 | TRAVELING WITH A TOUR GUIDE   p.042

수년간 우리의 생활 방식이 향상됨에 따라, 오늘날 사람들이 해외로 널리 여행을 하는 것을 보는 것은 드문 일이 아니다. 가장 인기 있는 두 가지 여행 방법은 여행 가이드와 함께 하는 것과, 그리고 책과 대중매체로 인해 가능하게 된, 혼자서 하는 여행이다. 비록 몇몇 사람들은 홀로 여행하는 것을 선호하지만, 나는 더 체계적이고 안전하기 때문에 가이드와 함께 여행하는 것을 강하게 선호한다.

첫째, 가이드는 중요한 장소나 위치를 알기 때문에, 적절한 시간에 가장 유명한 곳으로 여행객들을 데려갈 수 있다. 예를 들어, 한 번은 가이드와 함께 프랑스를 여행할 기회가 있었다. 가이드가 내가 방문하고 싶어했던 모든 유명한 미술 박물관을 보여 주어서 여행은 정말 훌륭했다. 게다가, 가이드의 도움으로 시간을 절약할 수 있었다. 그는 위치를 잘 알고 있었기 때문에 한 곳에서 다른 곳으로 나를 데려갈 때마다 가장 빠른 경로를 택했다. 반대로, 만약 혼자서 여행을 했더라면, 나는 그 지역의 한쪽 끝에서 다른 쪽 끝으로 배회하느라 시간을 낭비했을지도 모른다.

뿐만 아니라, 가이드는 특정한 장소에 익숙한 사람들이다. 따라서, 관광객들은, 특히 응급 상황에서, 언어나 현지 관습에 대해 걱정하지 않아도 된다. 예를 들면, 내 친구가 태국으로 여행을 갔을 때 뱀에 물린 적이 있었다. 하지만 가이드의 신속한 도움으로 그녀는 곧 병원을 찾아서 빠른 치료를 받을 수 있었다. 그러므로 안전과 응급 상황을 대비하여 가이드와 함께 있는 것은 여행하는 동안에 마음을 안심시켜준다.

몇몇 사람들은 홀로 여행하는 것이 새로운 사람들을 만나고 문화를 직접 경험할 수 있는 기회가 된다고 말한다. 하지만 대부분의 사람들은 다른 나라의 문화에 친숙하지 않기 때문에, 여행하는 동안 위험에 맞닥뜨릴 수 있다. 그러므로, 보다 더 안전하고 체계적인 여행을 하기 위해, 나는 홀로 여행하는 것보다는 가이드와 함께 해외 여행을 하는 것을 선호한다.

Actual Test 04

TASK 1 · INTEGRATED TASK

Anthropology: Native Americans

READING   p.045

유럽인들이 신대륙에 도착했을 때, 그들은 이미 많은 부족들이 그곳에서 살고 있다는 사실을 깨달았다. 대부분의 전문가들은 이들의 조상이 아시아의 시베리아와 북미의 일부를 연결했던 얼음 다리를 건너 미대륙에 도착하게 되었다고 믿게 되었다. 시간이 흐르면서, 그들은 북미와 남미 전역으로 퍼져 나갔다. 하지만, 오늘날 미 원주민들이 아시아가 아닌 유럽에서 왔다는 증거가 존재한다.

약 13,000년 전쯤, 미대륙에는 고고학자들이 클로비스인이라고 부르는 부족이 있었다. 이들이 사용했던 독특한 석창의 뾰족한 끝은 북미 전역에 걸쳐 몇몇 지역에서 발견되고 있다. 흥미롭게도, 이러한 창 끝은 솔류트레인이라고 불리는 유럽인들의 창 끝과 유사하다. 이들은 약 19,000년부터 15,000년 사이에 프랑스의 일부 지역에서 살았다. 몇몇 고고학자들은 클로비스인의 창끝이 솔류트레인의 것에 바탕을 두고 있다고 믿는다. 이들은 클로비스인들이 솔류트레인들의 후손이거나 적어도 그들과 접촉했을 것이라고 주장한다.

초기 미국인들과 솔류트레인들 사이에서 또 하나의 비슷한 점은 신체적 유사함이다. 미대륙에서 발굴된 일부 고대인들의 유해는 유럽에서 발견된 솔류트레인들의 것과 유사한 모습을 보이고 있다. 특히, 두개골의 모양은 거의 동일한데, 이는 둘 사이에 같은 조상이 있었다는 점을 시사한다.

솔류트레인들은 배를 타고 대서양을 건너 미대륙으로 갔을 것이다. 성공하기 힘든 여행이었겠지만, 그들은 대양을 건널 수 있을 만큼 튼튼한 선박을 건조할 수 있었을 것이다. 솔류트레인들은, 불과 몇 주 후에, 유럽을 떠나 미대륙에 도착하여 새로운 삶을 시작했을 수도 있다.

LISTENING   🎧 04-01

W Professor: Around 13,000 years ago, people first arrived in the Americas. During the last great ice age, the sea level was much lower, so a land bridge was exposed between the lands that are modern-day Russia and Alaska. Nomads following herds of animals crossed the bridge and subsequently populated North and South America. That's the widely accepted theory. Recently, some experts have proposed that a group of people from Europe named the Solutreans made it to the Americas first. I find this theory erroneous for several reasons.

First, they base their evidence on ancient spear points. Near Clovis, New Mexico, archaeologists found some spear points that are the oldest manmade objects unearthed in the Americas. These spear points are said to have belonged to the Clovis people. The spear points resemble those used by the ancient Solutrean people of Western Europe. But the Solutreans had died out thousands of years before the Clovis people arose in America. There's no way the two of them could have been connected. The similarity is a mere coincidence.

Next, the remains of some early Americans and Solutreans show that they shared some physical characteristics. For instance, their skulls have some identical features. But that's not enough evidence to make a connection between the two. After all, you could probably find similarities in the skull shapes of people from multiple unconnected cultures all around the world.

Now, here's the worst argument that they make . . . Some experts claim the Solutreans built ships and sailed them across the Atlantic. That's impossible. First, the Solutreans lived more than 15,000 years ago. Back then, no one built ships that could sail across an ocean. Plus, the Atlantic is known for its rough weather. Any ship made in prehistoric times would have sunk soon after reaching deep water.

교수: 약 13,000년 전, 사람들이 최초로 미대륙에 도착했습니다. 마지막 대빙하기 동안, 수면이 훨씬 낮아졌고, 그 결과 오늘날의 러시아와 알래스카의 육지 사이에 육교가 드러나게 되었습니다. 동물의 떼를 따라가는 유목민들은 그 다리를 건너 이후 북남미에 정착하게 되었죠. 이것이 널리 인정받고 있는 이론입니다. 최근, 일부 전문가들이 솔류트레인이라 불리는 유럽인의 한 무리가 미대륙에 처음 도착했다고 주장하고 있습니다. 저는 이 이론이 몇 가지 이유들 때문에 옳지 않다고 생각합니다.

첫째, 그들은 고대의 창 끝을 근거로 삼고 있습니다. 고고학자들은 뉴멕시코 근처의 클로비스에서 미대륙에서 발굴된 것 중 가장 오래된 인공 물품들인 창 끝을 발견했습니다. 이 창 끝은 클로비스 사람들의 것이라고 말해지고 있습니다. 창끝의 모양은 서유럽에서 살던 고대 솔류트레인의 것들과 유사합니다. 하지만, 솔류트레인들은 미 대륙에서 클로비스인들이 생기기 전 이미 수천 년 전에 사라졌습니다. 두 민족들이 서로 연관되었을 가능성은 전혀 없습니다. 그러한 유사점은 단순히 우연의 일치인 것이죠.

다음으로, 일부 초기 미국인들과 솔류트레인들의 유골은 신체적 특징의 유사성을 보여 줍니다. 예를 들어, 그들의 두개골들은 몇 가지 동일한 특성을 가지고 있습니다. 하지만, 그것이 그 둘 사이를 연결시켜 줄 만큼의 충분한 증거는 되지 못합니다. 어쨌든, 전세계에 걸쳐 있는 여러 무관한 문화권의 사람들의 두개골 모양에서도 유사성을 찾아낼 수가 있을 것입니다.

자, 몇몇 전문가들이 만들어 낸 최악의 주장을 알려드리겠습니다… 그들은 솔류트레인들이 선박을 건조하여 항해를 해서 대서양을 건넜다고 주장합니다. 이는 불가능합니다. 첫째, 솔류트레인들은 15,000년보다도 훨씬 전에 살았습니다. 당시, 대양을 건널 수 있는 배를 만들 수 있는 사람은 없었습니다. 게다가, 대서양은 거친 기후로 유명합니다. 선사 시대에 만들어 진 선박이라면 깊은 물에 도달했을 때 곧 가라앉았을 것입니다.

교수는 솔류트레인들이 미 원주민의 조상이라는 이론이 타당하지 않다고 주장한다. 이는 미 원주민이 아시아로부터 왔다는 명제는 잘못된 것으로 판명되었다는 지문의 주장을 직접적으로 반박한다.

첫째, 두 집단의 사람들이 비슷한 창 끝을 가지고 있었지만, 그들은 관계가 없었을 것이다. 이 주장은 클로비스인들의 출현과 솔류트레인들의 소멸 시점이 수천 년의 차이를 두고 발생했다는 사실에 의해 뒷받침된다. 이는 독특한 석창끝 때문에 두 집단 사이의 사람들이 같은 조상을 가지고 있다는 것이 증명되었다는 지문의 주장을 부인한다.

둘째, 교수는 서로 관련이 없는 사람들 사이에서도 두개골 모양에 있어서 여러 유사점들이 있을 수 있기 때문에 두개골 모양의 유사점만 보고서 그들의 조상이 동일하다는 결론을 내리는 것은 너무 성급한 것이라고 주장한다. 이러한 점은, 신체적인 유사성이 조상이 같다는 주장에 힘을 실어 준다는 지문의 주장을 반박하는 것이다.

마지막으로, 솔류트레인들이 항해를 해서 대서양을 건너 미대륙으로 왔다는 주장은 비합리적이다. 그 시대에 누구도 그러한 기능을 갖춘 배를 만들 수 없었으며, 대서양의 거친 기후 때문에 누구도 대양을 건너지 못했을 것이다. 이는 솔류트레인들이 선박을 건조하여 대서양을 건너 미대륙까지 항해를 했다는 지문의 주장을 반박한다.

TASK 2 · INDEPENDENT TASK

Living Environment

유년기는 아이들이 사회성, 다양한 주제에 대한 지식, 그리고 성격 등의 다양한 분야에서의 많은 도구를 개발하고 발전시키는 중요한 시기이다. 그런 기술과 능력을 발전시킬 수 있는 환경이 아이들의 성장에 영향을 끼치는 요인들 중 하나이다. 일부 사람들은 아이들은 대도시에서 자라야 한다고 주장하지만, 나는 아이들이 대도시보다 시골에서 자라는 것이 낫다는 명제에 강하게 찬성한다. 두 가지 이유는 아이들이 스트레스를 덜 받고, 자연에서 시간을 보낼 수 있기 때문이다.

첫째, 대도시의 많은 아이들은 건강과 관련된 문제를 겪고 있다. 많은 연구는 과도한 스트레스와 압박감 때문에 대도시의 아이들 중 70% 이상은 정서적 문제뿐 아니라 신체적 문제를 겪고 있다는 것을 보여준다. 반면, 아이들이 많은 열린 공간에서 뛰어 노는 동안 또래 친구들과 협동하고 화합하는 것을 배우기 때문에 시골에서 아이들은 더 행복한 경향이 있다.

뿐만 아니라, 아이들이 느긋한 환경에서 배울 수 있는 자연적인 환경에 노출되는 것은 중요하다. 예를 들면, 곤충, 식물, 그리고 동물 등의 자연을 직접 경험한 아이들은 학과목에 대해 내재적 동기를 보여주었다는 것이 연구 결과 밝혀졌다. 이는 아이들의 자연과의 상호 작용이 아이들로 하여금 더 깊이 있는 지식을 얻는 것을 흥미로워 했기 때문에 벌어졌다. 이는 동기 부여가 되기 위해 경쟁이 치열한 학생들로 가득한 교실에서 보상을 받아야 했거나 배움에 대한 압박을 가졌던 아이들과 대조적이다.

대도시에서는 아이들에게 많은 기회가 있다는 것이 사실이다. 하지만, 더 많은 기회는 종종 더 치열한 경쟁과 압박과 관련이 있다. 느긋한 환경에서의 배움은 아이들이 성적이나 보상 등의 요소로 인해 동기 부여를 받게 만들기 보다는 내재적 동기를 세우도록 돕는다. 나아가, 아이들은 또래 친구들과 놀고 협력과 화합을 하는 방법을 배울 기회를 더욱 많이 가진다. 그러므로, 나는 아이들이 대도시에서보다 시골에서 자라는 것이 낫다고 굳게 믿는다.

유년기는 아이들이 사회성, 다양한 주제에 대한 지식, 그리고 성격 등의 다양한 분야에서의 많은 도구를 개발하고 발전시키는 중요한 시기이다. 그런 기술과 능력을 발전시킬 수 있는 환경이 아이들의 성장에 영향을 끼치는 요인들 중 하나이다. 일부 사람들은 아이들은 시골에서 자라야 한다고 주장하지만, 나는 아이들이 대도시보다 시골에서 자라는 것이 낫다는 명제에 강하게 반대한다. 두 가지 이유는 아이들이 대도시에서는 더 많은 기회를 가지고 있고, 도시에는 많은 자원이 있기 때문이다.

첫째, 배우고 경쟁할 수 있는 기회가 많이 있다. 도시들에 인구가 밀집됨에 따라, 많은 교육 기관들은 다양한 종류의 수업들을 제공한다. 아이들은 미래를 준비하기 위해 경쟁력이 있도록 배울 필요가 있다. 다양한 대회, 콘테스트, 혹은 운동 경기에 적극적으로 참가함으로써, 아이들은 그들의 관심사를 발견하고 개척할 뿐 아니라, 다른 이들과 경쟁하고 협력하는 것을 배우기도 한다.

뿐만 아니라, 도시는 아이들이 여러 문화를 경험할 기회를 준다. 예를 들면, 대도시에서는 대부분, 세계 각지에서 온 많은 여행객들과 주민들이 있다. 따라서, 시골에서는 음식의 선택이 제한되는 반면 도시에서는 다른 종류의 음식을 제공하는 수많은 식당을 찾을 수 있다. 또한, 아이들은 박물관이나 콘서트장을 방문하는 등의 문화 생활에 더 많이 노출된다. 이러한 경험들은 삶의 기본 토대를 형성하는데 있어 매우 귀중하다.

시골이 아이들에게 더욱 느긋한 환경과 덜한 경쟁을 제공해 주는 것은 사실이다. 하지만 경쟁은 아이들에게 그들의 기량을 발달시키도록 동기를 부여한다. 게다가, 대도시에서는 아이들이 이용할 수 있는 많은 기회가 있고, 문화 생활에 노출되는 것은 아이들이 그들의 관심사와 미래에 대한 목표를 찾는데 도움이 될 것이다. 그러므로, 나는 아이들은 시골보다 대도시에서 자라는 것이 낫다고 굳게 믿는다.

Actual Test 05

TASK 1 · INTEGRATED TASK

Forestry: Prescribed Burns

한때 미국의 삼림 관리인들은 갑자기 발생하는 작은 산불조차도 예방하려고 노력을 했다. 하지만, 최근 몇 십 년간, 많은 삼림 기관들은 처방화입이라고도 불리는 통제화입을 허용하는 정책들을 입법화시키고 있다. 통제화입에서는, 삼림의 일부를 태우는 것이 허락되지만, 화재가 너무 확대되지 않도록 주의를 기울여야 한다. 처방화입은 오늘날 흔히 사용되고 있지만, 백해무익하다는 증거들도 많다.

처방화입의 가장 큰 단점 중 하나는 해당 지역의 야생 생물에 미치는 영향이다. 처방화입은 종종 직접적으로 사슴, 곰, 다람쥐, 그리고 토끼와 같은 숲속 생물의 죽음을 초래한다. 게다가, 화재로 인해 그곳에서 서식하는 대부분의 동물들의 보금자리가 파괴된다. 서식지를 잃어버린 동물들은 새로운 곳으로 옮겨 가야 한다. 그러한 지역에서는 보다 많은 동물들이 한정된 먹이 공급을 위한 경쟁을 하게 되므로 이는 해당 지역의 토착 생물들에게 부정적인 영향을 미친다.

국립 공원의 처방화입에는 하루 이틀만 소요되는 것이 아니다. 한 번에 수

일이 걸리는 경우도 많다. 따라서 나무와 기타 식물들을 태움으로써 생기는 연기로 인해 다량의 대기 오염이 발생한다. 이 연기는 상당히 짙고 재로 가득 차 있다. 이는 인근 지역에서 호흡을 하는 이들에게 해를 끼칠 뿐만 아니라, 대기를 통해 퍼져 나갈 수도 있는데, 이로써 산불 지역으로부터 멀리 떨어진 곳의 대기의 질도 떨어지게 된다.

다수의 삼림 관리인들은 대형 산불을 예방할 수 있기 때문에 처방화입이 필요하다고 주장한다. 하지만 산불은 종종 화재가 났던 부분을 우회해서 그 대신 다른 곳으로 번지기도 한다. 어떤 경우에는, 처방화입이 걷잡을 수 없게 되어, 큰 산불로 이어졌다. 따라서, 삼림 관리인 자신들이 산불로 인한 특정 지역의 막대한 파괴의 원인이 되기도 했다.

LISTENING   🎧 05-01

M Professor: In the American West, many large areas of land are covered by forests. So during these regions' dry seasons, forest fires sometimes break out. We see this every year in California as well as in other places. For years, authorities tried to put out these fires as soon as they started. However, these days, the authorities are actually the ones starting the fires. No, they're not arsonists . . . They're doing prescribed burns. The burns are intended to prevent larger forest fires from taking place and burning huge amounts of land. Now, there are some opponents of prescribed burnings, but most of their concerns are unfounded.

Some claim that prescribed burnings kill many forest animals. But interestingly enough, few animals get killed by them. Birds can easily escape. And forest mammals can flee fast enough to avoid the fires. Studies on prescribed burnings in Yellowstone National Park have also shown that displaced animals rarely encounter problems finding new homes since the forested areas are, well, enormous.

It's true that prescribed burns create air pollution due to the smoke from burning trees. Yet consider this . . . Prescribed burns affect small forested areas. And they're done to prevent much larger fires from breaking out. So, uh, sure, they pollute the air, but they release less smoke than a huge fire would. I'd say it's better to have a little of a bad thing than a lot of it.

Okay . . . In rare instances, prescribed burns have gotten out of control. But as a general rule, they're very carefully monitored. Additionally, before the burns start, forestry officials take precautions to ensure that the flames won't spread to areas they don't want burned. Considerable amounts of, um, thought go into these burns. They aren't begun until conditions are right, so the chances of them becoming raging infernos are slim.

교수: 미국의 서부에는, 많은 광범위한 지역들이 숲으로 덮여 있습니다. 그래서, 이들 지역의 건기 동안, 산불이 가끔 발생합니다. 다른 지역뿐만 아니라 캘리포니아에서도 해마다 산불을 보게 됩니다. 수년 간, 당국은 이러한 산불이 발생하자마자 진화하기 위해 노력을 했습니다. 하지만, 오늘날, 산불을 일으키는 것은 사실 관계 당국입니다. 아니에요, 당국이 방화범은 아닙니다. 그들은 처방화입을 실시하는 것입니다. 그 산불은 더 큰 산불로 엄청난 양의 토지가 불에 타는 것을 예방하고자 의도된 것입니다. 자, 처방화입에 대해 몇몇 반대론자들이 있기는 하지만, 그들의 걱정 대부분은 근거가 없는 것입니다.

일부는 처방화입으로 많은 삼림 동물들이 목숨을 잃는다고 주장합니다. 하지만, 흥미롭게도, 산불에 의해 죽는 동물들은 거의 없습니다. 새들은 쉽게 탈출할 수 있습니다. 그리고 숲 속의 포유 동물들은 산불을 피하기에 충분히 빠른 속도로 도망칠 수가 있습니다. 옐로우스톤 국립 공원의 처방화입에 대한 연구 역시 삼림이, 음, 거대하기 때문에, 쫓겨난 동물들이 새로운 집을 찾는데 문제가 발생하는 경우는 거의 없는 것을 밝혀냈습니다.

처방화입으로 나무가 타서 생기는 연기 때문에 대기 오염이 발생한다는 점은 사실입니다. 하지만 이러한 점을 생각해 보세요... 처방화입은 삼림의 작은 부분에만 영향을 미칩니다. 그리고 처방화입은 훨씬 더 큰 산불이 발생하는 것을 예방하기 위해 행해집니다. 그러니까, 음, 맞아요, 처방화입이 대기를 오염시키지만, 거대한 산불에 비하면 적은 양의 연기만을 방출합니다. 나쁜 것은 많이 가지고 있는 것보다 적게 가지고 있는 것이 낫다고 말씀드리고 싶네요.

좋아요... 거의 없는 경우인데, 처방화입을 통제할 수 없었던 적이 있었습니다. 하지만, 일반적으로는, 매우 신중히 관리됩니다. 게다가, 화재가 시작되기 전, 삼림 관리인들은 원하지 않는 부분으로 화염이 번지지 않도록 예방 조치를 확실히 취합니다. 이러한 화재에는 상당히 많은 음, 고려가 이루어집니다. 처방화입은 모든 조건에 맞지 않는 한 시작되지 않기 때문에, 불타오르는 지옥이 될 가능성은 매우 적습니다.

Sample Essay   p.058

교수는 처방화입이 더 큰 산불을 예방하려는 목적을 가지고 있다고 주장한다. 이는 여기에 장점보다는 단점이 더 많다는 지문의 주장을 직접적으로 반박한다.

첫째, 동물들은 도망칠 수 있는 충분한 시간이 있기 때문에 다만 몇 안 되는 동물들만이 산불로 인해 죽음을 맞는다. 게다가, 교수는 옐로우스톤 국립 공원에 대한 사례를 예로 드는데, 이 공원의 거대한 크기 덕분에 동물들은 새로운 서식지를 찾는데 어려움을 겪지 않는다. 이는 통제화입으로 숲 속 동물들이 죽고 먹이를 찾는 데 어려움을 겪는다는 지문의 주장을 반박한다.

그리고, 교수는 통제화입의 환경 파괴에 대한 오해가 있어 왔다고 말한다. 통제화입이 연기를 만드는 것은 사실이다. 하지만, 통제화입에서의 연기의 양은 큰 산불에서 발생하는 연기의 양에 비해 훨씬 적다. 이는 통제화입에 수일이 걸리는 경우가 많아서 통제화입에서 발생되는 연기가 대기 오염을 일으킨다는 지문의 주장을 반박한다.

마지막으로, 통제화입은 신중하게 실행된다. 삼림 관리인들은 의도적인 산불을 일으키기 전에 많은 생각과 노력을 기울인다. 그러므로 조건이 맞지 않는 경우, 삼림 관리인들이 산불을 일으킬 가능성은 낮다. 이는 예상치 못한 산불의 확산으로 통제화입이 큰 산불로 바뀔 수 있다는 지문의 내용에 반한다.

TASK 2 · INDEPENDENT TASK
Self-Discipline

Sample Essay 1 ı AGREE   p.061

침실은 하루가 시작되는 공간이다. 사람들은 방을 관리하는 다양한 방법을 가지고 있다. 어떤 이들은 특정한 주제로 방을 꾸미기도 하고, 어떤 이들은 실용성에 맞추어 방을 정돈하며, 또 어떤 이들은 자신의 방에서는 완벽한 편안함을 느껴야 한다는 이유로 물건을 정리하려 하지 않는다. 일부 사람들은 정리하는 능력과 성공에 상관관계가 없다고 하지만 나는 방 정리를 깔끔하게 하는 사람들이 정리 습관을 발전시킬 수 있고 강한 책임감을 가지기 때문에 자신의 목표를 달성하는 데 성공할 확률이 더 높다고 굳게 믿는다.

첫째, 정돈 능력은 대부분의 직업에서 필수적인 것이다. 본인의 물건들을 제자리에 정리해 둠으로써, 사람들은 중요도와 사용 빈도에 따라 물건들을 어떻게 분류하는지에 대해 배운다. 예로써, 장르에 따라 책을 분류하는 습관을 기른 사람들은 주어진 일을 효율적으로 정리하는 경향이 있어서 보다 우수한 관리 능력과 생산성을 보인다.

둘째, 자신의 방을 깔끔하게 유지하는 사람들은 규칙적으로 자신의 방을 정리해야 하기 때문에 책임감을 가지고 있으며, 그들이 발전시킨 훈련법은 직장에서 자신의 일을 수행하는데 도움이 된다. 예를 들어, 내 사촌은 피곤하더라도 이틀에 한 번씩 방을 정리한다. 이러한 책임감은 회사에서도 반영되었다. 그녀는 책임감 있는 직원으로 인정을 받아 부서의 매니저로 승진했다.

대부분의 사람들이 업무로 인해 바쁘고 집에 있는 동안은 쉬고 싶어하기 때문에 때때로 방을 정리하는 것이 어려운 것은 사실이다. 하지만, 개인의 물건들을 지저분하게 두는 것은 불편함을 초래한다. 뛰어난 정리 능력을 갖추는 것은 회사에서 유용하다. 더 나아가, 규칙적으로 방을 정리하는 것은 책임감을 가지는 데 도움이 된다. 위의 이유로, 나는 방 정리를 잘하는 사람들이 자신의 목표를 달성하는 데 성공할 확률이 더 높다는 진술에 강력히 동의한다.

Sample Essay 2 | DISAGREE   p.062

침실은 하루가 시작되는 공간이다. 사람들은 방을 관리하는 다양한 방법을 가지고 있다. 어떤 이들은 특정한 주제로 방을 꾸미기도 하고, 어떤 이들은 실용성에 맞추어 방을 정돈하며, 또 어떤 이들은 자신의 방에서는 완벽한 편안함을 느껴야 한다는 이유로 물건을 정리하려 하지 않는다. 일부 사람들은 방 정리를 깔끔하게 하는 사람들이 자신의 목표를 달성하는 데 성공할 확률이 더 높다고 주장하지만, 나는 이에 반대한다. 사람마다 먼저 해야 하는 일들이 다르고, 정리 능력과 성공의 상관관계는 특정 직업에서만 적용된다.

첫째, 모든 사람들은 다양한 업무에 다양한 가치를 부여한다. 우리 사회가 더욱 치열해지고 사람들은 회사에서 너무 바쁘기 때문에 방을 정리하느라 별도의 노력을 기울이는 것은 어렵게 되었다. 예를 들어, 나는 언제나 퇴근을 늦게 한다. 집에 도착할 무렵이면, 극도로 피곤해서 물건을 제자리에 놓을 시간이 없다. 방을 청소하는 것보다는 일이 더 중요하다고 생각했기 때문에, 나는 대신 가사 도우미를 고용했다.

둘째, 방을 깨끗하게 유지하는 것은 정리 능력을 가르쳐 주지만, 한 사람이 일부 직업에서 성공하기 위해 다른 능력이 요구된다. 예로써, 운동 경기에서 우승하는 것과 방을 정돈하는 능력 간에는 상관관계가 없기 때문에, 운동선수들은 정돈하는 능력을 기르는 것보다 연습을 하는데 시간을 보내는 것이 더 중요하다.

방을 정리하는 능력을 기르는 것이 성공에 기여할 수 있다는 점은 사실이다. 반대로, 성공하기 위해 요구되는 다른 많은 요인들도 있다. 그러므로, 자신의 정리 능력이 성공하는데 도움이 된다고 말하는 것은 성급한 것이다. 일이 바쁜 사람들은 자신의 방을 정돈할 시간을 내는 것이 어렵다. 더 나아가, 정리하는 능력은 특정 직업에만 도움이 된다. 위의 이유로, 나는 방 정리를 잘하는 사람들이 자신의 목표를 달성하는 데 성공할 더 높은 기회를 가진다는 진술에 결코 동의하지 않는다.

Actual Test 06

TASK 1 · INTEGRATED TASK
Geography: Carolina Bays

READING   p.065

미국의 델라웨어에서 플로리다 북부로 이어지는 동부의 연안을 따라가면, 통상 캐롤라이나 만이라고 불리는, 연속으로 함몰된 약 50만개의 지형이 있다. 이들은 대부분 타원형이며, 일부는 호수지만 대체로 건조하다. 또한 모래로 된 높은 가장자리가 함몰 지역을 둘러싸고 있는 모습도 종종 발견된다. 캐롤라이나 만의 기원은 불확실하지만, 하나의 이론에 따르면 우주의 물체들이 지구에 부딪쳐서 그들이 생겨났다고 한다.

이 운석 충돌설에 의하면, 소행성이 미국의 중서부 지역의 오대호 위에서 폭발했다고 한다. 그 후, 폭발로부터 나온 충격파와 소행성의 파편들이 캐롤라이나 만을 형성했다. 만의 형태가 그러한 기원에 대한 한 가지 단서가 된다. 만의 형태는 타원형이며 북서쪽부터 남동쪽까지 뻗쳐있고, 남동쪽의 끝자락은 둥글기보다는 뾰족한 편이다. 이는 오대호가 발견되는 북서쪽에서 그러한 물체들이 지구와 충돌했다는 것을 보여 준다.

지질학자들은 일부 만으로부터 코어 샘플들을 채취했다. 그들은 주로 다른 유명한 운석 충돌 지역에서 나오는 광물과 암석의 몇몇 흔적들을 발견했다. 또한 이러한 표본들의 모래에는 보기 드물게 철이 부족하다. 일부 전문가들은 지구에 충돌했던 소행성 파편들의 압력에 의해 철이 파괴되었을지도 모른다고 가정하고 있다.

또 한 가지 이상한 점은 일부 캐롤라이나 만에서 탄소의 드문 형태인 버키볼이 존재하고 있다는 사실이다. 버키볼은 1985년 우주 공간에서의 실험 도중 처음 발견되었다. 따라서 많은 과학자들은 캐롤라이나 만의 버키볼의 존재가 지구 밖의 물체와 지구가 충돌했음을 나타낸다고 생각한다. 종합해 보면, 이 모든 요인들은 충돌로 인해 캐롤라이나 만이 만들어졌다는 주장에 무게를 실어준다.

LISTENING   🎧 06-01

M Professor: Take a look at this aerial photograph . . . Notice the oval shapes on the land . . . ? These are Carolina bays. There are more than half a million of them in the Atlantic coastal states in the United States. There are two main theories concerning their origins. Some believe, well, an asteroid striking the Earth made them. Others believe that the actions of the wind and water made them. Personally, I doubt the impact theory. Here's why . . .

The impact theory is partially based on the shapes of the bays. They're oval, long, and pointed at their southeastern ends. It looks like something hit the land from the northwest. But not all are shaped that way. Some in Virginia and Georgia are almost circular. Additionally, if an impact event had really created them, then they all would have been made simultaneously. But scientists dating the material in different bays have determined that some were created thousands of years apart.

An examination of the bays' rocks and soil also disproves the impact theory. There are no common materials in Carolina bays and known impact craters around the planet. An example is, ah, shocked quartz, which is formed by sudden massive impacts. No one has ever discovered shocked quartz in any Carolina bay. In addition, while Carolina bays lack iron, this may be the result of a chemical process, not an asteroid impact.

Finally, supporters of the impact theory cite the presence of buckyballs in some Carolina bays as proof. A buckyball is a rare form of carbon first discovered in outer space. Yet some experts believe lightning strikes can make buckyballs, meaning that they aren't always extraterrestrial in origin. The region of the U.S. that has Carolina bays often gets severe thunderstorms, so that could explain why so many buckyballs are there.

교수: 상공에서 찍은 이 사진을 보세요... 땅에 있는 타원 모양에 주목해 봅시다... 이것이 바로 캐롤라이나 만입니다. 미국의 대서양 해안 주에 50만개 이상이 있죠. 그것의 유래에 관해서는 두 개의 주요한 이론이 있습니다. 몇몇 사람들은 음, 지구에 충돌했던 소행성이 이들을 만들었다고 믿고 있습니다. 다른 이들은 바람과 물의 작용으로 만들어졌다고 합니다. 개인적으로는, 충돌 이론에 의문을 가지고 있습니다. 그 이유는 다음과 같습니다...

충돌 이론은 부분적으로 만의 형태에 기초하고 있습니다. 타원형이고 길며 남동쪽 끝은 뾰족합니다. 마치 북서쪽에서 무엇인가 땅에 충돌한 것처럼 보입니다. 하지만 모든 형태가 다 그렇지는 않습니다. 버지니아와 조지아에 있는 일부는 거의 원형입니다. 게다가, 만약 충돌로 인해 만들어졌다면, 모두가 동시에 만들어졌어야 합니다. 그렇지만 여러 만에 있는 물질들의 연대를 측정한 과학자들은 이들 일부가 수천 년의 차이를 두고 만들어 졌다는 결론을 내렸습니다.

만의 암석이나 토양에 대한 조사 역시 충돌 이론을 반증하고 있습니다. 캐롤라이나 만에는 흔한 물질들이나 지구의 이곳저곳에 있는 충돌 구덩이들이 없습니다. 예로써, 충격 석영은 갑작스러운 커다란 충돌에 의해 형성됩니다. 캐롤라이나 만의 어떤 곳에서도 충격 석영을 발견한 사람은 없었습니다. 또한, 캐롤라이나 만에는 철이 부족한데, 이는 소행성 충돌이 아닌 화학 작용의 결과일 수도 있습니다.

끝으로, 충돌 이론의 지지자들은 캐롤라이나 만의 버키볼의 존재를 그 증거로서 언급합니다. 버키볼은 우주 공간에서 처음 발견되었던 탄소의 드문 형태입니다. 하지만 일부 전문가들은 번개가 버키볼을 만들어 낼 수 있다고 믿고 있습니다. 버키볼이 항상 우주에 그 기원을 두고 있다고만 할 수는 없는 것이죠. 캐롤라이나 만이 있는 지역에는 종종 극심한 뇌우가 발생하기 때문에 왜 그곳에 버키볼이 많은지에 대해서는 설명이 될 수가 있습니다.

Sample Essay | p.068

교수는 캐롤라이나 만이 생겨난 유래에 관해 일부 전문가들이 가정하고 있는 충돌 이론에 의문이 제기되고 있다고 주장한다. 이는 캐롤라이나 만이 과거 우주로부터의 물체와 지구가 충돌했던 결과라는 지문의 주장을 직접적으로 반박한다.

첫째, 교수는 캐롤라이나 만의 형상은 충돌 이론이 타당하지 않다는 것을 증명해 준다고 말한다. 교수에 따르면, 모든 캐롤라이나 만이 같은 형상을 가진 것은 아니다. 이러한 사실은 만의 형태가 소행성 분화구의 형태와 같으며 외계의 물체가 미 북서쪽으로부터 떨어졌다는 지문의 주장에 의문을 제기한다.

뿐만 아니라, 교수는 알려진 모든 충돌 구덩이에 있는 흔한 물질들이 발견되지 않았다고 주장한다. 예를 들면, 충돌 지역에서 일반적으로 발견되는 충격 석영은 전혀 발견되지 않았다. 게다가, 철의 결핍은 화학 작용의 결과로서 설명될 수 있다. 이는 핵심 샘플들이 다른 충돌 지점과의 유사성을 보여 주고, 철은 소행성 파편의 압력에 의해 파괴되었다는 지문의 주장과 반대된다.

마지막으로, 버키볼은 번개로 인해 생길 수 있다. 이는 극심한 뇌우가 종종 발생하는 캐롤라이나 만의 지역들을 살펴봄으로써 확실히 설명될 수 있다. 이러한 주장은 버키볼의 존재가 지구 밖의 물체가 지구에 충돌했다는 점을 증명해 준다는 지문의 주장을 반박한다.

TASK 2 · INDEPENDENT TASK
Monetary Value

Sample Essay 1 | AGREE | p.071

수년에 걸쳐 생활 방식이 향상됨에 따라, 개인이 돈을 어떻게 사용해야 하는가에 대한 질문이 다양한 방법으로 제기되고 있다. 어떤 이들은 여행에 돈을 쓰고, 어떤 이들은 새로운 취미 개발에 돈을 쓰며, 다른 이들은 미래를 위해 저축을 하고 있다. 미래나 예기치 못한 상황을 대비하여 저축을 하는 것은 언제나 현명한 일이지만, 여행을 하는 동안 스트레스를 해소할 수 있기 때문에, 나는 휴가와 여행에 돈을 써야 한다고 굳게 믿는다. 게다가, 여행을 함으로써 관점을 넓힐 수도 있다.

첫째, 여행은 직장의 고된 일에서 비롯되는 스트레스를 덜어줄 수 있다. 여행이 제공해 주는 놀랄 만큼의 아름다운 경치와 특별한 순간들로 인해, 사람은 일상으로부터 벗어날 수가 있다. 예를 들면, 나는 작년 여름 회사에서 주어진 새로운 업무에 대한 압박감으로 불안감을 느낀 적이 있었다. 그래서, 나는 한국의 몇몇 작은 마을들을 여행하기로 결심했다. 여행을 하는 동안, 나는 신선한 공기와 아름다운 경관으로 가득한 마을에서 전통 음식과 온천을 즐겼다. 그 결과, 다시 원기를 회복한 기분을 느끼게 되었으며 새로운 업무를 성공적으로 시작할 수 있었다.

둘째, 우리는 다른 곳을 여행하면서 우리의 시야를 넓힐 수 있다. 다양한 사람들을 만나고 다양한 경험을 함으로써, 새로운 관습을 배우고 미지의 곳을 탐험해 볼 수 있다. 예를 들면, 내 사촌은 해마다 휴가 철에 다른 나라로 여행을 간다. 새로운 곳을 방문 할 때마다, 그녀는 그 지역의 새로운 문화를 경험하고 익숙하지 않은 관습을 이해하려고 노력한다. 이는 그녀의 마음을 열어 주며 타인에 대한 이해심을 길러 준다. 그녀가 이러한 능력을 얻지 못했다면, 특정한 사람이나 상황을 다루는데 어려움을 겪고 있을 것이다.

미래를 위해 저축하는 것이 안정감을 느끼게 해 주는 것은 사실이다. 하지만, 소중한 추억과 경험을 얻는 것도 그만큼 중요하다. 여행을 통해서, 사람들은 직장의 스트레스로부터 벗어날 수 있고, 더 열심히 일해야겠다는 동기 부여도 받을 수 있다. 게다가, 사람은 직접적인 경험으로부터 배움을 얻고 생각의 폭을 넓힐 수도 있다. 이상의 이유들 때문에, 나는 미래를 위해 저축하는 것보다는 휴가를 보내며 여행을 하는데 돈을 사용하는 것이 더 낫다는 주장에 강력히 동의한다.

Sample Essay 2 | AGREE | p.072

수년에 걸쳐 생활 방식이 향상됨에 따라, 개인이 돈을 어떻게 사용해야 하는가에 대한 질문이 다양한 방법으로 제기되고 있다. 어떤 이들은 여행에 돈을 쓰고, 어떤 이들은 새로운 취미 개발에 돈을 쓰며, 다른 이들은 미래를 위해 저축을 하고 있다. 비록 여행은 소중한 경험을 가져다 주지만, 돈은 사람들이 추구하는 장기적 목표를 뒷받침해 줄 수 있기 때문에, 나는 미래를 위해 저축을 해야 한다고 굳게 믿는다. 게다가, 저축을 하면 긴급 상황에서도 항상 재정적으로 안정감을 느낄 수 있다.

첫째, 집을 사거나 학비를 내는 것과 같은 추구해야 할 많은 기본적인 목표들이 있다. 여행이 재미를 주는 것은 사실이다. 하지만, 미래를 위해 저축하는 것이 보다 더 의미가 있다. 예를 들면, 나는 휴가에 돈을 쓰는 것 대신 미래에 주택을 구입하기 위해 저축을 하고 있다. 휴가에 쓰는 돈은 휴가 후에 없어지지만, 주택은 내가 가지고 있는 한 남아 있을 것이다. 게다가, 여행에 돈을 지출하면, 주택을 구매할 때까지 소요되는 시간이 더 길어질 것이다.

둘째, 긴급 상황을 포함한 예기치 못한 상황에 대비하여 항상 저축을 해야 한다. 그럼으로써, 재정적으로 안정되고 대비가 잘 되어 있다는 느낌을 받을 수 있다. 예를 들면, 내 친구는 교통 사고를 당해서 2주간 입원을 했다. 큰 수술에 많은 비용이 필요했지만, 저축 습관 덕분에 그는 필요한 돈에 대해 걱정을 하지 않고 수술을 받을 수 있었다. 만약 그가 저축을 하지 않았더라면, 다른 사람이나 금융 기관으로부터 돈을 빌려야 했을 것이고 수술은 지연되었을 것이다.

여행이 다시 직장으로 돌아왔을 때 원기를 회복시켜 주는 것은 사실이다. 하지만, 예상치 못한 상황이 많기 때문에, 삶을 즐기고 싶은 욕구만을 따라갈 수는 없다. 장기적인 목표를 달성하기 위해 열심히 노력하는 것은 중요하다. 게다가, 긴급 상황을 대비해 저축을 하는 것은 항상 현명한 일이다. 그렇게 하면, 재정적인 면에 대해 안심할 수 있다. 이상의 이유로, 나는 미래를 위해 저축하는 것보다 휴가를 보내며 여행을 하는데 돈을 사용해야 한다는 주장에 강력히 반대한다.

Actual Test 07

TASK 1 · INTEGRATED TASK

American History: Robert E. Peary

READING   p.075

20세기 초반, 많은 탐험가들이 북극에 도달하기 위해 경쟁을 했다. 차후 몇몇이 그 목적을 달성했다고 주장을 했는데, 이는 누가 그 곳에 먼저 도달했는가에 대한 질문을 다소 논쟁적으로 만들었다. 하지만, 다양한 증거로 주장이 뒷받침되는 까닭에, 미국인인 로버트 피어리라는 탐험가가 육로로 1909년 4월 9일 북극에 도착했다는 인정을 받게 되었다.

피어리가 북극 여행에서 돌아왔을 때, 그보다 일 년 전 북극에 도달했다고 주장하는 프레드릭 쿡이라는 또 다른 탐험가가 있다는 것이 알려졌다. 피어리는 자신의 증거를 명망 높은 단체인 국립 지리 협회에 보냈다. 그의 기록을 면밀히 검토한 후, 그 협회는 쿡은 그렇지(도달하지) 않은 반면, 피어리는 북극에 도달했다고 결론지었다.

피어리의 보고서에서는, 그가 마지막 베이스캠프로부터 북극까지 도달하는 데 약 37일이 걸렸다고 진술되어 있다. 많은 북극 전문가들은 여정에서 피어리가 견뎌야 했던 혹독한 조건들을 고려해 보았을 때 여정이 너무 짧았다고 믿었다. 그러나, 2005년 또 다른 탐험가인 톰 에이버리가 피어리의 여정을 그대로 반복해 보았다. 그의 팀은 1909년 당시의 개 썰매 복제품을 사용했고, 가능한 최고로 피어리가 직면했던 조건들을 반영했다. 에이버리의 팀은 37일이 조금 못되게 북극에 도착했으며 이는 피어리의 주장이 타당하다는 것을 증명해 주었다.

피어리 자신은 능숙한 항해사였고 여행하는 동안 많은 것을 목격했으며, 그래서 그는 언제 북극에 다다랐는지를 알고 있었다. 또한 그곳에 있는 동안

사진도 몇 장 찍었다. 사진을 찍었던 날 하늘에 있던 태양의 위치와 얼음 위의 그림자 길이를 조사함으로써, 국립 지리 협회의 전문가들은 이 사진들을 찍었을 때 피어리가 정말로 북극에 서 있었다는 결론을 내렸다.

M Professor: According to your textbook, American Robert E. Peary was the first man to reach the North Pole. However, many historians, including myself, disagree and don't believe that Peary made it there. In fact, the evidence shows that Peary's claim is shaky at best.

Peary and Frederick Cook, another adventurer, both said they had reached the North Pole. The National Geographic Society examined the evidence and supported Peary's claim. Case closed, right? Well . . . not exactly. The society wasn't filled with impartial observers since Peary was friends with the people examining his records. He was also a big donor to the society. Furthermore, the society took only two days to examine the evidence, which Peary himself admitted was, uh, problematic.

You're probably wondering what evidence Peary submitted, right? First, there were his navigation records. Keep in mind, however, that Peary was the lone member of his team schooled in navigation, so no one on site could confirm his figures. Second, his trip to the North Pole only took thirty-seven days. That's too short. Now I'm aware that Tom Avery duplicated this feat in 2005, but his experiment was flawed. After all, the weather conditions were much different. And the weights of the sled loads may have differed, too. It simply wasn't an accurate test.

I'm also aware that Peary claimed to have taken some photos at the North Pole. However, Peary's camera was manufactured to fit six different lenses. Depending on which lens Peary used, the lengths of the shadows would have varied. Since we don't know what lens his camera had, we can't trust the photographic evidence. It may have appeared he was at the North Pole when he really wasn't. As for me, I believe that Peary was near the North Pole yet never actually got there.

교수: 여러분의 교재에 의하면, 미국인인 로버트 피어리가 북극에 도달했던 첫 번째 사람이었습니다. 하지만, 저를 포함한 많은 역사가들은 이에 동의하지 않으며, 피어리가 그곳에 도달했다는 것을 믿지 않습니다. 사실, 그러한 증거는 피어리의 주장이 기껏해야 불확실하다는 점을 보여 주고 있습니다.

피어리와 또 다른 모험가인 프레드릭 쿡은 둘 다 북극에 도달했다고 말했습니다. 국립 지리 협회는 그 증거를 검사하고 피어리의 주장을 지지했습니다. 사건이 종료되었어요, 그렇죠? 자... 꼭 그렇지만은 않습니다. 피어리는 기록을 검사하는 사람들과 친구였기 때문에, 그 협회는 공정한 감독관들로 채워져 있지 않았습니다. 그는 또한 그 협회의 중요한 후원자였어요. 게다가, 그 협회가 증거를 검토하는 데는 이틀밖에 걸리지 않았으며 이는 피어리 자신도 어, 의심스럽다고 인정을 했을 정도지요.

피어리가 어떤 증거를 제출했는지 아마 궁금할 거예요, 그렇죠? 첫째, 그의 항해 기록이 있습니다. 그런데 기억해 두세요, 피어리는 그의 팀에서 항해에 관한 교육을 받았던 유일한 구성원이었기 때문에 현장에서 누구도 그의

수치를 확인해 줄 수 없었습니다. 둘째, 그의 북극 여행은 37일밖에 걸리지 않았습니다. 그것은 그야말로 너무 짧아요. 자, 톰 에이버리가 2005년에 이 위업을 재현했다는 것을 알고 있습니다만 그의 실험에는 결함이 있었습니다. 아무튼, 기후 조건이 상당히 달랐습니다. 그리고 썰매 짐의 무게도 달랐을 수 있고요. 그것은 그저 정확한 검증이 아니었습니다.

또한 저는 피어리가 북극에서 몇 장의 사진을 찍었다고 주장했던 점도 알고 있습니다. 하지만, 피어리의 카메라는 6개의 서로 다른 렌즈를 설치하도록 제작되어 있었습니다. 피어리가 어떤 렌즈를 사용했느냐에 따라서, 그림자의 길이는 달라졌을 것입니다. 그의 카메라에 어떤 렌즈가 있었는지 모르기 때문에, 우리는 사진의 증거를 믿을 수 없습니다. 그는 실제로 (북극에) 있지 않았지만 북극에 있었던 것처럼 보였을지도 모릅니다. 저로서는 피어리가 북극 근처에 있었지만, 절대로 그 곳에 도달하지 않았다고 믿습니다.

Sample Essay   p.078

교수는 많은 전문가들이 로버트 피어리가 북극에 성공적으로 도달한 최초의 인간이었다는 것을 확신하지 않는다고 주장한다. 이는 그러한 단정을 입증하는 많은 증거가 있다는 지문의 주장을 직접적으로 반박한다.

첫째, 국립 지리 협회의 조사관들이 그의 동료들이었기 때문에 피어리의 주장은 유효하지 않다. 게다가 검사관들은 피어리가 북극에서의 첫 번째 탐험가였다고 결정을 내리기 전에 서둘러 이틀 만에 그의 기록을 조사했다. 이는 피어리의 기록이 그 협회에의해 신중히 검토되고 승인되었다는 지문의 주장과 모순된다.

다음으로, 교수는 피어리가 원정에서유일한 숙련된 구성원이었기 때문에, 북극에 그가 있었음을 확인해 줄 사람이 없었으며 피어리의 항해 기록에는 설득력이 없다고 주장한다. 더욱이, 다른 조건들이 다른 이들에 의해 행해진 여정과 비교하기 어렵게 만든다. 이는 톰 에이버리가 여정을 더 짧은 시간 안에 반복했을 때까지 피어리의 여정이 겨우 37일 걸렸다는 점에 전문가들이 회의적이었다는 지문의 내용에 의문을 제기한다.

마지막으로, 카메라에 다른 이미지들을 보여 줄 수 있는 6개의 서로 다른 렌즈들을 설치할 수있었기 때문에, 사진 증거는 신뢰할 수 없다. 이는 태양의 위치와 그림자의 길이를 보여 주는 피어리의 사진들이 국립 지리 협회로 하여금 그가 정말로북극에 갔다는 주장에 대해 확신하도록 이끌었다는 지문의 주장을 반박한다.

TASK 2 · INDEPENDENT TASK
Media

Sample Essay 1 | AGREE   p.081

학습 방법에는 여러 가지가 있다. 어떤 이들은 수업을 들으며 배우고, 어떤 이들은 텔레비전 등의 대중매체를 이용해 배우며, 또 다른 이들은 독서를 통해서 배운다. 각각의 방법에는 장점뿐만 아니라 단점도 있지만, 나는 TV를 보며 배움을 얻는 것이 가장 효과적이라고 굳게 믿는다. 내가 이런 믿음을 가진 데에는 두 가지 이유가 있다. TV 시청에 의한 학습은 시간을 절약해 주며, 시각적 내용은 이해를 보다 용이하게 해 준다.

우선, 텔레비전을 시청함으로써 지식을 얻는 시간을 절약할 수 있는데, 이는 TV가 통상 역사, 천문학, 또는 지질학 등의 분야에 있어서 요약된 주제를 보여 주기 때문이다. 이는 짧은 시간 내에 많은 정보를 얻을 수 있도록 해 준다. 예를 들어, 내 사촌은 17세기의 위대한 철학자들에 대해서 공부를 해야만 했다. 비록 과제를 수행하는데 한 달간의 시간만이 있었지만, 그녀는 해낼 수 있었다. 이러한 성취는 당면한 사안에 대한 요약을 그녀에게 제공해 준 TV프로그램을 시청함으로써 가능했다. 그녀가 독서를 통해서 철학자들을 공

부를 하려고 했다면, 훨씬 더 많은 시간이 걸렸을 것이다.

덧붙여, TV는 정보를 보다 더 효과적으로 얻을 수 있도록 해 주는 시각적 효과를 제공한다. 다시 말해서, 시청자들은 연속적인 이미지로서 보게 될 때 어려운 개념들을 더 잘 이해할 수 있다. 예를 들어, 내 친구는 하나의 실험을 이해하는데 어려움을 겪은 적이 있었다. 하지만 한 교수가 실험 절차를 보여 주는 TV 프로그램을 시청하여 큰 어려움 없이 실험 과정을 이해할 수 있었다. 그 결과, 교수가 실험을 진행하는 것을 시청한 후, 내 친구는 실험 지시에 따라 실제 스스로 실험을 진행할 수가 있었다.

독서를 함으로써 여러 세부적인 정보를 얻을 수 있다는 점은 사실이다. 그럼에도 불구하고, 다양한 분야에서 폭넓은 정보를 얻으려고 하는 이들에게 이는 시간이 너무 오래 걸리는 일일 수 있다. 이렇게 볼 때, 시청자들은 TV를 시청함으로써 많은 지식을 얻는 동시에 시간도 절약할 수 있다. 게다가, 텔레비전은 시청자가 더 효율적으로 주제를 이해하는데 도움이 된다. 상기 이유들로 인하여, 나는 책을 읽으며 배우는 것보다는 TV를 시청하며 배우는 것이 더 낫다는 진술에 강력히 동의한다.

Sample Essay 2 | DISAGREE   p.082

학습 방법에는 여러 가지가 있다. 어떤 이들은 수업을 들으며 배우고, 어떤 이들은 텔레비전 등의 대중매체를 이용해 배우며, 또 다른 이들은 독서를 통해서 배움을 얻는다. 각각의 방법에는 장점뿐만 아니라 단점도 있지만, 나는 독서를 통해 배움을 얻는 것이 가장 효과적이라고 굳게 믿는다. 이러한 확신에는 두 가지 이유가 있다. 책은 훨씬 더 많은 세부적인 정보들을 제공해 주며, 그리고 책을 읽음으로써, 분석 및 해석과 같은 능력을 습득할 수 있기 때문이다.

우선, 책은 독자들에게 풍부한 통찰과 세부적인 내용들을 제공해 준다. 다시 말해서, 독자들은 책을 통해 깊이 있는 지식을 얻을 수 있다. 예를 들자면, 내 사촌은 세계의 화산에 관한 텔레비전 프로그램을 시청했다. 화산에 대한 일반적인 정보는 얻을 수 있었던 반면, 그에 대한 구체적인 지식은 얻을 수 없었다. 이후, 그녀는 해당 주제에 관한 책을 찾고 나서야 화산을 보다 깊이 있게 이해할 수 있었다. 이러한 사례는, TV를 보는 것보다 더 많은 시간이 걸리기는 하지만, 배우는데 있어서는 독서가 더 효과적인 방법임을 입증해 준다.

덧붙여, 사람들은 책을 읽음으로써 분석과 해석 능력을 배운다. 예를 들어, 내가 Sea World의 돌고래에 대한 TV쇼를 시청했을 때, 포획된 돌고래들은 돌고래 쇼에서 공연을 잘 하기 위해 평생을 보내는 것처럼 보였다. 그러나, 그에 대한 책을 읽으면서, 나는 그 TV 프로그램이 오직 환경론자들의 관점에서만 만들어졌다는 것을 깨달았다. 그 소재에 대한 많은 책을 읽으며 나는 다양한 관점으로 생각하는 것을 배웠다. TV에서만 돌고래를 보았다면, 나는 Sea World에 대해 편견을 가졌을 것이다.

TV가 시청자들에게 이미지를 제공해 줌으로써 좀 더 나은 이해를 도울 수 있다는 것은 사실이다. 하지만, 여러 도서에는 개념에 대한 독자의 이해를 도와줄 수 있는 사진들이 포함되어 있다. 책은 보다 상세한 내용들을 독자에게 제공한다. 게다가, 독자들은 상상, 분석, 해석의 능력을 개발할 수 있는 기회를 갖는다. 상기 이유들로 인하여, 나는 책을 읽으며 배움을 얻는 것보다 TV를 시청하며 배우는 것이 더 낫다는 진술에 강력히 반대한다.

TASK 1 · INTEGRATED TASK

Music: Instruments

음악은 약 40,000년의 역사를 가지고 있다. 그것은 예술적 표현은 물론이고 기분 전환이나 의식의 목적으로 사용되어 왔다. 음악은 항상 우리 주변에 존재해 왔고, 어릴 적에 악기를 배우는 것은 종종 필수라고 여겨진다. 하지만, 음악을 감상하기 위해 악기를 연주할 줄 알아야 하는 것이 정말 필요한가? 많은 연구들은 어린 시절에 악기를 배우는 것이 생각하는 만큼 도움이 되지는 않을 수도 있다는 것을 밝혀 냈다.

악기를 연주할 때 신체 부상을 겪기 쉽다. 사람이 어릴 때, 고통이 진전되면서 후에 심각한 문제를 유발할 수 있다. 예를 들면, 일부 악기들은 악기를 다룰 때 아이들이 머리를 기울이게 하기 때문에 많은 아이들은 목이나 어깨 통증을 겪는다. 또 음악인들이 직면하는 하나의 일반적인 신체적 어려움은 마른 입이다. 관악기는 일반적으로 호흡 조절과 유지가 필요하고, 입을 굉장히 건조하게 만든다. 이런 점에서 아이가 악기를 하도록 강요하는 것은 불합리하다.

아이들이 어릴 때 악기를 연주하게 만드는 것에 대한 또 하나의 우려는 그들이 감정적인 어려움으로 고통 받을 수 있다는 것이다. 아마추어들, 심지어 전문 음악가들도 콘서트를 준비하거나 자격증 시험을 준비하는 동안 많은 스트레스에 시달린다. 다른 아이들은 공연이나 오디션 같이 중요한 행사에서 실수를 저질렀을 때 좌절감을 느낄 수 있는 반면에, 어떤 아이들은 그런 모든 압박을 견디지 못할 수 있다.

신체적, 감성적 어려움 외에도, 어린 나이에 악기를 배우는 것은 시간 낭비일 수 있다. 모든 아이들이 악기를 연주하는 것을 배우는데 필요한 책무와 책임감을 견딜 수 있는 것은 아니다. 악기를 배우는 것은 매일 연습을 요하고 아이들로 하여금 포기하기 쉽게 만든다. 이는 학생이 악기의 기초를 이해하지 않고서는, 배운 대부분의 지식을 잃어버릴 가능성이 높다는 이유에서 시간 낭비일 수 있다.

M Professor: Childhood is a period of tremendous growth in all areas of development. So it's very important to provide kids with stimulating environments. Many studies have been conducted and have discovered that pleasurable music affects reinforcement learning. Learning a musical instrument not only provides positive physical and emotional support, but it also helps children in the future. Let's look at this more closely.

I've noticed there are some people who worry about injuries caused by learning an instrument . . . Well . . . there is an even higher possibility of being injured while playing sports . . . Some of the most common injuries include fractures, ankle sprains, and knee problems. Even sitting still and studying can cause serious neck or back pain. A lot of research has, in fact, shown the benefits of music while patients undergo treatment or surgery . . . like lowering blood pressure, slowing heart rates, and reducing the levels of stress hormones. So music can actually help bodies heal.

We all get stress in our lives . . . Even babies experience stress starting the moment when they are born, so it's not just musical instruments that give kids pressure or stress. Rather, learning an instrument can help people overcome emotional problems. For instance, it's known that pleasing music causes increased levels of dopamine, which is the primary neurotransmitter associated with cognitive, behavioral, and emotional functioning. Hmm . . . By learning to play an instrument, children are naturally exposed to a medium which can help them overcome negative emotions, grief, and trauma.

Gaining creativity and confidence by learning musical instruments teaches children with invaluable lessons. Students also learn responsibility, dedication, and patience while putting time and effort into practice. Even if they quit playing the instrument, the commitment and the discipline they have learned during lessons, practices, and performances will aid them throughout their lifetimes. So it really is hard to say that learning a musical instrument during childhood is time consuming.

교수: 아동기는 모든 발달 분야에 있어 엄청난 성장의 시기입니다. 그래서 아이들에게 자극을 주는 환경을 제공하는 것은 아주 중요하지요. 많은 연구들이 실행되었고 유쾌한 음악은 강화 교육에 영향을 끼친다는 것을 발견했어요. 악기를 배우는 것은 긍정적인 신체적, 감성적 버팀목을 제공할 뿐 아니라 아이들에게 미래에 도움이 되기도 합니다. 좀더 자세히 보도록 하지요.

저는, 악기를 배움으로써 발생하는 부상에 대해 걱정하는 일부 사람들이 있다는 것을 알아챘어요... 글쎄요... 스포츠를 하는 동안 부상을 입을 가능성이 심지어는 더 높아요... 가장 흔한 부상은 골절, 발목 삠, 그리고 무릎 문제 등이요. 심지어는 가만히 앉아서 공부하는 것도 심각한 목이나 허리 통증을 유발할 수 있습니다. 많은 연구들이, 사실, 환자들이 치료나 수술을 받는 동안 (누리는) 음악의 이점을 보여 줍니다... 이를테면 혈압을 낮추고, 심장 박동수를 줄이고, 스트레스 호르몬의 수치를 감소시키는 그런 거요. 그러니까 음악은 사실상 몸이 낫도록 도움을 줄 수 있는 거지요.

우리는 모두 삶에서 스트레스를 받아요... 심지어는 아기들도 태어나는 순간부터 스트레스를 경험하지요. 그러니까 악기만이 아이들에게 압박과 스트레스를 주는 것은 아니에요. 악기를 배우는 것은 감정의 수치를 극복하도록 도움을 줄 수 있어요. 예를 들면, 유쾌한 음악은 도파민의 수치를 증가시키지요. 도파민은 인지, 행동, 그리고 감정 기능과 연관된 주된 신경 전달 물질이에요. 흠... 악기 연주하는 것을 배우며 아이들은 자연스럽게 부정적인 감정이나 슬픔, 그리고 정신적 충격을 극복할 수 있도록 도움이 되는 매개체에 노출이 되는 겁니다.

악기를 배우며 창의력과 자신감을 얻는 것은 아이들에게 귀중한 교훈을 가르쳐 줍니다. 학생들은 연습에 시간과 노력을 쏟으며 책임감, 헌신, 그리고 인내심도 배우게 되지요. 악기를 중단한다 할지라도 수업, 연습, 연주하는 동안 배워 온 책무와 훈련은 그들의 삶 내내 도움을 줄 거예요. 그러니, 아동기에 악기를 배우는 것은 시간 낭비라고 말하기는 힘듭니다.

교수는 어린 나이에 악기를 배우는 것은 아이들에게 활기찬 환경을 제공해 주기 위해 필요하다고 주장한다. 이는 악기를 배우는 것은 이상적이지 않다는 지문의 의견을 반박한다.

첫째, 부상은 아이들이 가만히 앉아있을 때조차도 일어날 수 있고, 사실, 음악은 몸이 회복하는데 도움을 준다. 좀 더 자세히 말하면, 악기를 배우는 것은 치료나 수술하는 동안 혈압을 낮추고 스트레스 호르몬의 양을 낮추는 것 같은 많은 이점이 있다. 이는 어린 나이에 악기를 배우는 것은 부상을 초래할 수 있다는 주장을 직접적으로 반박한다.

게다가, 교수는 음악을 배우는 것은 아이들로 하여금 정서적인 문제를 극복하도록 도울 수 있다고 주장한다. 그에 따르면, 유쾌한 음악을 연주하고 듣는 것은 인지, 행동, 그리고 정서적 기능과 관련이 있는 도파민을 분비한다. 이는 악기를 배우는 것은 아이들에게 많은 압박과 스트레스를 준다는 지문의 내용에 반한다.

마지막으로, 아이들은 악기를 배우면서 창의력과 자신감을 기르면서 스스로를 단련하게 된다. 아이들이 악기를 끊더라도, 그들이 쏟은 헌신과 노력은 헛되지 않는다. 이는 악기를 배우는 것은 큰 부담을 주기 때문에, 아이가 그만두겠다고 결정한다면 시간 낭비가 될 수도 있다는 지문의 주장에 반대한다.

TASK 2 · INDEPENDENT TASK
Hobbies

Sample Essay 1 | AGREE | p.091

정도의 차이는 있지만, 대부분의 사람들은 일에서 스트레스를 받는다. 따라서, 일에서 잠시 벗어나 취미나 신체 활동을 하며 휴식을 취한다. 어떤 이들은 직장에서 하는 일과 유사한 종류의 취미나 운동을 즐겨야 한다고 주장한다. 하지만, 새로운 것을 시도해 봄으로써, 사람들은 다른 배경을 가진 다른 이들을 만나볼 기회를 가질 수 있기 때문에, 나는 그러한 의견에 반대한다. 또한, 다양한 분야를 경험해 볼 수도 있을 것이다.

첫째, 다른 취미를 시도하는 것은 사람들이 다른 배경을 가진 다른 이들과 어울릴 기회를 제공한다. 예를 들면, 과학자인 내 사촌은 매 주말마다 암벽 등반을 한다. 그는 사무실로부터 벗어나 신체 활동을 할 뿐만 아니라 다양한 직업을 가진 사람들과 만남으로써 스트레스를 해소할 수 있다고 말한다.

둘째, 직업과 다른 활동을 함으로써, 사람들은 다양한 경험에 참여할 수 있다. 예로써, 내 친구는 고고학자로 일하고 있는데, 그녀는 주로 동료들과 함께 유물과 유골을 발굴하는 교외에서 일한다. 하지만, 그녀는 플라멩코 춤을 배우기 시작했다. 춤을 배움으로써, 내 친구는 새로운 기술을 습득하고 음식을 비롯한 스페인 문화를 경험해 보는 기회도 가졌다.

사실 직업과 유사한 취미를 가지면, 결국 스트레스만 받고 시간과 돈을 낭비하는 상황이 되어버리는, 이후 그다지 재미있지 않은 것으로 판명되는 취미를 가지게 될 위험성은 없다. 반대로, 도전은 종종 사람들로 하여금 다른 직업을 가진 사람들과 만날 수 있는 기회를 찾도록 새로운 세상을 열어 준다. 더 나아가, 자신의 직업과 연관성이 없는 활동을 선택함으로써 다양한 경험을 즐길 수도 있다. 그러므로, 나는 사람들이 직장에서 하는 일과 매우 다른 취미나 신체 활동을 하며 휴식을 취해야 한다는 주장에 전적으로 찬성한다.

Sample Essay 2 | DISAGREE | p.092

정도의 차이는 있지만, 대부분의 사람들은 일에서 스트레스를 받는다. 따라서, 일에서 잠시 벗어나 취미나 운동을 하며 휴식을 취한다. 어떤 이들은 직장에서 하는 일과 상당히 다른 종류의 취미나 운동을 즐겨야 한다고 주장한다. 하지만, 사람들은 자신의 관심사와 관련된 직업을 갖는 경향이 있기 때문에 나는 그러한 의견에 반대한다. 게다가, 일과 비슷한 활동을 하는 것은 시간과 돈을 절약해 준다.

첫째, 대부분의 사람들은 관심 분야에 기반하여 직업을 선택한다. 그러므로, 자신의 직업과 밀접한 관련이 있는 활동을 즐길 가능성이 더 크다. 예로

써, 환경 보호 단체에서 일하는 95퍼센트 이상의 사람들이 골프나 환경을 해치는 다른 취미 활동을 하는 것을 꺼린다고 말했다. 대신, 그들 중 다수는 자연 보호 운동과 관련된 연극 및 미술 활동 등에 참여하고 있다.

둘째, 새로운 취미를 시도하는 것은 재미있는 경험을 제공하기 보다는 스트레스를 만들어 낼 수 있다. 예를 들면, 세계 여행을 좋아하는 여행사 직원은 할인된 가격에 여행을 할 수 있는 기회를 많이 접한다. 반대로, 만약 여행사 직원이 악기를 배우려 시도하다가 나중에 자신이 재능이 없다는 것을 알게 된다면, 그는 스트레스를 견디는 것은 말할 것도 없고, 시간과 돈 낭비를 한 셈이 될 것이다.

새로운 활동에 참여하는 것이 새로운 사람들과 만날 기회를 줄 수 있는 것은 사실이다. 하지만, 대인 관계를 넓히는 것이 삶에서 반드시 필요한 것은 아니다. 대부분의 사람들의 직업들은 그들의 관심사와 관련이 있기 때문에, 그들은 직업과 비슷한 활동을 즐길 것이다. 더 나아가, 직업과 밀접한 관계가 있는 취미를 갖는 것은 사람들이 시간과 돈을 절약하게 해 줄 것이다. 그러므로, 나는 사람들이 자신의 일과 매우 다른 취미를 시도하는 것은 무의미하다고 굳게 믿는다.

Actual Test 09

TASK 1 · INTEGRATED TASK
Sociology: The Privatization of Infrastructure

READING | p.095

20세기의 상당 부분 동안, 미국의 여러 주 및 시 정부뿐만 아니라 연방 정부 역시 국가의 사회 기반 시설, 특히 전기, 수도, 그리고 운송 산업을 관리했다. 그러나, 지난 30년간, 미국의 많은 산업이 민영화되었다. 결과는 대부분 긍정적이었다.

정부는 여러 기반 시설 사업과 프로젝트들을 매각해서 상당한 이득을 얻었다. 예를 들어, 1987년, 철도 Conrail은 17억 달러에 매각되었다. 1997년에는 Elks Hill Petroleum Reserve가 37억 달러로 민영화되었다. 많은 북부의 주에서 주 정부들은 유료 도로의 관리 권한을 수십 억 달러에 팔았다. 대부분의 주 정부가 예산 부족을 겪고 있는 시기에, 민간 부문으로부터의 이러한 자금의 유입은 대단히 필요하다.

사기업들은 일반적으로 기반 시설 프로젝트들을 정부보다 더 잘 운영한다. 첫째로, 사기업들은 이익을 내는 데에 집중해서, 정부 운영 체제하에 존재했던 비효율성을 없앤다. 예를 들면, 불필요한 부서들을 정리하고, 생산적인 근로자에게는 보상을 주고 승진을 시키는 반면, 생산성이 없는 근로자는 해고한다. 공공 기관들이 민영화될 때마다 근로자의 생산성이 극적으로 증가한다는 점을 많은 연구들이 입증해 주고 있다. 우수한 관리법으로 인하여, 기업은 더욱 효율적이게 된다.

사기업들은 국영 기업들에 비해 신기술을 도입할 가능성이 더 높다. 하나의 예가 텍사스이다. 그곳에서는, 민간 기업들이 에너지 생산에 앞서고 있다. 수십 억 달러의 여러 전력 프로젝트들, 특히 풍력과 같은 녹색 에너지를 활용하는 것들이 현재 시행되고 있거나 개발 단계에 있다. 결과적으로, 산업 발전소로써 텍사스는 상당히 많은 에너지를 생산하여 그곳의 기업들을 위한 충분한 양의 에너지를 만들고 있을 뿐만 아니라 근접해 있는 주들에게도 전기를 수출하고 있다. 그 주가 그렇게 많은 양의 에너지 생산을 가능하게 만든 것은 텍사스가 신기술에 의존하고 있기 때문이다.

W Professor: All right, class, we've talked about the advantages of privatizing key infrastructure like power companies and waterworks. Now, let's focus on some disadvantages of doing so. I contend that it's better for the government to remain in control. Here's why . . .

Okay, yes, many governments need the influx of cash they get from selling a utility company. After all, they can net billions of dollars this way. But governments shouldn't worry about making money. Power companies and other utilities don't belong in the hands of private industry. Governments should run them for the good of all citizens. After all, what happens if a private electric company raises its rates? Since it has a monopoly, the people living nearby have no choice but to pay exorbitant rates to get electricity. That's not fair.

And remember what happened when the state sold the power company last year? That's right. The new owners immediately laid off twenty percent of the workforce. They fired 300 people. Many are still unemployed. The company claimed those workers were unneeded, but they all had families to support. The government was their source of income. The state let them down by privatizing that company.

I know people love talking about how private companies are innovators, especially when it comes to using new technology. Sure, companies like Apple, Amazon, and Microsoft are great at that. But it's not a bad thing that governments are slow to adopt new technology. Why . . . ? Well, new technology often has a plethora of unexpected problems that make it break down or perform poorly. Remember that awful new computer operating system from two years ago? By the time government utilities incorporate new technologies, the problems with them have been worked out. So, uh, they operate more smoothly and with fewer issues.

교수: 좋아요, 여러분, 우리는 전력 회사 및 수도 회사와 같은 핵심 기반 시설의 민영화의 장점에 대해 이야기를 했어요. 이제 그렇게 하는 것의 몇몇 단점들에 초점을 맞추어 봅시다. 저는 정부가 계속 관리하는 것이 더 좋다고 주장해요. 이유를 말씀드리죠...

좋아요, 그래요. 많은 정부가 공익 기업을 매각함으로써 얻어지는 현금의 유입을 필요로 하죠. 어쨌든, 이러한 방법으로 수십 억 달러의 순익을 올릴 수 있으니까요. 하지만, 정부는 돈을 버는 것에 대해 걱정하지 말아야 합니다. 전력 기업과 다른 공익 기업들은 사기업에 해당되지 않습니다. 정부는 모든 시민의 이익을 위해 그 사업들을 운영해야 합니다. 결국 민간 전기 회사가 요금을 올리면 어떻게 될까요? 그것은 독점권을 가질테니 근처에 사는 사람들은 전기를 얻기 위해 과대한 요금을 지불하는 것 외에는 선택의 여지가 없습니다. 그건 공정하지 않습니다.

그리고 작년에 주가 전력 회사를 매각했을 때 무슨 일이 생겼는지 기억하나요? 맞아요. 새로운 소유주들이 인력의 20퍼센트를 바로 해고시켰습니다. 300명을 해고한 것입니다. 다수가 여전히 실직 상태고요. 회사는 그 노동자들이 필요 없었다고 주장하지만, 그들 모두에게는 부양해야 할 가족이 있었습니다. 정부는 그들의 수입의 원천이었어요. 주가 회사를 민영화시키면서 그들을 저버린 것입니다.

사람들은 특히나 신기술의 사용에 관한 한 얼마나 사기업이 혁신자인지에 대해 말하길 좋아한다는 것을 알고 있습니다. 물론, Apple, Amazon, 그리고 Microsoft와 같은 기업들은 신기술에 뛰어납니다. 하지만, 정부가 천천히 신기술을 도입하는 것도 나쁘진 않아요. 왜냐고요? 자, 신기술은 고장이 나거나 제대로 작동하지 않는 등의 다양한 예상치 못한 문제들을 종종 가지고 있습니다. 2년 전 그 끔찍했던 신 컴퓨터 운영 시스템을 기억하나요? 정부 공익 기관에서 신기술늘을 통합시킬 때쯤, 그러한 문제들이 해결되었죠. 그래서 음, 훨씬 더 원활하게 그리고 더 적은 문제를 가지고 운영되고 있습니다.

Sample Essay p.098

교수는 민간 부분의 조직이 그러는 것보다 정부가 기반 시설 산업을 관리하는 것이 더 낫다고 주장한다. 그녀는 민영화의 세 가지 단점을 들어 자신의 주장을 뒷받침한다. 이는 기반 시설의 민영화가 많은 혜택을 가져다 준다는 지문의 주장을 직접적으로 반박한다.

첫째로, 정부의 목적은 이윤 창출이 아니라 자국민의 이득이다. 만약 사기업이 독점의 지위를 남용해서 과도한 요금을 부과한다면, 그러한 제도로부터 고통을 받는 것은 시민일 것이다. 이 사실은 기반 시설의 민영화가 특히 경제 위기를 겪는 정부에게 재정적 도움을 제공해 줄 수 있다는 지문의 주장을 반박한다.

게다가, 교수는 기반 시설의 민영화가 취업 기회를 낮출 것이라고 주장한다. 사례에서 보여지듯이, 많은 노동자들은 전력 회사가 민영화된 후 직장을 잃었다. 이는 수익 창출이라는 목적을 위한 노동력의 청산이 생산력을 향상시킨다는 지문의 주장과 모순된다.

마지막으로, 교수는 새로운 과학 기술의 빠른 도입으로 심각한 문제들을 비롯한 많은 문제들이 일어날 수 있다고 주장한다. 따라서 혁신 시스템을 상대적으로 신중히 도입하는 것이 문제의 가능성을 줄여 줄 것이다. 이는, 성공적인 풍력 시스템을 갖춘 텍사스에서 볼 수 있듯이, 끊임없는 최신 기술의 도입이 필요하다는 지문의 견해에 반대된다.

TASK 2 · INDEPENDENT TASK
Shopping Malls

Sample Essay 1 | AGREE p.101

도시들은 끊임없이 발전과 개발을 겪기 때문에, 마을 주변에서 건설 현장을 보는 것은 흔히 않은 일이 아니다. 새로 지어지는 건물 중 하나는 쇼핑몰이다. 사람들이 더 많은 가게를 원하지만, 일부 사람들은 그들이 사는 지역에 가게들을 짓는다는 생각에 반대한다. 내게 선택권이 있다면, 나는 내가 사는 동네에 쇼핑몰이 있기를 원한다. 이유는 강화된 보안과 경제적 이점을 제공하기 때문이다.

첫째, 그 지역에서 운영하는 업체들 덕분에 보안이 강화될 것이다. 대형 쇼핑몰이 지어지면, 지역 경찰과 CCTV 이외에 사설 보안 업체가 건물들의 전반적인 안전을 관리하여 별도의 안전을 제공한다. 예를 들면, 연구가 보여주길 새로운 쇼핑센터가 막 세워진 지역에서는 높게는 90%까지 범죄율이 줄어들었다.

뿐만 아니라, 대형 쇼핑몰은 미용실, 요가 센터, 그리고 식당 등의 다른 종류의 서비스 사업들이 있게 될 것이므로 경제 성장으로 이어질 것이다. 예를 들어, 스탠포드 쇼핑센터에서 진행되었던 연구에 따르면, 다른 가게들을 방문한 후에 소비자들의 75% 이상이 식사나 음료 중 하나를 구입하여 더 많은 지출을 하는 결과로 이어지게 된다. 편리성과 다양한 선택들은 많은 소비자들을 유치할 것이고 다수의 취업의 기회를 제공하여, 결국 지역 단체에 경제적 이득을 가져올 것이다.

우리 동네에 대형 쇼핑몰이 들어오는 것이 수많은 사람들과 자동차로 인한 교통 혼잡을 일으킨다는 것은 사실이다. 하지만, 그것은 휴일에만 일어나고, 사실, 동네에 휴일 느낌을 더해 준다. 대형 쇼핑센터는 보안 순찰차 활동을 통해 그 지역에 별도의 안전을 제공해 준다. 더 나아가, 더 많은 소비자들을 유치하는 것은 경제적인 상황을 개선시킬 수 있다. 그러므로 나는 동네에 대형 쇼핑센터를 건설하는 것을 적극 지지할 것이다.

Sample Essay 2 | DISAGREE
p.102

도시들은 끊임없이 발전과 개발을 겪기 때문에, 마을 주변에서 건설 현장을 보는 것은 흔치 않은 일이 아니다. 새로 지어지는 건물 중 하나가 쇼핑몰이다. 사람들은 더 많은 가게를 원하지만, 일부 사람들은 그들이 사는 지역에 가게들을 짓는다는 생각에 반대한다. 나에게 선택권이 있다면, 나는 쇼핑몰이 내가 사는 곳에서 멀리 있었으면 좋겠다. 이유는 범죄, 그리고 교통 관련 문제들 때문이다.

첫째, 많은 가게들이 있는 지역에는 항상 범죄율이 높다. 초대형 몰은 극장, 스포츠 경기장, 그리고 심지어는 호텔도 포함할 수 있고, 그런 장소들에서 범죄가 일어나는 것은 불가피하다. 연구에 따르면 대형 쇼핑몰은 파괴, 절도, 그리고 대중 소란에 항상 노출되어 있다. 더 나아가, 소비자들의 유입은 많은 쓰레기를 만들 것이고, 쓰레기를 버리는 것보다 치우는 것에 더 많은 시간이 걸릴 수 있다.

뿐만 아니라, 그 지역의 주민들은 교통 관련 문제들을 겪을 것이다. 예를 들면, 더 많은 소비자들이 쇼핑몰에 더 많은 차를 운전하고 올 것이다. 따라서, 더 많은 주차 공간이 필요할 것이다. 쇼핑센터가 특히나 도시에서는 돈이 많이 들어가는 굉장히 넓은 공간 혹은 커다란 주차 건물을 세우지 않는 이상, 주차난이 생길 것이다. 이 문제에 더하여, 교통 위반, 자동차 사고, 그리고 소음이 생길 것이다.

대형 쇼핑몰이 편리할 것이라는 것은 사실이다. 하지만, 그 어떤 것도 동네의 안전과 비교될 수는 없다. 범죄 증가율의 가능성이 높아, 동네 전체는 끊임없는 위험에 노출될 수 있다. 덧붙여, 쇼핑몰 주변의 주민들은 주차난, 교통 위반, 그리고 소음 등의 교통과 관련된 문제들에 대처해야 할 것이다. 그러므로 나는 대형 쇼핑 센터의 건설을 적극 반대할 것이다.

Actual Test 10

TASK 1 · INTEGRATED TASK

Archaeology: The Construction of the Pyramids

READING
p.105

고대 이집트인이 피라미드를 어떻게 지었는지에 대한 의문은 역사가들과 고고학자들을 오랫동안 미궁에 빠뜨려 왔다. 각각의 피라미드는 커다란 돌덩어리로 이루어져 있다. 몇몇 경우, 하나의 피라미드에 수백만 개의 돌덩어리가 있는 경우도 있다. 하지만, 이집트인들은 첨단 장비 없이도 어떤 식으로든 이러한 돌덩어리들을 제자리로 옮기고 지탱시키는데 성공했다. 그들이 어떻게 이러한 위업을 이루었는지에 대한 답은 공학의 다음 세 가지 측면에 있는 것처럼 보인다. 경사로, 기중기, 그리고 콘크리트가 그것이다.

첫째, 이집트인들은 돌을 더 높이 올리기 위해 피라미드 주위에 흙으로 된 경사로를 사용했다. 건설이 진행됨에 따라, 경사로는 더욱 높게 지어졌다. 각 돌덩어리는 통나무 위에서 굴려지거나 사람과 동물이 팀을 이루어 이를 끌

어 올렸다. 그리고 나서, 돌덩어리들은 제자리로 올려졌다. 이집트인들은 한쪽 면에 하나의 길고 높은 경사로를 짓거나, 양쪽 면에, 나선 모양으로 꼭대기까지 이르는, 일련의 짧은 경사로들을 연속해서 만들었다.

둘째, 이집트인들은 힘든 위치 안으로 일부 돌들을 옮기기 위해 밧줄과 도르래가 있는 기중기를 사용했다. 이러한 장치들은 나무로 만들어졌는데, 돌덩어리들을 붙들기 위해서는 가죽 끈이 사용되었다. 그리고 나서, 일꾼들은 돌덩어리를 들어올리기 위해 긴 밧줄을 잡아당긴 후 제자리에 내려 놓았다. 기중기의 사용은 이집트인들이 – 일부 60톤까지 무게가 나가는 – 거대한 돌덩어리들을 어떻게 몇몇 내부의 방으로 옮겨져 놓았는지를 설명해 준다.

마지막으로, 이집트인들이 일종의 콘크리트를 가지고 있었을 가능성도 있다. 석회암과 다른 광물들로 만들어져 콘크리트는 돌덩어리들 사이의 공간들을 메우는데 사용되었다. 이는 전체적인 구조를 강화시켰으며 피라미드들이 높게 지어질 수 있도록 했다. 콘크리트를 사용하지 않았다면, 엄청난 무게 때문에 피라미드가 붕괴되었을 수도 있을 것이다.

LISTENING
10-01

W Professor: The Great Pyramid of Giza in Egypt is estimated to be made of two million stone blocks, some of which weigh several tons. Okay. I know what you're thinking . . . You want to know how people in a society with limited technology moved those stones and put them into place while building the pyramids. Well . . . there are lots of theories, but none so far seems satisfactory.

One of the most accepted theories is that the Egyptians built ramps which let them push or pull the stones into place. It sounds plausible, yet there's no evidence of ramps ever existing in Egypt. In addition, many experts believe the pyramids were too tall for ramps. For instance, the Great Pyramid of Giza stood 146 meters high. The ramps would have been so heavy that they would have fallen down before they ever reached anywhere near that height.

Once the blocks got onto the pyramids—however that happened—we're now faced with the question of how they were moved into the correct positions. One theory is that cranes moved them. Yet there's no record anywhere of the Egyptians having built cranes. Nor have any cranes ever been found in Egypt. Finally, the cranes would have been made of wood, which was scarce in Egypt during the time the pyramids were built.

Some have claimed that the Egyptians used concrete to fill in the gaps between the stones. While some evidence of concrete has been found, the Egyptians had no knowledge of how to make it. The Romans, however, were using concrete by the first century B.C. In all likelihood, the Romans, who occupied Egypt during their history, tried to repair the pyramids with concrete. So it wasn't the Egyptians using concrete but people who came centuries after them who utilized it instead.

교수: 이집트 기자의 거대 피라미드는 일부 무게가 수 톤이나 나가는 2백만 개의 돌덩어리들로 만들어졌다고 추정됩니다. 좋아요. 여러분이 무슨 생각을 하는지 알고 있습니다... 제한된 기술만을 가지고 있던 사회에서 어떻게 사람들이 피라미드를 만드는 동안 그와 같은 돌들을 이동시켜 제자리에 두었는

지 알고 싶어하는군요. 음… 많은 이론들이 있지만, 지금까지 그 어느 것도 만족스러운 것은 없습니다.

가장 인정받는 이론 중 하나는 이집트인들이 경사로를 만들어서 돌들을 밀고 끌어 당길 수 있도록 했다는 것입니다. 가능한 것으로 들리지만, 이집트에서 경사로가 존재했다는 증거는 없습니다. 게다가, 많은 전문가들이 경사로를 만들기에는 피라미드가 너무 높았다고 믿고 있습니다. 예를 들면, 기자의 거대 피라미드는 높이가 146미터입니다. 경사로의 무게가 너무 많이 나가서 그 정도의 높이의 근처에 가기도 전에 무너져 버렸을 수도 있습니다.

돌덩어리들이 피라미드 쪽으로 도달했다 하더라도, 일단 도달한 후 돌덩어리들이 어떻게 적절한 위치까지 옮겨졌는지에 대한 의문에 직면하게 됩니다. 한 가지 이론에 따르면 기중기가 돌덩어리들을 옮겼다고 합니다. 하지만, 이집트인들이 기중기를 만들었다는 기록은 어디에도 없습니다. 이집트에서 발견된 기중기도 전혀 없고요. 마지막으로, 기중기는 나무로 만들어졌을 텐데, 피라미드가 지어진 당시의 이집트에는 나무가 드물었습니다.

어떤 이들은 이집트인들이 돌 사이의 틈을 메우기 위해 콘크리트를 사용했다고 주장합니다. 콘크리트에 대한 일부 증거는 발견이 되었지만, 이집트인들은 그것을 만드는 방법에 대한 지식을 가지고 있지 않았습니다. 하지만 로마인들은 기원전 1세기경에 콘크리트를 사용했습니다. 십중팔구, 역사상 이집트를 점령했던 로마인들이 콘크리트로 피라미드들을 보수하려 했을 것입니다. 그러니까 콘크리트를 사용했던 것은 이집트인들이 아닌, 수세기 후에 온 사람들이었던 것이죠.

Sample Essay   p.108

교수는 기자의 거대 피라미드에 관한 이론 중 그 어느 것도 타당해 보이지 않는다고 주장한다. 이러한 주장은 이집트인들이 공학의 세 가지 측면을 이용하여 돌덩어리들을 성공적으로 제자리에 옮겨다 놓고 고정시킬 수 있었다는 지문의 주장을 정면으로 반박한다.

첫째, 피라미드 건설에서 경사로의 사용은 증명될 수 없다. 교수에 따르면, 피라미드가 너무 높기 때문에 경사로를 만드는 것은 불가능했을 것이다. 이는 이집트인들이 흙으로 만든 경사로를 이용하여 돌덩어리들을 더 높은 곳까지 옮길 수 있었다는 지문의 내용과 모순된다.

뿐만 아니라, 교수는 기중기의 사용에 관한 또 다른 이론이 비현실적이라고 주장한다. 이집트에서는 실제 기중기나 기중기의 사용에 대한 어떠한 관련 기록도 발견되지 않았다. 게다가, 나무는 피라미드가 건설될 당시 드물었다. 이는 크레인으로 이집트인들이 거대한 돌덩어리들을 들어올릴 수 있었다는 지문의 주장에 의문을 제기한다.

마지막으로, 이집트인들에게는 콘크리트의 사용에 대한 지식이 없었다는 것이 밝혀졌다. 로마인들이 이집트를 지배했기 때문에, 아마도 그들이 피라미드를 보수하기 위해 콘크리트를 사용했을 것이다. 이는 이집트인들이 피라미드의 틈을 메우기 위해 콘크리트를 사용했다는 지문의 의견에 반한다.

TASK 2 · INDEPENDENT TASK
Teachers' Roles

Sample Essay 1 | AGREE   p.111

대학교는 학생들이 자신의 학구적인 목표를 추구하는 고등 교육과 연구 기관이다. 대학교가 학생들의 배움이 이루어지는 곳이기도 하지만, 교수들은 그들의 연구에도 많은 시간과 노력을 쏟는다. 어떤 이들은 교수들은 연구에 매진해야 한다고 주장하지만 나는, 교수들은 가르치는데 집중해야 한다고 굳게 믿는다. 나는 배움의 목적과 연구에 매진하고 싶어하는 이들을 위한 다른

직위가 있기 때문에 이렇게 느낀다.

첫째, 교육 기관의 목적은 학생들이 그들의 학구적 목표를 달성하도록 도와주는 것이다. 자세히 말하자면, 다양한 과목에서 기초 지식의 토대를 쌓은 고등학교에서 졸업한 후, 학생들은 흥미가 있는 특정 분야에서 더욱 깊이 있는 지식을 쌓기 위해 대학교에 입학한다. 하지만, 만약 교수가 대부분의 시간을 연구하고 자신의 프로젝트를 하는데 사용한다면, 그 교수는 자신의 일은 성취할 수 있어도 학생들은 스스로 연구하고 배우게 될 것이다. 이는 학교의 전반적인 학문적 수준 및 명성에 영향을 끼칠 것이다. 그러므로, 자신의 지식을 학생들에게 전달하는 것은 학교에서 교수의 최우선 사항이어야 한다.

뿐만 아니라, 연구 교수라고 불리는 직책이 있고 이는 교수가 가르칠 의무 없이 오로지 자신의 연구에 집중할 수 있도록 해준다. 연구나 프로젝트를 시작하기 위해서 교수는 정부나 회사로부터 지원금을 필요로 하고 준비에는 많은 시간과 노력을 들여야 것이다. 교수는 또한 안식년을 가질 수 있어서 자신의 연구에 더 집중할 수 있다. 교수에게 안식년을 제공하는 목적은 그가 연구를 하도록 장려하기 위함이다.

교수들에게 있어 연구가 그들의 전문 분야에서 자신의 지식을 개발 및 발전시키는 것은 사실이다. 하지만, 교육 기관의 목적은 학생들에게 올바른 지도하에 교육시키는 것이다. 학생들에게 지식을 전달하는 것이 교수들에게 최우선 과제이다. 학생들이 대학 기간 동안 그들의 교육 목표를 추구할 수 있도록 특정 전공에서 더욱 깊이 있는 지식을 제공하는 것은 교수의 책임이다. 나아가, 교수가 연구에 몰두하고 싶다면, 연구 교수직에 지원하거나 안식년을 가질 수 있다. 그러므로 나는 교수들은 연구보다는 가르치는데 집중해야 한다는 명제에 강력히 찬성한다.

Sample Essay 2 | DISAGREE   p.112

대학교는 학생들이 자신의 학구적인 목표를 추구하는 고등 교육과 연구 기관이다. 대학교가 학생들의 배움이 이루어지는 곳이기도 하지만, 교수들은 그들의 연구에도 많은 시간과 노력을 쏟는다. 어떤 이들은 교수들은 연구에 오히려 매진해야 한다고 주장하는 반면 어떤 이들은 교수들에게는 가르치는 것이 우선시 되어야 한다고 생각한다. 내 의견으로는, 교수들은 연구하는데 집중해야 한다. 이는 교육자 자신들도 학구적으로 개발과 발전을 할 필요가 있고, 연구의 끊임없는 작업은 후의 프로젝트들에 지원금을 얻는 것을 수월하게 해 주기 때문이다.

첫째, 연구를 하는 것은 교수의 학구적 성장과 발전뿐 아니라 개인적 성장과 발전을 위해서도 필요하다. 수업을 하는 동안 교수들은 자신이 연구를 통해 얻은 지식을 강의실로 가져와 공유한다. 연구는 대부분 새로운 질문을 불러일으키고, 결국 전문적 공동체를 형성한다. 예를 들면, 매일 수많은 새로운 연구 결과가 발표되고, 연구에 연루되는 것은 교수들이 가르치는 방법과 능력을 향상시키는데 중요하다. 게다가, 학자로서, 교수는 학계에 흔적을 남길 수 있는 가능성을 가질 것이다.

뿐만 아니라, 교수들은 정부나 기업으로부터 자금을 얻기 위해 수행한 연구에 대한 이력을 가지는 것이 필요하다. 예를 들어, 만약 교수가 새로운 DNA 구조를 찾기 위해 연구를 실행하고 싶으면, 교수는 함께 일할 팀과 연구실을 갖기 위해 충분한 재정적 지원이 필요하다. 만약 교수가 그의 능력과 생각을 증명하기 위한 이전의 연구 이력이 없다면, 정부나 기업들이 위험을 안고 많은 돈을 투자하는 것은 하지 않을 것이다.

교수들에게 안식년이 있는 것은 사실이다. 하지만, 그 특정한 해는 연구만 하라는 것이 아니며, 교수들이 새로운 교수법, 프로그램, 그리고 교과 과정을 개발할 수 있는 시기이다. 오랫동안 연구를 하는 것은 교수들에게 학문적 발전을 제공한다. 나아가, 프로젝트나 연구를 하기 위한 충분한 지원금을 받는 것은 필수이다. 그러므로 나는 교수들은 연구에 집중해야 한다고 강력히 믿는다.

Actual Test 11

TASK 1 · INTEGRATED TASK

Psychology: Reasons for Sleep

READING p.115

대부분의 사람들이 매일 밤 수면을 취하고 가끔은 낮에도 잠을 잔다. 의학 분야에 있는 학자들이 답을 내리려고 노력했던 한 가지 질문은 왜 사람들에게 수면이 필요한가이다. 이에 대해서는 세 가지 이유가 있는 것으로 보인다. 첫째는 수면이 기억력 기능을 향상시켜 준다는 것이다. 다음으로, 에너지를 보존하기 위해 수면을 취한다는 것이다. 마지막으로, 신체로부터, 특히 뇌에서, 유해한 독성 물질들을 제거하기 위해서 수면을 취한다는 것이다.

수십 년 동안, 과학자들은 수면과 기억력에 초점을 맞추어 실험을 진행해 왔다. 이러한 실험들을 통해 그들은 규칙적이고 충분히 길게—보통 밤에 6시간이나 7시간 동안—수면을 취하는 사람들이, 수면을 충분히 취하지 못하는 사람들에 비해 훨씬 더 뛰어난 인지 능력과 기억력을 가진다는 점을 배웠다. 게다가, 일반적으로 렘수면 동안 이루어지는 꿈을 많이 꾸는 사람들은 렘수면을 덜 취하는 사람들에 비해 기억력이 더 좋다.

수면을 취할 때, 신체는 회복되며, 에너지가 보충된다. 수면은 신체의 에너지를 보존시켜 주는 동시에 신체가 스스로 복구되도록 해 준다. 사람이 잠을 잘 때 그 사람의 신체는 적은 양의 에너지만을 사용한다. 따라서, 사람은 깨어날 때 더 많은 에너지를 갖게 된다. 이는 곰 같은 일부 동물들이 왜 겨울잠을 자는지에 대한 설명을 가능하게 해 준다. 곰은 비축해 놓은 적은 양의 에너지만으로 장기간 동안 생존할 수 있는 것이다.

인간을 대상으로 한 실험에 따르면 뇌는 깨어있을 때 보다 장시간의 수면 후에 더 적은 양의 독성 물질을 갖게 된다. 뇌에서 독성 물질이 제거됨으로써 사람들은 보다 더 명확하게 사고를 할 수 있다. 게다가, 충분한 양의 수면을 취한 후에는 깨어날 때 보다 더 상쾌한 기분을 느낀다. 이는 사람들로 하여금 맑은 정신으로 일상적인 기능에 참여하는 것을 가능하게 해 준다. 반대로, 잠을 덜 자면, 그런 개인의 뇌에는 더 많은 독소가 남아 있게 된다. 그 결과, 사람들은 머리가 멍해지고 생산성은 떨어진다.

LISTENING 🎧 11-01

W Professor: Sleep is a normal human function. But why do we sleep . . . ? There's actually a good amount of uncertainty surrounding this question. Some sleep experts believe that sleeping helps people in several ways. Let me go over a few of them now.

First is memory function. Does sleep help improve it . . . ? In several experiments done with human test subjects, the answer appears to be, uh, yes. But there's contradictory evidence. For instance, many experts believe REM sleep is essential to improving memory retention. Yet some experiments on people who got little or no REM sleep showed that they still had good memories. So it's entirely possible that REM sleep doesn't help improve everyone's memories.

It's true that sleep helps improve the bodily conditions of ill or injured people. But what about restoring people's energy levels? Remember that most living things get their energy from food. Yet while we're sleeping, we can't eat, so, naturally, we can't build up any energy. And when most people wake up, they immediately eat to restore lost energy. As far as energy is concerned, I'd say the only thing that's true is that we use less energy when we're asleep than when we're awake.

Some scientists state that toxins get removed from the brain while a person is sleeping. Is that true . . . ? Hmm . . . It's hard to say. See, uh, not everyone is the same. People get exposed to various amounts of toxins. And people's bodies absorb different amounts as well. There was one experiment in which people were deprived of sleep for several days. Then, they were allowed to sleep for a longer period than normal. Afterward, those people's toxin levels were lower than normal. However, that's not a normal sleep pattern, so the experiment was inconclusive. Clearly, more research is necessary.

교수: 수면은 인간의 정상적인 기능입니다. 하지만 우리는 왜 잠을 잘까요...? 이 문제에 관해서는 사실 상당히 많은 불확실한 점들이 있습니다. 일부 수면 전문가들은 수면이 여러 가지 측면에서 도움이 된다고 믿고 있습니다. 그 중 몇몇에 대해 검토를 해 보도록 하죠.

첫째는 기억력에 관한 것입니다. 수면이 기억력을 향상시키는데 도움이 될까요...? 인간을 대상으로 한 다수의 실험에서의 대답은 음, 맞는 것 같아 보입니다. 하지만 모순되는 증거가 있어요. 예를 들어, 많은 전문가들은 렘수면이 기억력 향상에 필수적이라고 믿고 있습니다. 그렇지만 적은 양의 렘수면 혹은 전혀 렘수면을 겪지 않은 사람들을 대상으로 한 몇몇 실험에서는 그들도 여전히 훌륭한 기억력을 보인다는 점을 나타내 줍니다. 따라서 렘수면이 모든 이들의 기억력을 향상시키는데 도움이 되지는 않는다는 것이 전적으로 가능해요.

수면이 아프거나 부상당한 사람들의 몸 상태를 좋아지게 만든다는 것은 사실입니다. 하지만 에너지 수치를 회복하는 것은 어떨까요? 대부분의 생물들은 음식으로부터 에너지를 얻는다는 점을 기억하세요. 하지만 우리는 잠을 자는 동안 음식을 먹을 수 없기 때문에 당연히 어떤 에너지도 축적할 수가 없습니다. 그리고, 대부분의 사람들이 잠에서 깨어나면 없어진 에너지를 보충하기 위해 바로 음식을 먹습니다. 에너지에 관해 유일하게 사실이라고 말씀드릴 수 있는 점은 우리가 깨어있을 때보다 수면 시 더 적은 양의 에너지를 소모한다는 것입니다.

몇몇 과학자들은 사람이 잠을 자는 동안 뇌에서 독성 물질이 제거된다고 주장합니다. 사실일까요...? 음... 그렇게 말하기는 힘듭니다. 자, 음, 보세요, 모든 사람들이 똑같지는 않습니다. 사람들은 다양한 양의 독성 물질에 노출이 됩니다. 그리고 인간의 신체 역시 다른 양의 독성 물질을 흡수하죠. 사람들에게 수일 동안 수면을 취하지 못하게 했던 실험이 있었습니다. 그런 다음 정상 때보다 더 긴 시간의 수면이 허락되었죠. 후에, 이 사람들의 독소 수치는 평균보다 낮았습니다. 하지만, 이는 일반적인 수면 패턴이 아니기 때문에 실험 결과는 결정적이지 않습니다. 명백한 것은, 더 많은 연구가 필요하다는 점입니다.

Sample Essay p.118

교수는 사람들이 왜 수면을 취하는지는 불확실하다고 주장한다. 그녀는 수면의 이유에 대해 세 가지 진술을 한다. 이러한 주장은 사람들에게 잠이 필요한 확실한 이유가 있다는 지문의 주장을 직접적으로 반박한다.

첫째, 교수는 렘수면과 기억력 향상 사이에는 상관관계가 없다고 말한다.

적은 양의 렘수면을 경험하거나 전혀 렘수면을 경험하지 않은 사람들도 기억력 면에서 어떤 차이점도 나타나지 않았다. 이는 충분한 시간 동안 수면을 취한 사람들이 충분히 수면을 취하지 않은 사람들보다 더 나은 인지 능력과 기억력을 가지고 있었다는 지문의 주장에 반대된다.

둘째, 그녀는 사람들이 수면을 취하는 동안 에너지가 회복된다고 말하는 것은 정확하지 않다고 강조한다. 이는 생명체들이 음식 섭취로부터 에너지를 얻고, 사람들은 일어나자마자 음식을 먹는다는 사실이 이를 뒷받침해 준다. 이러한 점은 수면을 취하는 동안 에너지가 보충되기 때문에 신체는 원기를 회복하게 된다는 지문의 내용에 반한다.

마지막으로, 사람들에게 노출되는 독성 물질의 양과 우리의 신체가 받아들이는 독성 물질의 양은 개인에 따라 다르다. 게다가, 실험은 일반적인 수면 패턴 하에서 실행된 실험이 아니었다. 따라서, 어느 누구도 수면이 독소의 제거를 하게 하는지에 대해 확신할 수 없다. 이는 자는 동안 우리 뇌는 독성 물질을 제거한다는 지문의 의견을 반박한다.

TASK 2 · INDEPENDENT TASK
Life Expectancy

Sample Essay 1 | TECHNOLOGICAL IMPROVEMENTS   p.122

수십 년 전에는, 많은 나라들의 평균 수명이 45세 정도였기 때문에 한 사람이 50세가 되면 많은 문화의 사람들이 축하했다. 사람들의 생활 양식의 향상 덕분에 지금 세계적인 평균 수명은 70세가 넘는다. 평균 수명의 증가에 기여한 많은 요소 중에서 나는 기술의 발달이 이 현상에 대해 가장 잘 설명해 준다고 굳게 믿는다. 주요한 이유로는 의료 장비의 발달과 인터넷의 등장을 들 수 있다.

첫째, 의료 장비가 이렇게 발달하지 않았던 시대와 비교해서 지금은 수술을 집도하는 로봇까지 있다. 이는 많은 환자들이 더 오래 사는 것을 가능하게 해주었다. 예를 들어, 과거에는 암에 걸리는 것은 거의 언제나 죽음을 뜻했다. 하지만, 오늘날에는 초기에 찾아내면 대부분의 암으로부터 생존할 가능성이 높다. 그러므로, 의료 장비의 발달은 전보다 인간이 더 오래 사는 것을 가능하게 해 주었다.

게다가, 사람들은 특정 질병으로부터 자신을 어떻게 지켜야 하는지에 대한 방대한 지식을 가지고 있다. 과거에는 사람들이 겪는 증상에 대한 그 어떤 조언도 얻는 게 힘들었다. 따라서, 사람들은 치료를 받을 수 있는 적절한 시기를 종종 놓쳤다. 예를 들면, 뇌졸중은 종종 방치되고 심지어는 죽음을 초래하기도 했다. 반면, 많은 사람들이 인터넷에서 뇌졸중의 신호에 대해 찾아본 이후에 즉각적인 조치를 취해서 그들의 생명을 구했다.

일부는 사람이 더 오래 사는 건 식단의 개선 때문이라고 주장한다. 하지만 같은 음식이 과거에도 있었다. 어떤 종류의 음식이 자신의 건강에 가장 좋은지 알아내기 위해 검색하는 것을 가능케 하는 건 인터넷이었다. 게다가, 의료 기술이 수년간 많은 사람들의 생명을 지켜왔다. 따라서, 나는 기술 발달이 인간의 평균 수명의 연장을 설명해 준다고 굳게 믿는다.

Sample Essay 2 | CHANGES IN EDUCATION SYSTEMS   p.123

수십 년 전에는, 많은 나라들의 평균 수명이 45세 정도였기 때문에 한 사람이 50세가 되면 많은 문화의 사람들이 축하했다. 사람들의 생활 양식의 향상 덕분에 지금 세계적인 평균 수명은 70세가 넘는다. 평균 수명의 증가에 기여한 많은 요소 중에서 나는 교육 제도의 변화가 이 현상에 대해 가장 잘 설명해 준다고 굳게 믿는다. 주요한 이유로는 사람들의 전반적인 건강에 대한 지식과 불치병에 대한 연구 때문이다.

첫째, 과거에는, 일반적인 사람들은 건강에 관한 지식이 거의 없었고, 사람들은 스스로 진단을 내리기 힘들었다. 하지만, 적절한 교육으로 사람들은 증상과 예방 방법 등을 포함해 흔한 질환에 대해 더 잘 알게 되었다. 예를 들면, 아이들이 예방 접종을 할 때, 부모는 부작용이 있을 때 어떻게 해야 하는지 뿐만 아니라 그 예방 접종에 대한 정보가 모두 들어있는 인쇄된 종이를 받는다. 이는 사망을 줄이고 평균 수명이 연장되도록 이끌었다.

뿐만 아니라, 늘어나는 의료 연구소의 수가 사람의 생명을 지키는데 지대한 기여를 했다. 예를 들면, 많은 사람들은 오래 전에 홍역으로 죽었다. 하지만, 정부는 많은 예산을 연구소 설립에 할당했고, 연구원들은 감염으로부터 다른 이들을 예방하기 위한 백신을 개발했다. 따라서, 과거에는 치명적이었지만 이제는 쉽게 치료되어 더 이상 생명을 위협한다고 여겨지지 않아 장수를 초래하는 많은 질병들이 있다.

일부는 사람들이 더 오래 살게 된 것이 식단의 개선 때문이라고 주장한다. 하지만 같은 음식이 과거에도 있었다. 올바른 교육 없이는, 사람들은 건강을 유지하기 위해 그들이 무엇을 먹어야 하는지 알아내기 위한 지식이 없을 것이다. 게다가, 질병과 세균에 관한 끝없는 연구는 과학자들이 불치라고 여겨졌던 일부 질병에 대한 치료법까지 알아내게 했다. 그러므로 사람들의 평균 수명 연장은 교육 제도 덕분이라고 볼 수 있다.

Sample Essay 3 | IMPROVEMENTS IN PEOPLE'S DIETS   p.124

수십 년 전에는, 많은 나라들의 평균 수명이 45세 정도였기 때문에 한 사람이 50세가 되면 많은 문화의 사람들이 축하했다. 사람들의 생활 양식의 향상 덕분에 지금 세계적인 평균 수명은 70세가 넘는다. 평균 수명의 증가에 기여한 많은 요소 중에서 나는 식생활의 개선이 현상에 대해 가장 잘 설명해 준다고 굳게 믿는다. 주요한 이유로는 사람들의 더욱 균형 잡히고 영양분이 풍부한 식사와 건강 보조 식품 때문이다.

첫째, 건강과 관련된 많은 문제들은 그것이 지식의 부족이나 식량 부족으로 인한 부적절한 식사에 의해 발생한다. 건강한 식사는 사람들에게 생존과 건강 유지를 위한 영양소와 에너지를 공급한다. 예를 들면, 혈액의 칼슘 수치가 낮으면 갑작스런 심장 마비의 위험 가능성을 높일 수 있다. 이는 많은 칼슘이 들어 있는 음식을 섭취함으로써 쉽게 예방할 수 있다. 그러므로 적절한 양의 다양한 종류의 음식을 먹는 것은 장수를 가져다 준다.

게다가, 많은 이용 가능한 건강 보조 식품이 있다. 예를 들면, 우리는 광범위한 상표의 비타민 상점을 쉽게 찾을 수 있다. 나이, 성별, 기능에 따라 세분화 된 많은 종류의 비타민들이 있다. 이는 사람들이 자신의 건강을 관리하거나 개선시키는 것을 돕는다. 이렇게, 건강 보조 식품의 도움으로 사람들은 건강을 유지하고 더 오래 사는 것이 가능하다.

일부는 교육 제도의 변화들 덕분에 사람들이 더 오래 산다고 주장한다. 하지만, 과거에도 책은 널리 보급되었고 대부분의 사람들은 건강에 대한 기본 지식이 있었기 때문에 교육의 부족이 낮은 평균 수명을 야기했다는 것은 믿기 힘들다. 대신 균형 잡힌 식단과 비타민을 포함한 건강 보조 식품은 사람들의 몸이 더 효과적으로 작동할 수 있도록 해준다. 그러므로 위에서 언급된 이유들이 신체가 질병들을 극복하게 도와주며 결과적으로 연장된 평균 수명으로 이끈다.

Actual Test 12

TASK 1 · INTEGRATED TASK
Zootechnics: Cows

READING p.127

지구는 그 어느 때보다도 가장 급격한 기후 변화를 겪고 있다. 세계의 일부 지역들에서는 일부 사람들이 홍수로 죽어가는 반면 또 다른 지역들에서는 산불로 인해 사람들이 자신의 집에서 대피해야 한다. 많지 않은 사람들만이 소, 닭, 그리고 돼지가 기후 위기의 주된 원인이라는 것을 알고 있다. 다수의 과학자들과 환경 보호론자들이 지구가 최악의 상황에 도달하기 전에 소의 숫자를 줄여야 할 필요성에 대해 경고하고 있다.

많은 연구에 따르면, 소는 온실가스의 14%를 차지하고 지구의 문제를 일으키는 주요 원천이다. 소는 장의 발효라고 불려지는 과정을 통해 메탄가스를 생산한다. 이는 미생물이 동물들에 의해 섭취되는 식물 성분을 분해하고 발효시키는 것을 포함하며 부산물로 메탄가스를 생산한다. 식물 섬유는 모든 식물들에게 찾아지므로, 소가 더 많은 식물을 먹을수록, 더 많은 메탄가스를 생산하고, 이는 환경 문제에 큰 원인이 된다.

과도한 방목은 기후 변화에 기여하는 또 다른 요소이다. 미국의 거의 1/3 정도의 땅은 방목에 사용된다. 과도한 방목은 비와 바람에 의해 땅의 압축과 침식을 일으킨다. 압밀은 식물이 자라고 물이 스며드는 것을 방해하여, 결국 사막화를 일으킨다. 과도한 방목의 또 다른 문제점은 토종 대신 외래 식물이 확산되어 생물 다양성의 손실을 일으킬 것이라는 것이다.

이 문제에 대한 해결책이 있다. 식품 공학의 발달 덕분에 배양육은 소고기의 대안이 될 수 있다. 연구실에서 배양된 고기는 전통의 고기와 보기에도 같고, 맛도 같다. 배양육은 소에서 키우는 것이 아닌, 미생물의 균체의 성장과 보급을 하기 위해 특별히 만들어진 배양용 병에서 자란다. 배양육으로의 변환은 소로 인한 온실가스 배출을 최대 90%까지 줄일 수 있다. 다른 이점은 물과 땅의 사용 감소와 배설물 양의 감소이다.

LISTENING 🎧 12-01

W Professor: There are about one billion cows in the world. Cows are raised for their meat, milk, and hides . . . Their hides are used to make leather . . . So can we live without cows? The answer is no . . . hmm. . . at least not for the next several years. It is true that cows contribute to greenhouse gases that lead to climate change. But we can't just make them go extinct. Let's be more rational and find some ways that could actually work in real life.

Environmentalists are very concerned about methane produced by cattle. But where is the methane coming from? It comes from the fiber in plants that cows eat . . . Then why not change their diets and make cows more sustainable and less gassy? In one experiment, scientists fed cattle seaweed and found that their methane emissions were reduced by up to sixty percent by making seaweed just one percent of their diet. They also learned that seaweed doesn't make milk taste bad. Hmm . . . This is promising, isn't it? It is the most inexpensive and easiest solution.

Overgrazing is said to cause soil erosion, which leads to

desertification . . . and eventually climate change. But this, too, can be readily solved with good herd management. For instance, rotating herds between pastures can give plants time to recover and will maintain a diversity of native grasses. This ultimately restores the soil by making it healthy and enhances the soil's overall ecological functions. Proper grazing management can even help alleviate climate change.

About cultured meat . . . It was a great attempt made for the environment . . . but there are obvious downsides to it. It is believed that it will produce more carbon dioxide than methane, and carbon dioxide takes a very long time to dissipate. On top of that, it is too pricey. Producing the meat is costly, so the amount produced has a limit . . . making the product too expensive for the average consumer. In other words, cultured meat won't be widely available anytime soon.

교수: 지구에는 약 10억마리의 소가 있습니다. 소는 고기, 우유, 그리고 (소의) 가죽을 위해 키워지고... 이 가죽은 우리가 아는 (무두질을 거친) 가죽을 만들기 위해 이용되는데요... 이러니, 우리가 소 없이 살 수 있을까요? 대답은 아니요... 입니다... 적어도 향후 몇 년 간은요. 소들이 기후 변화를 일으키는 온실가스에 한 몫 한다는 것은 사실이에요. 하지만 우리가 소를 멸종시킬 수는 없잖아요. 좀 더 이성적으로 현실 생활에서 실제로 할 수 있는 몇 몇 방법을 찾아봅시다.

환경학자들은 소들에 의해 배출되는 메탄가스에 대해 상당히 걱정을 합니다. 그런데 메탄가스는 어디서 올까요? 그건 소들이 먹는 섬유 식물에서 온답니다. 그렇다면, 식단을 변경해서 소를 더 지속 가능하게 하고 조금 덜 가스를 배출하도록 하는 건 어떨까요? 한 실험에서 과학자들은 소들에게 해초를 먹였고 그들의 식단에서 단 1%를 해초로 만듦으로써 60%까지 메탄가스 방출을 줄였다는 걸 알아냈습니다. 그들은 또한 해초는 우유의 맛도 해치지 않는다는 걸 배웠어요. 흠... 전망이 밝지 않나요? 그것은 가장 저렴하고 쉬운 해결책이에요.

과도한 방목이 흙의 침식을 일으키고 사막화로 이끌지요. 그리고 결국 기후 변화까지요. 하지만 이 역시 올바른 방목축 관리로 쉽게 해결될 수 있어요. 예로서 목초지 간에 소 떼를 회전시키는 것은 식물이 회복할 수 있는 시간을 주며 토종 풀들의 다양성을 유지하게 해주지요. 이것은 궁극적으로 그것을 건장하게 만듦으로써 회복시키고 토양의 전체적인 생태학적 기능을 강화시켜 줘요. 올바른 방목 관리는 심지어는 기후 변화를 완화시키는 데에도 도움이 될 수 있습니다.

배양육 말인데요... 그것은 환경을 위한 굉장히 좋은 시도였어요. 하지만 분명한 단점이 있지요. 배양육은 메탄가스보다 더 많은 이산화탄소를 생산한다고 예상이 되요. 그리고 이산화탄소는 분산시키는 데 아주 오랜 시간이 걸린답니다. 뿐만 아니라, 배양육은 너무 비싸요. 고기를 생산하는 것은 비용이 많이 들고 생산되는 양이 제한적이에요... 일반 소비자에게 배양육은 너무 비싼 거지요. 다시 말해서, 배양육은 빠른 시일 안에 널리 보급될 수 없다는 것입니다.

Sample Essay p.130

교수는 소를 가축으로 기르는 데 환경친화적인 방법이 고려되어야 한다고 주장한다. 이는 심각한 환경 영향을 일으킬 수 있기 때문에 소의 숫자가 현저히 감소되어야 한다는 지문의 주장을 정면으로 반박한다.

첫째, 소에서 나오는 메탄가스 양의 감소는 소의 식단을 바꿈으로써 해결할 수 있다. 또한, 바뀐 식단에서 나오는 우유는 맛이 나쁘지도 않아서 과정 전체는 추진하기 쉽다. 이는 소들이 식물 섬유를 먹음으로 인해서 지구에 해로운 메탄가스를 많이 생산해서 전 지구적인 문제를 일으킨다는 지문의 내용을 반박한다.

게다가, 교수는 올바른 방목축 관리가 식물들이 회복하게 해줄 뿐 아니라 토종 식물들의 다양성을 유지하면서 기후 변화를 늦춰 줄 것이라고 말한다. 이는 과도한 방목이 생물의 다양성의 손실뿐만 아니라 사막화의 원인이 될 수 있다고 설명하는 지문의 내용에 반대한다.

마지막으로, 배양육은 소고기를 대체할 수 없다. 사실, 이산화탄소는 분산하는데 메탄가스보다 더 오랜 시간이 걸리기 때문에 더 많은 이산화탄소를 생산하는 배양육이 환경에 더욱 나쁠 수 있다. 그리고, 배양육은 소고기보다 더 비싸다. 그러므로 일정 수의 사람들만이 그것을 살 수 있다. 이는 소고기와 같은 맛을 낼 뿐 아니라 더 적은 물과 땅을 사용하는 배양육은 소고기의 훌륭한 대안일 수 있다는 지문의 주장을 반박한다.

TASK 2 · INDEPENDENT TASK
Past vs. Present

Sample Essay 1 | AGREE   p.133

농업 기술과 요리법의 발달 덕분에, 수년에 걸쳐 식품은 커다란 변화를 겪었다. 게다가, 최근의 웰빙 유행은 식품 산업에도 영향을 끼치고 있다. 몇몇 사람들은 현대인들이 보다 건강에 좋은 음식을 먹는다고 주장한다. 하지만 나는 과거 사람들이 섭취한 음식이 오늘날 섭취되는 음식보다 훨씬 더 몸에 좋았다고 굳게 믿는다. 이는 현재 인간에게 매우 해로울 수 있는 유전자 변형 음식이 존재하고 있기 때문이다. 게다가 과거에는 오염되지 않은 환경이 건강에 보다 좋은 농작물을 생산해 냈다.

농업 기술은 우리가 먹는 농작물에 많은 변화를 가져왔다. 첫째, 오늘날 많은 사람들이 유전자 변형 음식을 먹고 있을 수 있다. 유전자 변형 농작물을 사용하는 두 가지 이유는 농작물의 성장을 촉진시키고 음식물 부패의 과정을 늦추기 위해서이다. 둘째, 익는 속도를 늦추기 위해, 사과 등의 과일은 방사선 처리 과정을 거치는데, 이로써 영양학적인 가치가 감소될 수 있다. 이러한 기술의 장기적 영향은 아직 확실치 않다.

게다가, 과거에는 환경이 오염되지 않았다. 따라서, 농작물, 가축, 그리고 다른 동물들이 자라는 환경이 오늘날에 비해 해롭지 않았기 때문에 과거의 음식은 섭취하기에 보다 더 안전했다. 예를 들면, 막대한 해상 기름 유출 사고로 많은 어류가 오염 물질을 먹어야만 했다. 그 결과, 많은 물고기들이 죽었고, 가까스로 살아남은 물고기들은 독성을 띤 유해한 식량 자원이 되었다. 그러한 피해를 복구하기 위해 많은 노력이 행해지고 있지만, 앞으로 사람들이 과거와 같은 신선한 물고기를 먹을 수 있을 것인지에 대해서는 장담할 수 없다.

발달된 기술로 식품의 이용 가능성을 넓히고, 특정한 음식에 요구되는 기후 조건과 상관없이 다양한 음식을 즐길 수 있게 되었다는 것은 사실이다. 하지만, 기술은 유전자 변형 식품 및 방사선 처리 식품 또한 생산해 냈다. 게다가, 농작물과 다른 생산품을 과거만큼 신선하게 생산하기에는 오늘날의 환경이 너무 오염되어 있다. 이상의 이유들로, 나는 과거의 사람들이 오늘날의 사람들이 그런 것보다 건강식을 섭취했다는 주장에 강력히 동의한다.

Sample Essay 2 | DISAGREE   p.134

농업 기술과 요리법의 발달 덕분에, 수년에 걸쳐 식품은 커다란 변화를 겪었다. 게다가, 최근의 웰빙 유행은 식품 산업에도 영향을 끼치고 있다. 몇몇 사람들은 과거의 사람들이 더 건강한 음식을 먹었다고 주장한다. 하지만 나는 현

대인들이 섭취하는 음식이 과거의 음식에 비해 훨씬 더 건강에 좋다고 굳게 믿는다. 이에 대한 이유는 음식을 신선하게 유지하는 보관 방법이 보다 개선되었기 때문이다. 게다가, 사람들은 건강식에 관한 정보에 더 많이 노출되어 있다.

첫째, 과거의 보관 방법은 현재의 보관 방법보다 비교적 열악했다. 따라서, 수확 당시에는 음식이 신선했더라도, 주방에 배달될 때쯤에는 종종 상하곤 했다. 따라서, 식품은 구할 수 없거나 신선하지가 않았다. 예를 들면, 한국 사람들은 뇌기능에 대한 블루베리의 효능에 대해 오래 전부터 알고 있었다. 하지만, 그 당시 신선한 블루베리를 수입하는 것은 기술의 부족으로 인해 과거에는 불가능했다. 오늘날에는, 보관 방법의 개선으로 블루베리를 쉽게 먹을 수 있다.

또한, 수십 년 전 특히 전쟁이나 경제적 어려움을 겪었던 나라에서는 많은 사람들이 건강식에 대해서 주의를 기울이지 않았다. 오히려, 대부분의 사람들은 먹을 수 있다는 것만으로도 만족했다. 예를 들면, 전쟁을 겪었던 내 할머니는 구할 수 있었던 것이면 무엇이든지 먹을 수 밖에 없었다고 말씀하셨다. 명백하게도, 건강식은 사치였다. 반대로, 책뿐만 아니라 대중 매체가 식품이 건강에 얼마나 직접적인 영향을 끼치는지에 대해 끝없는 정보를 제공해 주고 있기 때문에, 나의 엄마는 나의 가족이 먹는 음식의 영양 가치에 대해 관심이 있다.

환경 파괴가 식품의 악화를 초래했으며, 그 결과 새로운 질병이 나타난 것은 사실이다. 하지만, 의학 기술의 발달로 학자들은 대응책을 찾는데 도움을 받아 왔다. 게다가, 보관 방법과 식단에 대한 관심은 사람들을 건강식에 노출시켜 왔다. 이상의 이유로, 나는 과거의 사람들이 요즘 사람들에 비해 건강식을 섭취했다는 주장에 강력히 반대한다.

Actual Test 13

TASK 1 · INTEGRATED TASK
Zoology: Marsupials

READING   p.137

유대류의 동물들은 포유 동물로 간주되는 동물들이다. 유대류 중에는 캥거루가 가장 잘 알려진 유대류이다. 이들은 주로 호주에서 서식한다. 하지만, 몇몇 종은 뉴기니, 남미, 그리고 북미에서 발견되고 있다. 그러나, 화석 증거에 따르면, 유대류들은 한때 지구의 사실상 모든 지역에서 살았다. 그렇지만, 환경에 적응하는데 문제가 있어서, 이들은 대부분의 지역에서 사라져 버렸다.

유대류 동물들은 태반을 가지고 있지 않다는 점에서 다른 포유류들과 차이를 보이는데, 어미들은 새끼를 몸속에 갖고 있다가 출산하지 않는다. 대신, 유대류 동물의 새끼들은 완전히 성숙되기 전에 태어난다. 태어나자마자, 유대류 동물의 새끼는 어미의 신체에 있는 주머니로 기어들어 가는데, 여기서 성숙할 때까지 지내게 된다. 안타깝게도, 조산은 대부분의 유대류 동물들이 미발달된 면역 체계를 가졌다는 것을 의미한다. 이러한 사실은 유대류 동물들을 감염 및 조기 사망에 보다 취약하게 만들며, 감염 및 조기 사망은 상당히 빈번한 형태로 발생하고 있다.

유대류 동물들은 다른 포유 동물들에 비해 낮은 신진대사율을 가지고 있다. 포유 동물은 체온을 조절하기 위해, 에너지를 공급해 줄 수 있는 음식을 섭취해야만 한다. 하지만, 유대류 동물들의 신진대사율이 낮다는 점은 온도가 떨어졌을 때 이들이 체온 유지에 어려움을 겪게 된다는 점을 의미한다. 그 결과, 이들은 추운 지역에서 대부분 사라졌으며 지금은 호주나 남미와 같은

더 따뜻한 환경에서 주로 발견되고 있다.

또한, 유대류들은 포유류들과의 경쟁에서 밀려났기 때문에 오늘날 많은 지역에서 발견되지 않는다. 통상 동일한 생태계 내에 있는 동물들은 식량과 서식지를 둘러싸고 서로 경쟁을 한다. 면역 체계와 추운 날씨에 대한 부적응으로 약해진 유대류들은 훨씬 더 강하다고 입증된 포유류들에 의해 여러 지역에서 쫓겨 났다. 그 결과, 오늘날 유대류들은 전 세계 소수의 지역에서만 서식한다.

W Professor: Marsupials include animals such as kangaroos, koalas, and opossums. In the past, they lived everywhere, but today they're mostly found in Australia and South America. Some zoologists believe marsupials died out in other places because they were less able to adapt than placental mammals, yet I disagree with this notion. After all, remember that marsupials thrive in places where mammals don't. I'd say that hardly makes them weaker than mammals.

Marsupials have one big advantage over most other mammals: They lack placentas. Placental mammals carry their babies until they're mature, which could take several weeks or months. During that time, the mother is quite vulnerable. Marsupials such as kangaroos and opossums, meanwhile, give birth much more quickly. Their babies then mature outside the body in their mothers' pouches. This way, the babies are more easily protected by their mothers, and they can strengthen their immune systems by feeding and drinking their mothers' milk. This makes them strong and healthy as babies.

Marsupials create energy from the food they eat more slowly than other mammals. This has enabled them to adapt to harsh environments. For instance, in Australia, the land is dry, so it's sometimes hard to find food. Few mammals can survive in those conditions, but marsupials, which can go without food for long periods of time, aren't bothered at all. Marsupials can also regulate their body temperatures better than mammals, which stops them from overheating in hot, dry conditions.

The fossil evidence in Australia shows that placental mammals once lived there in great numbers. But those mammals couldn't handle Australia's harsh environment. Kangaroos, koalas, and other marsupials outcompeted them, so most mammals vanished from the land. I contend that marsupials are suited for certain types of land while placental mammals are more suited for other types.

교수: 유대류 동물에는 캥거루, 코알라, 그리고 주머니쥐 같은 동물들이 포함됩니다. 과거, 이들은, 어디에서나 살고 있었지만, 오늘날에는 주로 호주나 남미에서 발견되고 있습니다. 일부 동물학자들은 유대류 동물들이 태반을 가진 포유 동물들보다 적응 능력이 떨어졌기 때문에 다른 지역에서 사라졌다고 믿지만, 저는 이 견해에 동의하지 않습니다. 어찌됐건, 유대류들은 포유 동물들이 살지 않는 곳에서 번성하고 있죠. 그렇다고 해서 유대류 동물들이 포유 동물들보다 더 약하다고 할 수는 없다고 말씀드리고 싶습니다.

유대류 동물들은 대부분의 다른 포유 동물들에 비해 한 가지 큰 장점을 가

지고 있습니다. 그들에게는 태반이 없습니다. 태반을 가진 포유 동물들은 자신의 새끼들이 성숙할 때까지 수주나 수개월 동안 새끼들을 몸에 지니고 다닙니다. 이 시기 동안, 어미는 매우 취약하게 됩니다. 한편, 캥거루나 주머니쥐 같은 유대류 동물들은 훨씬 더 빨리 새끼를 낳습니다. 그들의 새끼들은 어미의 몸 밖에 있는 주머니에서 성장을 하죠. 이런 식으로 새끼들은 어미에 의해 훨씬 더 쉽게 보호를 받고, 어미의 젖을 먹음으로써 면역 체계를 강화시키게 됩니다. 이로써 새끼인 그들은 강하고 건강해집니다.

유대류들은 그들이 다른 포유 동물들보다 더 느리게 먹는 음식으로부터 에너지를 만들어 냅니다. 이는 혹독한 환경에 적응할 수 있도록 해 주었습니다. 예를 들면, 호주에서는 육지가 건조해서 때때로 음식을 구하기가 힘듭니다. 포유 동물들은 그러한 조건에서 거의 살아남을 수 없지만, 장기간 식량 없이 지낼 수 있는 유대류 동물들은 전혀 어려움을 겪지 않습니다. 유대류들은 또한 다른 포유 동물들에 비해 체온 조절을 더 잘하는데, 이는 덥고 건조한 기후에서도 신체가 과열되지 않도록 해줍니다.

호주에서 발견된 화석에 의하면 태반을 가진 많은 포유류들이 한때 그곳에 살고 있었다는 점을 알 수가 있습니다. 하지만, 그러한 포유 동물들은 호주의 혹독한 환경을 견딜 수 없었습니다. 캥거루, 코알라, 그리고 다른 유대류 동물들이 그들을 압도해서, 대부분의 포유 동물들은 그 지역에서 사라졌습니다. 저는 다른 종류의 지역에서는 포유류들이 보다 더 적합한 반면, 특정 지역에서는 유대류 동물들이 더 적합하다고 생각합니다.

Sample Essay
p.140

교수는 각각의 종들은 서식지로서 가장 적합한 지역을 가지고 있다고 주장한다. 따라서, 유대류 동물들은 포유 동물들보다 약한 것이 아니다. 이는 혹독한 환경에 적응할 수 있는 능력이 없었기 때문에 유대류 동물들이 대부분의 지역에서 사라졌다는 지문의 내용을 직접적으로 반박한다.

첫째, 유대류 동물들은 태반을 가지고 있지 않다는 이점이 있다. 반대로, 유대류 동물들은 태어난 직후 새끼들을 주머니에 넣어 다니기 때문에 그들의 안전 및 모유 수유로부터 오는 건강이 보장된다. 이 사실은 유대류 동물들의 조산이 종종 감염이나 조기 사망을 초래한다는 지문의 내용과 반대된다.

그리고, 교수는 차후 에너지로 변환되는 음식을 천천히 섭취하는 유대류들의 습관이 유대류 동물들로 하여금 서서히 혹독한 조건에서도 견딜 수 있도록 해 주었다고 주장한다. 이러한 점은 그들이 식량 없이도 오랜 기간을 견디는데 도움이 되는데, 건조하기 때문에 음식을 구하기가 어려운 호주에서는 유리하다. 게다가, 유대류들은 체온을 조절하는 능력이 다른 동물들보다 뛰어나다. 이러한 사실은 낮은 신진대사율 때문에 이들이 대부분의 지역에서 사라졌다고 설명하는 지문의 주장에 의문을 제기한다.

마지막으로, 화석에 대한 검증을 통해, 많은 포유 동물들이 과거 호주에서 살았다는 것이 입증되었다. 하지만, 그들은 혹독한 환경을 극복하지 못하고 그 지역을 떠나야만 했다. 이는 적자생존의 법칙에 따라 현재 포유 동물들이 사는 곳에서 유대류들이 사라졌다는 지문의 주장을 반박한다.

TASK 2 · INDEPENDENT TASK
Training

Sample Essay 1 | EVERYONE TOGETHER
p.143

얼마나 직원이 유능하고 숙련되었든지 간에, 회사는 새로운 기술을 사용할 때 항상 직원들을 교육시킨다. 직원들은 최신 방법을 배우고, 생각을 공유하고, 연수 과정 동안 피드백을 받는다. 일부 회사들은 연수 프로그램에 모든 직원들이 다 같이 참여하게 한다. 반면, 다른 곳은 일부는 프로그램에 참여하게 하고, 나중에 그들이 배운 것을 동료 직원들에게 전하게 한다. 둘 다 장단

점이 있으나, 나는 전자를 선호한다. 나는 협동심과 효율적인 의사소통 때문에 이렇게 느낀다.

첫째, 연수를 같이 받음으로써, 직원들은 서로 협력하고 의견을 공유하는 것을 배운다. 교육 시간에 모두가 참여하는 것은 일체감도 준다. 예를 들면, 만약 회사가 실행하는 새로운 기술이 너무 어려울 경우, 직원들은 다른 부분에서 노움을 받은 반면, 그들이 잘 하는 부분에서는 다른 이들에게 도움을 줌으로서 서로 도울 수 있다. 따라서, 직원들이 다른 부서에서 일할지라도, 그들은 여전히 다양한 직무를 수행하는 방법에 대한 전반적인 이해력을 가지고 있다.

게다가, 같은 교육자에게서 교육을 받으면 의사소통 착오의 가능성이 없어진다. 자세히 말하자면, 직원이 정보를 어떻게 전달하느냐에 따라 다른 결과가 생길 수 있다. 예를 들면, 통상 전화 게임에서 (단어 뜻 참조) 일어나듯이, 개인은 지식이나 설명을 자신만의 방식으로 인지할 수도 있다. 따라서, 만약 새로운 기술을 배워서 자신만의 어휘로 설명한다면, 다른 직원은 굉장히 다른 방법으로 이해할 수 있다.

한 직원이 다른 동료에게 자신이 배운 지식을 전달함으로써 배운 내용을 복습할 수 있는 것은 사실이다. 하지만, 연수 과정 동안 자신이 배운 것을 이해하는 것은 각 직원들의 책임이다. 같이 훈련에 참가하며 직원들은 서로 협동하는 것을 배울 수 있다. 게다가 직원들 간에 의사소통 착오가 발생할 가능성은 매우 낮다. 그러므로 직원들이 새로운 기술을 사용하게끔 훈련시킬 때, 나는 회사가 모든 직원이 연수 과정에 다 같이 참여하게 하는 것을 선호한다.

Sample Essay 2 | ONLY SOME   p.144

얼마나 직원이 유능하고 숙련되었든지 간에, 회사는 새로운 기술을 사용할 때 항상 직원들을 교육시킨다. 직원들은 최신 방법을 배우고, 생각을 공유하고, 연수 과정 동안 피드백을 받는다. 일부 회사들은 연수 프로그램에 모든 직원들이 다 같이 참여하게 한다. 반면, 다른 곳은 일부를 프로그램에 참여하게 하고, 나중에 그들이 배운 것을 동료 직원들에게 전하게 한다. 둘 다 장단점이 있으나, 나는 후자를 선호한다. 나는 직원은 실행을 통해 복습할 기회가 있고, 조정이 가능하기 때문에 이렇게 느낀다.

첫째, 배움의 가장 좋은 방법은 다른 이들에게 가르치며 배운 지식을 적용하는 것이다. 배운 것을 설명함으로써, 그는 그 개념을 완전히 이해할 수 있다. 예를 들면, 직원은 새로운 기술에 대한 정보를 이해했다고 느낄 수 있다. 하지만, 동료에게 새로운 기술을 보여주고 질의응답을 하면서, 그는 사실 완전히 이해하지 못한 일부가 있다는 것을 깨달을 수 있다.

뿐만 아니라, 이론이 항상 실제 상황에서 작동하는 것은 아니다. 동료에게 설명을 하며, 직원은 수정이 필요하거나 좀 더 자세히 설명이 되어야 하는 특정 부분을 발견할 수도 있다. 예를 들면, 동료에게 기술을 보여주면서, 그 직원은 새로운 기술은 조립하는 시간이 더 오래 걸린다는 것을 발견할 수도 있다. 그러면, 기업이 가능한 오류를 줄이는 데 도움이 되기 위한 조정이 행해질 수 있다.

같이 연수를 받는 것이 잘못된 전달의 가능성을 줄여준다는 것은 사실이다. 하지만, 연구하고 복습하는 것은 직원들의 책임이다. 무엇을 배웠는지를 동료에게 보여줌으로써, 직원들은 신기술에 대한 수업을 복습하고 완전히 이해할 수 있다. 게다가, 회사는 직원들이 동료에게 기술을 보여주는 동안 그 기술에 대한 의견을 얻을 수 있다. 그러므로 직원들이 새로운 기술을 사용하게끔 훈련시킬 때, 나는 회사가 몇몇 직원들이 연수 과정에 다녀오게 하여 나중에 그들의 동료들에게 자신들이 습득한 지식을 보여 주게 하는 것을 선호한다.

Actual Test 14

TASK 1 · INTEGRATED TASK
Engineering: Oil Sands

READING   p.147

오일 샌드는 모래, 진흙, 물 그리고 역청이라고 불리는 기름의 혼합물이고 지구에서 가장 큰 원유의 침전물이다. 그것은 캐나다의 알버타에서 발견되며 이는 캐나다를 미국에서 가장 큰 해외 원료 공급국으로 만들었다. 그것은 캐나다에 많은 경제적 이득을 가져왔지만, 오일 샌드에 의해 초래되는 손상의 규모는 엄청나다. 많은 전문가들은 캐나다의 오일 샌드 개발이 계속 가속화될 것이라 예측하며 올바른 제재가 시행되어야 한다고 주장한다.

첫째, 오일 샌드 추출에는 물이 반드시 필요하다. 무거운 원유인 역청은 모래, 진흙, 그리고 물로부터 분리되어야 한다. 이러한 분리 과정에서 상당량의 물과 화학 물질이 필요하며, 1베럴의 기름이 생산될 때 최대 4. 5갤론의 담수가 필요하다. 많은 사람들은 특히 가뭄 때, 농작물을 기르는 것보다 기름을 생산하는데 물을 사용할 가치가 있는지 의문을 품는다.

오일 샌드의 또 다른 심각한 문제는 잔해 물질을 가두는 테일링 폰드(tailing ponds), 댐, 그리고 제방 시설로부터의 유출이다. 이러한 유출은 많은 수중 생물들을 죽여 왔다. 예를 들어, 많은 오리들이 수은과 암모니아 같은 유독 물질에 노출되었으며 대부분은 죽었다. 오염된 잔해 물질의 호수는 많은 철새들도 죽였다.

게다가, 벌목, 수력발전 댐, 그리고 북부 수림대에서의 채광 같은 산업 발전은 아한대(亞寒帶) 생태계를 위험에 빠뜨렸으며 오일 샌드 개발 역시 예외는 아니다. 역청을 추출하는 것은 북부 수림대에 파괴적이다. 몇몇 부정적인 요소들은 수송관, 노천굴 광산, 그리고 도로들이며 이는 야생 동물종들을 내쫓는다. 캐나다의 북부 삼림대는 믿기 힘들 정도로 다양하며 단지 캐나다뿐 아니라 세계적으로 매우 중요하고 그것은 위험에 빠져 있다.

LISTENING   🎧 14-01

W Professor: Oil sands have caused major controversies among developers, the government of Canada, and environmentalists for many years. It is impossible to completely avoid environmental damage. However, the damage is barely noticeable considering the vast size of the land. The government of Canada has also enacted stringent rules that must be adhered to by every company. I would like to clarify some of the misconceptions on oil sands.

Many people are concerned about the use of water during the process. There is no need to be concerned. Most water used in oil sands development, uh, around ninety-four percent for in-situ recovery and eighty percent for established mining operations, is recycled. Of course, some new water is needed, but it comes from various sources like precipitation, rivers, and onsite drainage. Actually, less than one percent of the Athabasca River's annual flow is used. Again, there are strict regulations for water use, and businesses and governments continue to develop methods to minimize the use of water in the process.

Oil sands extraction leaves accumulations of residual

waste known as tailings, which contain some organic compounds that are toxic. The tailings are put in large ponds. While the water is recycled, the majority remains as mud almost permanently. In addition, oil sands mining companies as well as the government conduct close monitoring and are committed to high environmental standards to reduce potential environmental risks.

There is misinformation claiming that boreal forests are being destroyed. It is quite funny to hear that oil sands are destructive to the boreal forests in Alberta. According to Natural Resources Canada, only 0.2% of boreal forests in Alberta have been disturbed by oil sands mining over the past forty years. And after the bitumen is harvested, the materials that were once removed from the site are put back in the reserve to restore the land. So again, people should not be worried about boreal forests being destroyed by oil sands.

교수: 오일 샌드는 수년 간, 개발자들, 캐나다 정부, 그리고 환경 보호론자들 사이에서 많은 논란을 일으켜 왔어요. 환경적 손상을 완전히 막는 것은 불가능 합니다. 하지만, 땅의 광대한 지역을 고려하면 손상은 거의 알아차리기도 힘들 어요. 캐나다 정부는 또한 모든 기업이 반드시 따라야 하는 엄격한 규정을 제 정했어요. 저는 오일 샌드에 대한 몇 가지 잘못된 생각을 바로잡고 싶습니다.

많은 사람들이 과정 중의 물에 사용에 대해 걱정이 많아요. 걱정할 필요 가 없습니다. 오일 샌드 개발에 사용되는 대부분의 물은, 음, 원 위치에서는 약 94퍼센트, 그리고 채광 현장에서는 80퍼센트가 재활용되요. 물론 새로운 물이 조금 필요하긴 하지만 그건 다양한 원천 즉, 강수, 강, 그리고 현장의 배 수 에서 오지요. 사실, Athabasca 강의 1퍼센트도 안 되는 연간 강우량만이 사용됩니다. 다시 말하지만, 물의 사용에 대한 엄격한 규정이 있고, 사업체와 정부는 그 과정에 있어 물의 사용을 최소화하기 위한 방법을 끊임없이 개발 중이에요.

오일 샌드의 추출은 잔해물이라고 불리는 잔여 폐기물의 축적을 남기는 데 그것은 유독성의 일부 유기 혼합물을 포함하고 있어요. 잔해물은 커다란 호수에 둡니다. 물은 재활용이 되는 반면, 대부분의 잔여물은 진흙의 상태로 거의 영구적으로 놓이게 되고요. 게다가, 정부뿐 아니라 오일 샌드 채광 기 업들은 근접 관찰을 하고 잠재적인 환경 위험을 줄이기 위해 강도 높은 환경 기준을 결의합니다.

북부 수림대가 파괴된다는 주장하는 오보가 있어요. 오일 샌드가 알버타 에 있는 북부 수림대를 파괴시킨다는 걸 들으면 조금 웃기요. 캐나다 천연 자 원부에 따르면, 지난 40년 동안 알버타에 있는 북부 수림대의 0. 2%만이 오 일 샌드 채광에 피해를 봤습니다. 그리고 역청이 추출되면, 해당 지역에서 분리되었던 물질들이 땅을 복원하기 위해 보호 구역에 다시 놓이집니다. 그 러니까 다시 말하지만 사람들은 오일 샌드로 인해 북부 수림대가 파괴되는 것에 대해 걱정하지 않아도 되는 것이지요.

Sample Essay   p.150

교수는 오일 샌드로 인한 손상은 거의 알아차릴 수 없고 기업들은 캐나다 정부에 의해 세워진 엄격한 규칙을 따르고 있다고 주장한다. 이러한 주장들 은 캐나다의 오일 샌드가 환경 파괴에 주요 원인이라는 지문의 내용을 직접 적으로 반박한다.

첫째, 그녀는 오일 샌드에 사용되는 대부분의 물은 재활용된다고 강조한 다. 게다가, 새로운 물은 비와 강 같은 다른 원천에서 나온다. 이는 분리 과정

에서 엄청난 양의 물이 사용된다는 지문의 주장에 이의를 제기한다.

그리고 나서 교수는 오일 샌드 추출에서 폐기물인 잔해물이 유독 물질을 포함하고 있다고 주장한다. 하지만, 잔해물은 진흙으로서 영구적으로 남게 되고, 물은 재활용된다. 또한, 정부는 가능한 환경 위해를 줄이기 위해 엄중 히 감시할 것이다. 이는 잔해물의 유출이 철새뿐 아니라 많은 수생 동물도 죽 여왔다는 지문의 내용에 의문을 던진다.

마지막으로, 40년에 걸치는 동안, 알버타에 있는 북부 수림대의 0.2%만 이 오일 샌드 채광으로 인해 파괴되었다. 교수에 따르면, 역청이 추출된 후, 남은 물질들은 보호 구역에 다시 놓여진다. 이는 산업 발달이 세계에 매우 중 요한 북부 수림대를 위험에 빠뜨린다는 지문에서 보여진 주장을 논박한다.

TASK 2 · INDEPENDENT TASK
Problem Solving

Sample Essay 1 | AGREE   p.153

각 세대는 환경과 사회 문제를 포함한 다양한 문제로 인해 고통을 겪는 다. 특정 세대의 사람들이 이러한 이슈에 어떻게 대처하느냐는 미래에 막대 한 영향을 끼치며 사람들은 다음 세대를 위한 긍정적인 결과를 얻기 위해 많 은 노력을 한다. 일부 사람들은 우리의 문제들이 우리 세대에 의해 해결될 수 없다고 주장한다. 하지만, 나는 이러한 어려움들이 빠른 시간 내에 해결될 수 있다고 굳게 믿는다. 우선, 급속도로 발전하는 과학 기술이 해결책을 찾는데 도움을 줄 것이다. 게다가, 개인뿐만 아니라 많은 단체들이 최선을 다하여 이 러한 이슈들에 대처하고 있다.

첫째, 과학 기술의 발전으로 의학 및 환경 과학을 포함한 다양한 분야에서 문제 해결 속도가 빨라지고 있다. 따라서, 새로운 발견과 연구로 많은 문제들 이 해결되어 왔다. 예를 들면, 의료 기술에서는 말기 암 환자를 위한 치료법 이 개발되었다. 게다가, 건축의 발전 및 건설에서의 환경친화적인 접근법으 로 인해 오염을 일으켰던 문제들이 해결되고 있다. 그 결과, 다양한 이슈들을 해결해 줄 수 있는 수단들이 우리 세대의 문제들을 해소시켜 줄 것이다.

뿐만 아니라, 과거와 비교했을 때, 많은 단체, 기업, 그리고 개인들이 다양한 환경 및 사회 문제에 대해 점점 더 의식하고 있다. 따라서, 손상된 부분을 회복 시키기 위한 많은 노력이 가해지고 있다. 예로써, 환경 단체들은 환경 운동에 대한 참여를 장려하고 있으며, 대부분의 한국 사람들은 재활용 운동 및 비닐 대신 종이 가방을 사용하는 운동 등에 적극적으로 참여하고 있다. 이는 자연이 환경 파괴가 덜 했던 과거 시점의 수준을 회복하는데 도움이 될 것이다.

그 결과가 다음 세대까지 나타나지 않을 수도 있다는 점은 사실이다. 하지 만, 문제들은 해결될 것이고 다음 세대에는 계속되지 않을 것이다. 다양한 분 야에서의 빠른 과학 기술의 발전은 문제 해결을 촉진시켜 줄 것이다. 게다가, 대다수의 사람들과 단체들이 현재 우리가 겪고 있는 문제들을 해결하기 위 해 앞장 서고 있다. 위의 이유로, 나는 우리의 대부분의 문제들이 우리 세 대 안에 해결될 것이라는 주장에 강력히 동의한다.

Sample Essay 2 | DISAGREE   p.154

각 세대는 환경과 사회 문제를 포함한 다양한 문제로 인해 고통을 겪는다. 특정 세대의 사람들이 이러한 이슈에 어떻게 대처하느냐는 미래에 막대한 영 향을 끼치며 사람들은 다음 세대를 위한 긍정적인 결과를 얻기 위해 많은 노 력을 한다. 일부 사람들은 우리의 문제들이 우리 세대에 의해 해결될 수 있다 고 주장한다. 하지만, 나는 일부 문제들의 해결에 훨씬 더 많은 시간이 필요할 것이라고 굳게 믿는다. 우선, 몇몇 환경 피해는 복구하는데 상당히 많은 시간 이 필요할 것이다. 게다가, 일부 사회 문제는 결코 해결될 수 없는 것이다.

첫째, 과학 기술이 빠르게 진보하고 있지만, 모든 문제들을 비교적 짧은 시간 내에 해결할 수는 없다. 예를 들어, 시신세 당시 지구 온난화가 발생하였는데 그 열기가 방출되고 대기가 정상적인 온도로 돌아오는 데는 2천 년 이상의 시간이 걸렸다. 마찬가지로, 특정한 문제들, 특히 환경 문제들은, 많은 시간과 노력을 요하며 한 세대 안에는 해결될 수 없는 것이다.

뿐만 아니라, 몇몇 사회 문제들은 사회가 물질주의에 기반해 있는 한 지속될 것이다. 빈부의 격차가 존재하고 있기 때문에, 범죄는 사라지지 않을 것이다. 예를 들면, 절도를 포함한 범죄는 인간이 물건을 소유하고 저장하기 시작했던 이후로 계속 존재해 왔다. 굶주림 때문이던 혹은 욕심 때문이던, 절도는 해결해야 할 문제로 항상 남아 있을 것이다.

오늘날 사람들이 심각한 문제에 대한 인식이 더 커지고 이를 해결하기 위해 답을 찾으려 노력하고 있다는 점은 사실이다. 하지만, 몇몇 문제들은 장기간의 노력을 필요로 한다. 게다가, 시민 의식의 성숙과 엄격한 법률의 존재에도 불구하고, 사회가 자본주의에 바탕을 두는 한 특정 범죄는 지속될 것이다. 위의 이유로, 나는 우리의 대부분의 문제들이 우리 세대 안에 해결될 것이라는 주장에 강력히 반대한다.

Actual Test 15

TASK 1 · INTEGRATED TASK
Zoology: The Origins of Dogs

p.157

개들은 수천 년 간 인간의 곁에서 살며 일을 해왔다. 실제로, 개들은 인간이 사육한 첫 번째 동물이라고 알려져 있다. 그 때부터, 이 둘은 서로에게서 떨어질 수 없는 존재가 되었다.

개들이 늑대의 후손이라는 것은 명확하다. 어쨌든, 늑대들은 인간과 함께 살기 시작했다. 수 세대가 지난 후, 늑대들은 애완견들로 진화했다. 증거들이 이 이론을 뒷받침해 준다. 두 동물 모두 털, 긴 꼬리, 길고 뾰족한 주둥이, 커다란 치아, 그리고 쌍안시를 가지고 있는 네 발의 포유 동물이다. 그들은 한 배에서 낳은 새끼를 키우고, 자신들의 영역을 표시하며, 행동에 있어서도 기타 유사점을 보인다. 늑대와 개는 이종교배를 할 수도 있으며, DNA 연구는 그들이 밀접한 관련성을 지니고 있다는 점을 나타내 준다.

늑대와 인간이 정확히 어떻게 가까워졌는지는 추측으로만 알 수 있다. 아마도 일부 늑대들이 새끼 때부터 길러 졌거나, 혹은 인간이 굶주린 늑대에게 단순히 음식을 주었을 수도 있다. 어떤 경우이던, 늑대는 인간을 보다 더 신뢰하게 되었다. 이 늑대들은 선사 시대 사람들의 모닥불로 찾아왔을 가능성이 있으며 남은 고기 조각을 받아 먹었을 것이다. 서서히, 늑대들은 몇몇 인간 무리의 일부가 되어 갔다. 그들은 사람들이 커다란 사냥감을 사냥하는데 도움을 주었을 것이며 포식자와 적대 관계의 부족으로부터 사람들을 보호해 주었을 것이다. 그 과정에서, 늑대들은 길들여졌다.

선별적인 교배를 통해, 늑대는 보다 더 오늘날의 개와 닮아갔다. 이러한 교배는 오늘날 존재하는 엄청난 종류의 개들에 대한 이유가 된다. 인류학자들은 이러한 과정이 14,000년 전부터 시작되었다고 추측한다. 당시의 고대 무덤 일부가 발굴되었다. 그곳에서는 주인인 인간과 함께 묻혀있는 개가 있었는데, 이는 그 둘 사이에 이미 존재하고 있었던 강한 동료 의식을 명확히 보여 주었다. 수천 년 후 이집트 및 기타 고대 문명들이 생겨났을 무렵, 개들은 야생 동물이 아닌, 애완 동물로서 여겨지게 되었다.

W Professor: The origins of modern dogs are difficult to determine. You've probably heard people say that dogs are descendants of wolves, but that's not been proven. In fact, dogs may be completely unrelated to wolves. We know, of course, that dogs were domesticated, but exactly how and when this happened is unknown.

Dogs and wolves share many characteristics, but so do dogs and cats, and no one claims that one is descended from the other. So . . . did dogs descend directly from wolves? Perhaps not. Here's why . . . Wolves are larger and more aggressive than even the biggest species of dogs. Attempts to domesticate wolves have mostly failed, yet dogs that have grown up in the wild can still be tamed. It seems that they're from the same mammal family, but sometime in the far past, the two species diverged. The modern dog is probably descended from an ancestor similar to the wolf but smaller and less aggressive.

How did humans domesticate dogs? Perhaps by sharing food. Some dogs probably approached human camps, and if they posed no threat, they may have been given scraps of food by humans. The friendliest and most nonaggressive dogs got more food and may have been permitted to sleep with the humans. Gradually, these friendly dogs outcompeted the more aggressive ones and thus came to dominate the species.

So the final question is this . . . Why did humans domesticate the dog? We don't know for sure. Some remains . . . from 14,000 years ago . . . uh, these ancient remains of dogs have been found buried with humans, but human burial wasn't common until people abandoned their hunter-gatherer lifestyles and began settling in cities around, hmm . . . 8,000 to 10,000 years ago. So humans may have domesticated dogs before then, but without more evidence, we can't be certain.

교수: 오늘날 개의 기원은 확인하기가 힘듭니다. 여러분은 아마도 개가 늑대의 후손이라고 말하는 것을 들어 본 적이 있겠지만, 이는 입증된 바가 없습니다. 사실, 개들은 사람하고 전혀 연관이 없을지도 모릅니다. 우리는, 물론, 개들이 사육되었다는 점은 알고 있지만, 정확히 어떻게 그리고 언제 이런 일이 일어났는지는 밝혀지지 않았습니다.

개들과 늑대들은 여러 특성을 공유하고 있지만, 그것은 개들과 고양이들 사이도 마찬가지인데, 누구도 그것이 서로의 후손이라고 주장하지는 않습니다. 그러니까... 개들이 늑대의 직접적인 후손일까요? 아마도 아닐 것입니다. 여기 이유를 알려 드리면... 늑대는 개들 중 가장 큰 종 보다 훨씬 더 크고 훨씬 더 공격적입니다. 늑대를 사육하려는 시도는 대부분 실패했지만, 야생에서 자라난 개들은 여전히 길들여질 수 있습니다. 늑대와 개 모두 같은 포유류로부터 나왔다고 보이지만, 매우 오래 전에, 두 종은 나뉘어졌을 것입니다. 오늘날 개는 늑대와 비슷한 조상으로부터 나왔겠지만 보다 작고 덜 공격적 인종이었을 것입니다.

인간이 어떻게 동물을 길들였을까요? 아마도 음식을 나누어 주면서 그렇게 했을 것입니다. 몇몇 개들이 인간의 거주지에 나타났을 것이고, 그들이 위협적인 자세를 취하지 않는 이상, 인간들은 몇 조각의 음식을 주었을 것입니다. 가장 친근하고 호의적인 개들은 더 많은 음식을 얻었으며 인간과 함께 잠을 자도록 허락되었을 것입니다. 점차, 이러한 친근한 개들은 보다 공격적인 개들을 압도하여 종에서 우위를 차지하게 되었습니다.

이제 마지막 문제는 다음과 같습니다... 왜 인간이 개를 사육했을까요? 확실하게는 모릅니다. 몇몇 유골이... 14,000년 전으로부터의... 음, 고대의 개의 유골이 인간과 함께 매장되어 있는 것이 발견되었지만, 인간의 매장 풍습은 수렵 채집민의 삶의 방식에서 벗어나서 도시에 상주하기 시작한 후에나 흔해졌습니다... 8,000에서 10,000년 전입니다. 그러니까 인간들이 그 이전에도 개를 사육했을 수 있지만, 더 많은 증거 없이는 확신할 수가 없습니다.

Sample Essay   p.160

교수는 개의 기원을 알아내는 것이 불가능하다고 단정짓는다. 이는 인류 역사상 개가 첫 번째 애완 동물이라는 지문의 의견에 반대된다.

첫째, 늑대는 개의 가장 큰 종보다 더 크고 보다 적대적이기 때문에 개는 늑대와 다르다. 게다가, 야생에서 살았던 개들은 사육이 가능해서, 아마도 개가 크기가 조금 더 작고 덜 공격적인 늑대와 같은 동물로부터 유래되었을 것이라는 결론이 가능하다. 이는 외모, 행동, 그리고 DNA의 유사점에 근거하여 개가 늑대의 후손이라는 지문의 주장을 반박한다.

다음, 개들이 어떻게 길들여졌는지 역시 불확실하다. 더 붙임성 있는 개들은 더 적대적인 개들에 비해 유리했으며, 그 개체수는 공격적인 개들을 압도했을 가능성이 크다. 이는 인간과 늑대들 간에 호혜적인 관계가 나타났다는 지문의 주장을 반박한다.

교수가 지적하는 마지막 요점은 14,000년 전의 유물을 보면 개와 인간이 함께 매장되어 있다는 점이다. 하지만, 매장은 8,000년에서 10,000년 전 이후에야 일반적인 것이 되었다. 이는 무덤으로 이 둘 사이의 우정을 알 수 있다는 지문의 주장을 직접적으로 반박한다.

TASK 2 · INDEPENDENT TASK

Decision Making

Sample Essay 1 | AGREE   p.163

끝없는 사랑, 동기 부여, 그리고 신뢰를 제공하는 것 이외에도 부모들은 자신의 아이들을 올바른 길로 인도하는 사람들이다. 하지만, 아이들이 특정 나이에 도달하면, 부모가 아이들로 하여금 그들 자신의 목표를 정하게 해야 하는지에 대해서 말하는 것은 어렵다. 어떤 이들은 부모가 아이들이 자신의 미래를 결정할 수 있도록 해 주어야 한다고 주장하지만, 나는 부모가 아이들이 결정을 내리는 것을 도와야 한다고 굳게 믿는다. 이는 인생의 경험이 중요하기 때문이고, 부모는 아이들에 대해서 다른 누구보다 잘 알기 때문이다.

첫째, 부모들은 아이들보다 인생을 더 오래 살아온 사람들이다. 따라서, 종종, 그들은 착오를 겪거나, 좌절하거나 시간 낭비로부터 자신의 아이들을 구할 수 있는 더 쉽고 원활한 방향을 알고 있다. 많은 연구가 보여주길 부모와 함께 목표를 정하는 아이들은 스스로 목표를 정한 후 목표를 자꾸 바꾸는 아이들에 비해 그 목표를 고수하는 경향이 있다. 이는 결정을 하는데 있어 부모의 참여가 굉장히 중요한 역할을 한다는 것을 나타낸다.

덧붙여, 부모들은 더욱 객관적이고 이성적일 수 있다. 아이들은 그들의 관점에서만 보는 경향이 있어서 논리적이거나 통찰력이 있기 힘들다. 예를 들면, 요즘 많은 아이들은 연예 기획사로부터 주목을 받는 것이 얼마나 경쟁적이고 어려운 줄 모르기 때문에 가수가 되고 싶어한다. 만약 어떤 아이가 노래에 소질이 없다면 그 아이가 그것에 쏟아온 노력과 시간은 헛될 수 있다.

많은 활동을 시도해 보는 것은 아이들이 자신의 진정한 관심사와 강점을 찾을 수 있는 좋은 방법이다. 하지만, 그 분야에서 성공하지 못하는 것은 굉장한 좌절과 스트레스를 유발할 수 있다. 자기 아이들의 강점과 약점을 구분함으로써 부모들은 자신의 아이들과 협력하여 그들을 이끌어줄 수 있다. 아이들은 또한 그들의 미래를 결정하기에는 너무 어리다. 따라서 나는 부모가 자신의 아이들의 미래를 결정해야 한다는 주장에 찬성한다.

Sample Essay 2 | DISAGREE   p.164

끝없는 사랑, 동기 부여, 그리고 신뢰를 제공하는 것 이외에도 부모들은 자신의 아이들을 올바른 길로 인도하는 사람들이다. 하지만, 아이들이 특정 나이에 도달하면, 부모가 아이들로 하여금 그들 자신의 목표를 정하게 해야 하는지에 대해서 말하는 것은 어렵다. 어떤 이들은 부모가 결정을 내리는데 있어서 여전히 간섭을 해야 한다고 주장하지만, 나는 아이들이 자신의 미래를 결정해야 한다고 강력히 믿는다. 이는 사람들이 다른 관심사와 인생 목표를 가지고 있기 때문이다. 또한, 아이들은 자신의 실수로부터 배운다.

첫째, 누구도 다른 이의 삶을 대신 살아줄 수 없다. 다시 말해, 아이들은 자신의 흥미와 잠재력에 따라 미래에 어떤 것을 하고 싶은지 결정해야 한다. 예를 들면, 많은 부모들은 그들의 아이들이 더 도전적인 직업보다는 안전하고 안정적인 직업을 갖기를 바란다. 하지만, 전망이 밝은 직업이 아이의 행복을 보장하는 것은 아니다. 사람은 각각 삶의 특정 요소에 대해 다른 기준과 가치를 가지고 있기 때문에 자신에 대한 결정은 아이들에 달려 있다.

또한, 아이들이 어릴 때에는 고칠 수 있는 시간이 충분하기 때문에 실수가 허용되고 받아들여진다. 시행착오를 통해, 아이들은 마지막 결정을 내리기 전에 비판적이고 논리적으로 생각할 수 있는 법을 배운다. 반면, 만약 부모가 자신의 아이들을 위해 개입하고 결정을 한다면, 아이들은 조사하고, 결과를 예측하며, 대안을 제시하는 것을 결코 배우지 못할 것이다.

몇몇 부모들은 자신이 누구보다 아이들에 대해 잘 안다고 생각하지만, 아이들은 자신의 관심사와 재능에 기반하여 그들이 진정으로 하고 싶어하는 것을 해야 한다. 아이들이 하기로 결정한 것이 실패로 돌아가더라도 그들은 여전히 자신의 실수에서 배우며 더욱 훈련되고 자립적으로 될 것이다. 그러므로 나는 부모들이 아이들의 미래를 결정해야 한다는 주장에 반대한다.

Actual Test 16

TASK 1 · INTEGRATED TASK

Pharmacology: Pharmacy Automation

READING   p.167

정확함은 약학에 있어 가장 중요하다. 정확한 시간에 정확한 약을 환자에게 주는 것은 환자의 건강에 큰 영향을 줄 수도 있다. 약품 자동화의 발달은 약학업계에 큰 영향을 주었다. 몇몇 새롭게 전산화된 과정은 약물 조제, 약물 회수, 그리고 보관을 포함한다. 이런 새로운 기계화는 환자와 약국 모두에게 이점이 있다.

첫째, 인간은 실수를 하기 때문에, 약사가 오판하여 틀린 약이나 복용량을 줄 수 있다는 것은 때로는 불가피하다. 이는 매우 심각한 문제를 초래할 수 있으며 환자들을 위험에 빠뜨릴 수 있다. 실제로 미국에서는 약 7,000명의 사람들이 해마다 투약 오류로 사망한다. 자동화 해결책은 약에 관한 자세한 정보가 입력된 기계를 제공하며 정확도와 안정성을 보장한다.

약국 자동화는 처방약을 조제하는 과정만 바꾼 것이 아니라 약사들의 역할 역시 바꾸었다. 약사가 처방약을 조제하느라 바쁜 탓에 많은 이들이 긴 줄에서 자신의 차례를 기다리는걸 경험해 보았을 것이다. 로봇 덕분에 약사들은 이제 환자를 직접 돌볼 수 있는 시간이 더 많아졌으며 예방 접종 등의 병원 업무까지도 제공할 수 있으므로 환자들 사이에서 더욱 높은 만족감을 야기한다.

약품 재고를 관리하고 보관하는 것은 약국 업계에서 또 하나의 중요한 측면이고 이는 발달된 약국 기술로 혜택을 볼 수 있다. 로봇은 쉽게 유통 기한이 지난 약을 찾아내고 부족분을 확인할 수 있다. 이것은 약사가 약품을 제시간에 재주문할 수 있도록 돕는다. 재고를 확인하는 것은 매달 버려지는 엄청난 양의 약을 절약해 왔다. 그 시스템은 더 효과적인 직원 채용과 재고 관리를 가능케 하여 결과적으로 더 적은 낭비와 더 낮은 비용을 야기한다.

LISTENING 🎧 16-01

M Professor: Many of you probably think pharmacy automation is relatively new, but it was developed in the 1960s, and numerous pharmacies have already implemented some sort of automation. The main purpose of this growing trend is to reduce the risk of mistakes while increasing the efficiency of a pharmacy's operation. However, there are downsides that need to be taken into consideration.

It's true that humans make mistakes and that machines are more accurate and reliable. But who put all the information in the system in the first place? Input errors or simply the malfunctioning of the system can result in serious consequences. The number of deaths mentioned previously includes ones caused by wrong information put in the system.

It is great that pharmacists can spend more time with patients and provide more clinical services . . . and the overall quality of medical service will improve. But what if the machines break down? Hmm . . . If the pharmacy doesn't have an adequate backup plan, a breakdown can cause a chaotic situation. Preparing alternatives will take a lot of time and staffing . . . so I am skeptical that customers will be able to get better care from pharmacists.

Then there is the cost-effectiveness issue. It might seem that installing robots will save a lot of money . . . but that isn't necessarily true. Inventory management is required to refill the robots, and a pharmacist or authorized employee should be present for refilling and maintenance. So even though automation can identify expired medicine and items in inventory, it is humans who have to make decisions, dispose of expired medicine, and reorder stock. Besides, robots themselves cost a lot of money . . . They cost somewhere between $8,000 and $50,000 each depending on the model. Is it really worth investing that much money just to check on expired medicine?

교수: 여러분들 중 다수는 약품 자동화가 비교적 새롭다고 생각하겠지만, 사실 그것은 1960년대에 개발되었습니다. 그리고 많은 약사들은 이미 어떤 종류의 자동화를 실행해 왔어요. 이 증가 추세의 주요 목적은 약국 운영의 효율성을 높여주면서 실수의 위험을 낮추는 것입니다. 하지만, 고려되어야 할 필요가 있는 부정적 측면들이 있습니다.

인간이 실수를 하고 기계가 좀 더 정확하고 믿을만하다는 것은 사실이에요. 하지만 애초에 누가 그 시스템에 정보를 입력하나요? 입력 실수나 단순히 시스템의 오작동은 심각한 결과를 초래할 수 있습니다. 앞에서 언급된 사망자 수는 시스템에 입력된 잘못된 정보에 의해 발생한 것들까지 포함한 거예요.

약사가 환자와 더 시간을 보내고 병원 업무까지 제공할 수 있다는 건 훌륭해요. 그리고 전반적인 의료 서비스의 질이 향상되겠죠. 그런데, 기계가 고장나면 어쩌죠? 약국이 적절한 백업 계획을 가지고 있지 않으면, 고장은 혼란스러운 상황을 초래할 거예요. 대안을 마련하는 건 많은 시간과 인력을 요합니다... 그래서 저는 환자들이 약사들에게 더 나은 관리를 받을 수 있다는 점에 회의적이에요.

그리고 가격의 효율성에 관한 문제가 있지요. 로봇을 설치하는 것이 많은 돈을 절약하는 것처럼 보일 수 있어요... 하지만 그게 꼭 사실은 아니에요. 로봇을 다시 채우기 위해서는 재고 관리가 필요하고요. 약사나 혹은 관계자가 재고를 채우고 보수 유지를 위해 있어야 해요. 그래서 자동화가 유효 기간이 지난 약과 물품들의 재고를 확인할 수 있을지라도 결정을 내리고, 만료된 약을 폐기하고, 재고를 재주문하는 건 인간일 거예요. 게다가 로봇 자체도 굉장히 비싸요... 모델에 따라 한 개당 $8,000에서 $50,000 사이입니다. 유효 기간이 지난 약을 확인하기 위해 그 많은 돈을 투자하는 게 정말 가치가 있을까요?

Sample Essay p.170

교수는 약품의 자동화의 이점이 미심쩍다고 주장한다. 이는 약품의 자동화가 혁신적이고 약품 업계를 향상시킨다는 지문의 내용을 직접적으로 반박한다.

첫째, 만약 약사가 실수를 하면, 심각한 결과를 가져올 수 있다. 교수에 따르면, 지문에서 언급된 사망자 숫자는 약사와 로봇 둘 다에 의해 범해진 오류를 포함한다고 말한다. 이는 그 시스템이 제공하는 정확성과 안전성이 약품 오류로 인해 일어나는 사망을 감소시킬 거라는 지문의 주장에 반대한다.

뿐만 아니라, 교수는 기계가 고장날 가능성이 있음을 주장한다. 어떤 무질서한 상황도 피할 수 있도록 약국들은 대안을 마련하는 데 많은 시간과 인력을 할애해야 한다. 따라서, 준비에 매우 많은 시간이 걸릴 것이고, 이는 약사들이 환자들과 더 적은 시간을 이용 가능하게 할 것이다. 이는 로봇이 약사들로 하여금 환자에 관한 직접적인 관리 및 심지어는 병원 업무까지도 가능하게 할 수 있다는 지문의 주장에 대해 의구심을 제시한다.

마지막으로, 관계자 혹은 약사가 재고를 다시 채우거나 관리를 위한 점검을 해야 하기 때문에, 재고 관리는 여전히 필요하다. 나아가, 로봇은 구입하기 비싸다. 이는 자동화에 의한 효율적인 관리가 결과적으로 더 적은 낭비와 더 낮은 비용을 야기할 것이라는 지문의 주장에 반대한다.

TASK 2 · INDEPENDENT TASK
Technology

Sample Essay 1 | AGREE p.173

과학 기술의 발달로, 삶은 전보다 더욱 편리해졌다. 따라서, 사람들은 빠르게 변하는 세상에 적응하는 방법을 터득해 왔다. 일부 사람들은 과학 기술이 사람들의 삶을 더욱 어렵게 만들고 있다고 주장한다. 하지만, 두 가지 이유로, 나는 과학 기술로 사람들이 훨씬 더 행복해졌다고 굳게 믿는다. 첫째, 과학 기술은 삶을 더욱 편하게 만들고 있다. 게다가, 과학 기술의 진보 덕분에 세계화가 이루어지고 있다.

첫째, 과학 기술로 TV나 컴퓨터와 같은 수많은 전자 기기들이 생산되고 있다. 이런 상황은 그들의 삶을 더 편하게 만들었을 뿐 아니라 많은 사람을 막대한 양의 정보에 노출시켰다. 예를 들면, 요즘 많은 사람들이 스마트폰을 가지고 있다. 자신들의 전화로, 사람들은 길이나 특정 상품에 관한 정보 등 유용한 자료를 쉽게 접하고 있다. 많은 애플리케이션이 소비자의 요구를 충족시키기 위해 개발되고 있다. 예를 들어, 학생들은 학습에 도움을 얻기 위해 앱을 사용한다. 따라서, 전자 기기가 없는 삶을 상상하기는 어려울 것이다.

게다가, 다양한 배경을 가진 사람들 사이에서의 교류가 평범한 일이 되고 있다. 전자 통신 기기가 출현한 이래, 사람들은 세계의 다른 이들과 교제할 수 있게 되었다. 예를 들어, 대부분의 사람들이 이메일 계정을 가지고 있는데, 다수의 사람들은 하루에도 몇 번씩 이를 확인한다. 이메일은 멀리 떨어져 있을 때에도 서로 간의 의사소통을 가능하게 해 준다.

과학 기술이 사생활 침해를 포함한 몇몇 문제를 일으키고 있는 것은 사실이다. 하지만, 전문가들은 그에 상응하는 해결책을 고안해 내고 있으며 정부는 국민을 보호하기 위해 새로운 법안들을 통과시키고 있다. 많은 전자 기기들이 좀 더 편리한 삶의 방식을 즐길 수 있도록 사람들을 돕고 있다. 게다가, 과학 기술의 진보는 멀리 떨어진 곳에서도 서로 교제할 수 있도록 해 준다. 이상의 이유들로, 나는 과학 기술이 이전보다 사람들을 행복하게 만들었다는 주장에 동의한다.

Sample Essay 2 | DISAGREE   p.174

과학 기술의 발달로, 삶은 전보다 더욱 편리해 졌다. 따라서, 사람들은 빠르게 변하는 세상에 적응하는 방법을 터득해 왔다. 일부 사람들은 과학 기술이 사람들을 더 행복하게 만들었다고 주장한다. 하지만, 두 가지 이유로써, 나는 과학 기술이 삶을 더 어렵게 만들었다고 굳게 믿는다. 첫째, 일부 과학 기술로 인한 사생활 침해 문제가 부정적인 결과를 낳고 있다. 게다가, 환경 피해도 심각하다.

첫째, 많은 사람들이 서로에게 친근감을 느끼지 않는다. 인터넷이 사람들을 친밀하게 만든 것처럼 보이지만, 실제로는 많은 사람들로 하여금 사생활에 대해 더욱 경계하도록 만들었다. 예를 들어, 감시 카메라는 많은 사람들의 안전을 강화시켜 왔다. 하지만, 카메라들은 공공장소에서 하는 일을 감시함으로써 자유 또한 빼앗아 갔다. 따라서, 사람들은 끊임없이 자신이 다른 이들에 의해 감시 당하고 있다고 느끼며 스트레스를 받는다.

게다가, 과학 기술은 많은 환경 문제들을 일으켜 왔다. 다수의 전자 기기는 그 자체로서 해로운 전자기파를 발산하며, 제조 과정에서 해로운 물질들을 많이 만들어 낸다. 게다가, 기업들은 끊임없이 새로운 기기들을 생산하여 소비자들이 업데이트된 제품들을 구입하도록 부추긴다. 예를 들면, 핸드폰이나 텔레비전 등의 전자 기기를 작동시키기 위해 필요한 전기는 발전소에서 나오는데, 발전소는 지구의 평균 기온을 증가시켜 지구 온난화를 불러 일으키는 온실 가스를 만들어 낸다. 그 결과 격렬한 폭풍우와 해수면의 상승과 같은 자연 재해가 일어나고 있다.

끊임없이 발전하는 과학 기술 덕분에 삶이 매우 편리해지고 편안해진 것은 사실이다. 하지만, 그에 관해서는 이점보다 문제점이 훨씬 더 많다. 과학 기술은 사람들로 하여금 누군가가 자신들을 감시하고 있을지도 모른다는 불안감을 안겨다 주었다. 또한, 그것은 막대한 환경 파괴도 가져왔다. 이상의 이유로, 나는 과학 기술이 사람들을 이전보다 더 행복하게 만들었다는 주장에 확고히 반대한다.

Actual Test 17

TASK 1 · INTEGRATED TASK
Geology: The Little Ice Age

READING   p.177

약 1300년부터 1850년까지, 지구 대부분의 지역, 특히 북반구는 극심한 추위를 겪었다. 이 시기가 소빙하기라고 불리는 시기이다.

무엇이 소빙하기의 원인이 되었는지는 아무도 모른다. 멕시코 만류의 냉각이 온도 하강의 원인이 되었을 것이라는 몇몇 추측이 존재한다. 멕시코 만류는 북미의 동쪽 해안으로 흘러 들어 가서 대서양을 지나 북유럽에 도달하는 난류이다. 멕시코 만류가 지나가는 모든 지역, 인근 육지들은 평균 기온보다 따뜻한 온도를 경험하게 된다. 소빙하기 이전에는 중세 온난기라고 불리는 시기가 있었다. 이 기간 동안 따뜻한 온도가 빙하를 녹여서 멕시코 만류로 차가운 얼음물을 흘려 보냈을 수도 있다. 이 때문에, 멕시코 만류는 지나치게 되는 지역의 온도를 더 이상 따뜻하게 유지시켜 줄 수 없었을 것이다.

때때로, 화산 폭발은 전 세계적인 규모로 온도를 하강시키는 원인이 된다. 예를 들어, 크라카토아의 1883년 폭발과 탐보라의 1815년 폭발은 모두 전 세계의 기온을 하강시켰다. 하나의 화산이, 혹은 다수의 화산이 거대한 규모로 폭발함으로써 화산재 구름이 대기 속으로 들어가 태양빛이 차단됨으로써 소빙하기가 나타났다고 볼 수 있다.

1300년대의 하나의 주목할 만한 특징은 아시아와 유럽에서의 인구 감소이다. 이는 최소 유럽 인구의 1/3과 그 밖의 지역에서 수백 만 명의 목숨을 앗아갔던 전염병인 흑사병의 탓으로 돌릴 수 있다. 세계 인구가 감소하면서 일부 지역에 인간이 살지 않게 됨으로써 숲이 다시 자라기 시작했다. 나무들은 이산화탄소를 이용하여 영양분을 생성해 내는 과정인 광합성을 시작했다. 이처럼 많은 나무들은 대기의 이산화탄소 양을 급격히 감소시켰을 것이다. 이로 인해 지구 냉각화가 일어나서 소빙하기가 나타났을 수도 있다.

LISTENING   🎧 17-01

M Professor: During the late Middle Ages, there was a warming period. However, starting around 1300, for the next 550 years, much of the world experienced the Little Ice Age. It was a harsh, bleak period. But what caused it?

Some believe melting glaciers in the Atlantic Ocean caused the Gulf Stream to cool considerably. The Gulf Stream, by the way, lets many parts of Europe, including Ireland and Great Britain, experience unseasonably warm weather. I suppose this theory may account for the cooling in North America and Europe. But what about the Southern Hemisphere? New Zealand and South Africa, among other areas, experienced the Little Ice Age as well. The Gulf Stream flows nowhere near them. It's strictly in the Northern Hemisphere.

It's possible for the ash from a volcanic eruption to make global temperatures decline. For instance, in April 1815, Tambora, a volcano in Indonesia, violently erupted. It spewed so much ash that it created something called "the year without summer." Yet lower temperatures happened for just a year or two. The Little Ice Age lasted for centuries. So it would have taken the eruption of a supervolcano to have lowered temperatures that long. And geologists are positive that no supervolcanoes erupted back then.

Another theory is that the rapid reforestation of parts of the world decreased atmospheric carbon dioxide levels, which, in turn, caused global cooling. First, the forests didn't grow back quickly enough to have such a rapid effect on temperatures. Second, if this were true, then the Little Ice Age would have ended quickly. See, by 1450, Europe's population was back to pre-Black Death levels. And it continued rising. Thus many areas were deforested as people returned to them. So, ah, carbon dioxide levels should have subsequently increased, but they didn't. That rules out the tree theory.

교수: 중세 후반 동안, 따뜻했던 시기가 있었습니다. 하지만, 약 1300년을 시작으로 550년 동안, 세계의 많은 지역이 소빙하기를 겪었습니다. 혹독하고 황량한 시기였죠. 하지만 그것의 원인은 무엇이었을까요?

일부는 대서양에서 녹고 있던 빙하가 멕시코 만류를 냉각시켰다고 믿고 있습니다. 그건 그렇고, 멕시코 만류는 아일랜드와 영국을 비롯한 유럽의 많은 부분에 이상할 정도로 따뜻한 기후를 경험할 수 있게 해 줍니다. 저는 이 이론이 북미와 유럽의 냉각은 설명해 줄 수 있다고 생각합니다. 하지만, 남반구는 어떨까요? 다른 지역들 중 뉴질랜드와 남아프리카 역시 소빙하기를 겪었습니다. 멕시코 만류는 그들 지역 근처로 흘러 들어 가지 않습니다. 엄격히 말하자면 북반구 내에만 있는 것입니다.

전 세계의 기온을 떨어뜨린 것이 화산재라는 것이 가능할 수도 있습니다. 예를 들면, 1815년 5월, 인도네시아의 탐보라라는 화산이 격렬하게 폭발했습니다. 너무 많은 재를 뿜어냈기 때문에 '여름이 없는 해'라는 것을 만들어 내기도 했습니다. 하지만, 더 낮은 기온은 한 해 동안만 발생했습니다. 소빙하기는 수세기 동안 지속되었죠. 초대형 화산 폭발만이 온도를 그처럼 오랫동안 낮출 수 있었을 것입니다. 게다가 지질학자들은 그 시기 초대형 화산의 폭발이 없었다는 점을 확신하고 있습니다.

또 하나의 이론은 일부 지역에서의 급격한 재조림화가 대기의 이산화탄소 수치를 낮추어 결과적으로 지구 냉각이 이루어졌다고 합니다. 첫째, 산림은 온도에 그렇게 빠른 영향을 미칠 정도로 충분히 빨리 자라지 않았습니다. 둘째, 이것이 사실이라면, 소빙하기는 빨리 끝났을 것입니다. 자, 1450년경, 유럽의 인구는 흑사병 이전의 수준을 회복했습니다. 그리고 계속 증가했습니다. 따라서 다시 인구가 늘어남에 따라 많은 지역에서 벌목이 이루어졌습니다. 그렇다면, 음, 이산화탄소 수치가 이후 증가했어야만 했는데, 그렇지 않았습니다. 이로써 나무 이론은 배제되는 것이죠.

Sample Essay   p.180

교수는 소빙하기의 원인이 불확실하다고 주장하며, 이 시기 동안의 극한 추위에는 세 가지 이유가 존재한다는 지문의 주장을 반박한다.

첫째로, 그 이론은 지구의 특정 지역에만 적용될 수 있다. 유럽의 많은 지역이 멕시코 만류에 의해 이상할 정도로 따뜻한 날씨를 겪었다. 그럼에도 불구하고, 남반구 역시 소빙하기를 겪었다. 이는 중세 온난기 당시 따뜻한 날씨에 의해 녹은 빙하가 멕시코 만류로 차가운 물을 보내 지구의 전체적인 온도가 낮아졌다는 지문의 주장을 반박한다.

뿐만 아니라, 교수는 초대형 화산의 폭발만이 수세기 동안 온도를 낮출 수 있다고 주장한다. 하지만, 당시 초대형 화산 폭발에 관한 증거는 존재하지 않

는다. 이는 화산 폭발로 인해 재구름으로 뒤덮인 대기가 햇빛을 차단함으로써 심각한 기온 하락을 불러 일으켰다는 지문의 주장을 반박한다.

마지막으로, 숲의 재성장의 속도는 온도에 영향을 줄 수 없었을 것이고, 인구가 흑사병 전의 수준을 회복했을 때 소빙하기는 빠른 시간 내에 끝났어야 한다. 이는 줄어든 벌채로 인한 이산화탄소의 격감이 소빙하기를 야기시켰다는 지문의 수상과 반대된다.

TASK 2 · INDEPENDENT TASK
Method

Sample Essay 1 | AGREE   p.183

외국에 대해 배울 수 있는 방법들은 많다. 알고 싶어 하는 나라의 박물관을 방문하거나, 관련 서적을 읽거나, TV 프로그램을 시청할 수 있다. 일부 사람들은 한 나라를 방문하는 것이 그 나라에 대해 배울 수 있는 가장 효과적인 방법이라고 주장하지만, 나는 신문과 잡지를 읽는 것이 그 나라를 완전히 이해하는데 도움이 된다고 굳게 믿는다. 우선, 언론 보도는 한 나라의 현재 상황을 반영해 준다. 게다가, 신문과 잡지는 이용 가능한, 가장 최신의 정보를 담고 있는 출처이다.

첫째, 독자들은 신문과 잡지를 읽음으로써 한 나라에 대한 현재의 상황을 알 수 있다. 예를 들면, 나는 밴쿠버를 여행하기 전에 동계 올림픽 등 현지의 중요 행사들에 대해 알게 되었다. 신문 및 잡지들이 왜 캐나다 사람들은 겨울 스포츠에 뛰어난지에 대한 역사적이고 지리적인 이유들을 다루어 주었기 때문에, 나는 캐나다 문화에 대해 이해할 수 있었다. 신문은 밴쿠버에 사는 현지인들의 의견뿐만 아니라 정치적 쟁점에 대해서도 다루고 있었다. 만약 그 지역에 대한 책만 읽었더라면, 나는 당시 진행 중인 일들에 대해 알 수 있는 기회를 갖지 못했을 것이다.

뿐만 아니라, 잡지 광고는 한 나라를 알기에 중요한 자료가 된다. 이는 광고가 현지 생활 방식을 그대로 반영해 주기 때문에 사실이다. 예를 들면, 내가 요세미티로 여행을 준비하고 있었을 때, 잡지와 신문에서 스노타이어를 비롯한 눈 장비에 관련된 많은 광고를 보았다. 게다가, 자연 환경의 보호에 관한 기사도 많이 있었다. 그 지역에 실제로 갔을 때, 그곳에는 엄청난 양의 눈이 있었고, 천연 자원을 지키는 것에 대한 현지인들의 지대한 관심을 보고 놀라움을 느꼈다.

직접적인 경험이 한 나라에 대한 상세한 정보를 제공해 주는 것은 사실이다. 하지만, 한 나라의 모든 지방을 방문하는 것은 불가능할 수도 있고, 각 지방에는 고유의 문화가 있기 때문에, 지방의 문화에 관한 전체적인 그림을 얻는 것이 항상 가능한 것은 아니다. 반대로, 신문과 잡지는 한 나라의 가장 최근의 상황을 보여 준다. 게다가, 신문과 잡지의 많은 광고들은 특정 지역의 문화를 보여 준다. 이상의 이유들로, 나는 외국에 대해 알 수 있는 최선책은 신문과 잡지를 읽는 것이라는 의견에 강력히 동의한다.

Sample Essay 2 | DISAGREE   p.184

외국에 대해 배울 수 있는 방법들은 많다. 알고 싶어 하는 나라의 박물관을 방문하거나, 관련 서적을 읽거나, TV 프로그램을 시청할 수 있다. 일부 사람들은 신문과 잡지 등의 출판물을 읽는 것이 한 나라를 이해하는데 도움이 된다고 주장하지만, 나는 이 주장에 강력히 반대한다. 우선, 출판물이 나오기 전에 정부가 개입하는 경우가 종종 있다. 뿐만 아니라, 신문과 잡지는 작가나 편집자에 따라 편향되거나 주관적일 수 있다.

첫째, 신문과 잡지들이 항상 언론의 자유를 누리는 것은 아니다. 종종, 한 나라의 현지 상황뿐 아니라 정치적 상황에 의해서 통제를 받는다. 예를 들어,

모든 공산 국가는 언론을 통제하며, 정부가 인쇄되기 전 보도 자료를 면밀히 살펴 본다. 그러므로, 신문과 잡지는 사실을 반영하기 보다는, 시민들을 세뇌 시키기 위한 방법으로 사용될 수 있다.

뿐만 아니라, 신문과 잡지는 종종 편향되고 문제의 특정 부분만을 반영하는데, 이는 외국을 이해하는데 있어서 보충 자료로만 활용될 수 있다는 점을 나타낸다. 사실, 직접적인 경험을 얻는 것보다 더 나은 것은 없다. 예를 들면, 나는 캐나다에 휴가 차 방문하기 전, 현지 신문과 잡지를 읽었다. 하지만, 현지인들의 실제 생활과 의견은 그와 다르다는 점을 깨닫고 매우 놀랐다. 따라서, 작가나 편집자의 주관은 언론의 제약을 제기한다.

신문과 잡지가 한 나라의 현지인들을 위해 존재하는 것은 사실이다. 따라서, 그 지역의 특정 생각이나 취향을 나타낼 수는 있다. 하지만, 일부 기사와 광고는 사기업이나 개인에 의해 쓰여지거나 검토되기 때문에, 기사와 광고는 오히려 과장되거나 실제 사실을 외면하고 있을 수도 있다. 게다가, 정부의 개입과 언론의 주관성은 한 나라의 실제 상황을 이해하는 것을 더욱 어렵게 만든다. 이상의 이유들로, 나는 외국에 대해 알 수 있는 최선책은 신문과 잡지를 읽는 것이라는 의견에 강력히 반대한다.

Actual Test 18

TASK 1 · INTEGRATED TASK
Biology: Nomenclature

READING   p.187

지구상에는 800만 이상의 생물이 살고 있으며 120만 종 만이 확인되었다. 해마다 약 18,000개의 새로운 종이 발견되며 이름이 지어진다. 분류학에서는, 이런 이름을 붙이는 체계를 명명법이라고 하는데, 이는 새로 발견된 종에 대해 이름을 고르거나 고안하는 것이다. 이 절차에는 규칙이 있다. 이름은 고유해야 하고, 이름은 모욕적이지 않아야 하며, 해당 종은 그것을 발견한 과학자의 이름을 따라 지을 수 없다.

아마도, (새로운) 종의 이름을 짓는 가장 일반적인 방법은 그것의 특별한 특성을 선택하는 것일 것이다. 이는 사람들에게 생명체 자체에 대해 말해줄 수 있다. 특성이라 함은 그 종의 모양, 색깔, 크기, 혹은 주목할 만하면 어떤 것이라도 포함하기 때문에 다양한 조합과 가능성이 있다.

종을 위한 이름을 선정하는 또 다른 유명한 방법은 유명인의 이름을 사용하는 것이다. 예를 들면, 한 분야에 기여를 많이 한 사람이거나 유명 인사, 혹은 그 생물과 뭔가 비슷한 점이 있는 주목할 만한 사람 말이다. 어떤 생명체는 심지어 신화적 인물을 따서 이름이 지어진다.

일부 이름은 또한 그 종이 어디에서 왔는지 혹은 어디에서 발견되었는지 예상하는 것을 가능케 한다. 다른 종들은 좀 더 통찰력이 필요한 반면, 어떤 것들 즉, africanus, americanus, 혹은 madagascariensis 등은 구분하기 쉽다. 예를 들면, chinensis는 그 종이 중국에서 왔다는 것을 가리키고 indicus는 인도에서 왔다는 것을 가리킨다. 이름은 강, 마을, 혹은 동굴 같은 좀 더 세부적인 지역을 가리키기도 한다.

M Professor: Giving a new species a name is truly a fascinating moment for a scientist. But as exciting as it is, it is very important and could take more than a year for the whole process to take place. The three most common methods include naming a species according to its appearance, naming a species after a particular person, and naming a species according to where it's found or lives. Let's take a look at some examples.

There are some interesting . . . Well, I'd say rather playful names related to species' external features. One well-known example is Gelae, the genus of the round fungus beetle. These beetles got their names after their small, oval, and shiny bodies . . . and you can sort of tell from their names what they look like . . . Jelly beans, as we all know! The five new species include Gelae rol, Gelae fish, Gelae balae, Gelae donut, and Gelae baen. I am pretty sure those words sound familiar to most of you . . . and are easy to remember.

Some species are named after famous people. A relatively recently discovered moth species already has a proposed name: Dermophis donaldtrumpi. Right, the name refers to the former president of the United States, Donald Trump. As you can probably tell from the picture, the species got its name from its similar appearance to him. Um, it's head is covered with yellowish white scales.

The last one we are going to take a look at is how scientists name some species, especially plants, according to where they're discovered or where their habitat is. Let's look at a picture of this flower called the anemone hortensis. The word hortensis means "garden." So you can tell from its name that it's found in gardens. Let me give you another example. Here, take a look at this hedgehog called Erinaceus europaeus. Can you guess where it's from? Yes, it lives in Europe! Nice guess!

교수: 과학자에게 있어 새로운 종에 이름을 붙이는 일은 참으로 황홀한 순간입니다. 하지만 이름을 짓는 것은 흥미로운 만큼 매우 중요하며 모든 절차가 끝날 때까지 1년 이상이 걸릴 수도 있지요. 이름을 짓는 가장 흔한 세 가지 방법은 생김새에 따라 짓는 것, 특정 인물을 따라 이름 짓는 것, 그리고 그 종이 발견된 곳이나 사는 곳에 따라 이름을 짓는 것을 포함합니다. 몇몇 예들을 보도록 하지요.

좀 흥미로운, 음, 유쾌한 게 더 가깝겠군요. 특정 종의 외관의 특성과 관련된 유쾌한 이름들이 있어요. 가장 잘 알려진 예시 중 하나는 원형 곰팡이 딱정벌레의 한 종류인 '젤리'에요. 이 딱정벌레들은 그들의 작은 타원형의 빛나는 몸 때문에 그런 이름을 가졌고... 여러분은 어느 정도 그 이름으로부터 그들의 생김새를 알 수 있지요... 우리가 모두 아는 그 젤리 빈이요! 새로운 종 5개에는 젤리 롤, 젤리 피쉬, 젤리 밸리, 젤리 도넛, 그리고 젤리 빈이 있어요. 여러분들 대부분에게 저 단어들은 귀에 익숙하고... 기억하기도 쉬울 거라고 확신해요.

일부 종은 유명인의 이름을 따라서 지어요. 비교적 최근에 발견된 나방 종은 이미 제안된 이름이 있어요: 더모피스 도날드트럼피에요. 맞아요, 그 이름은 미국의 전대통령이었던 도날드 트럼프를 가리킵니다. 사진을 보고 여러분들도 말할 수 있듯이, 이 종은 그것의 그와 비슷한 외관에서 이름을 가져왔어요... 음. 그것의 머리는 누르스름한 하얀 비늘로 덮여 있어요.

우리가 살펴볼 마지막 방법은 과학자들이 몇몇 종, 특히 식물이 어디에서 발견되었는지 또는 그것들의 서식지가 어디인지에 따라 어떻게 식물들의 이름을 짓는가입니다. 아네모네 호텐시스라고 불리는 이 꽃의 사진을 봅시다. 호텐시스의 뜻은 '정원'이라고 합니다. 그러니까 그것의 이름만 듣고도 이 식물은 정원에서 찾아진다고 말할 수 있지요. 또 다른 예를 들어 볼게요. 여기요, 에리나수스 유로페우스라고 불리는 이 고슴도치를 보세요. 그것이 어디 사는지 짐작이 가나요? 맞아요. 그 고슴도치는 유럽에 살아요! 잘 맞췄어요!

Sample Essay   p.190

지문은 새로운 종이 어떻게 이름을 얻게 되는지, 그리고 그 과정에 어떤 절차가 필요한지에 대해 설명한다. 그리고 강의에서, 교수는 세 가지 방법을 예를 들어 설명한다.

첫째, 교수는 종의 외관과 연관이 있는 재미있는 이름의 예를 하나 든다. 즉, 곰팡이 딱정벌레에 사용되는 젤리류 말이다. 딱정벌레의 이름은 젤리 벨리, 젤리 도넛, 젤리 롤 등을 포함한다. 이들은 새로운 종에게 새로운 이름을 부여하는데 특별한 신체적 특징이 기여한다는 것을 보여주는 몇 가지 예이다.

게다가, (한 종류의) 나방이 최근에 발견되어 드디어 '더모피스 도널드트럼프'라는 정식 명칭을 받게 되었다. 그것의 머리는 노르스름한 하얀 비늘로 덮여 있다. 이는 새로운 종은 유명하거나 주목할 만한 인물을 따라 이름을 지을 수도 있다는 지문에서 설명된 의견을 뒷받침하는 훌륭한 예이다.

마지막으로, 교수는 아네모네 호텐시스라는 이름의 식물을 예로 제공한다. 호텐시스는 '정원'이라는 뜻이므로, 그 식물이 어디에 사는지 추측하는 것이 가능하다. 바로 정원에서다. 또 다른 예는 고슴도치인 에리나시어스 유로피어스이다. 그것의 이름이 말해주듯, 그 고슴도치는 유럽에서 왔다. 이러한 예들은 사람들이 그것의 명칭에 근거하여 종이 어디에 사는지와 어디에서 왔는지를 추측할 수 있다는 지문의 주장을 뒷받침한다.

TASK 2 · INDEPENDENT TASK
Society

Sample Essay 1 | AGREE   p.193

대도시 지역에는 수많은 사람들이 거주하고 있으며, 대부분의 사람들은 타인과 팔을 부딪치거나, 감정을 상하게 할 의도 없이 누군가를 툭 쳤던 경험을 몇 번쯤 가지고 있을 것이다. 일부는 사회가 바쁘고 복잡해졌음에도 불구하고 서로에게 예의를 기대해야 한다고 주장한다. 하지만, 나는 다음의 이유로 그 주장에 강력히 반대한다. 개인주의는 사람들을 무례함으로부터 덜 민감하게 만들며, 무례함에 반응하는 한계점도 변하고 있다.

첫째, 오늘날 사회는 매우 많은 것을 요구한다. 따라서, 사람들은 개인화되어 다른 이들에게 많은 신경을 쓸 여유를 가지고 있지 않다. 사실, 우리가 조밀한 세상에서 사는 것처럼 보이지만, 모두는 다른 이로부터 고립되어 있다. 예를 들면, 과거의 사람들은 길에서 다른 이들과 눈이 마주치면 인사를 했다. 반면, 오늘날에는 낯선 이들과 인사를 나누는 사람이 많지 않다.

둘째, 의도치 않게 반복적으로 불편함을 주는 타인들을 접하게 되면서, 무례함에 대한 관용이 생겨나게 되었는데, 이로써 사소한 영향에는 사람들이 별 반응을 하지 않게 되었다. 예를 들면, 오늘날 대중교통에서는 노인들에게 자리를 양보하지 않는 직장인들을 흔히 볼 수 있다. 이러한 상황은 직장인들이 회사로 인해 많이 지쳐 있으며 다른 이들에게 자리를 내어줄 의향이 없다는 점에서 비롯된다. 직장인들이 겪는 피곤을 이해하기 때문에 사람들이 그들을 비판하는 경우는 거의 없다.

다른 이들에 대한 예의와 매너가 사람들 사이에서 화합을 이루어 낸다는 점은 사실이다. 반대로, 특정 상황은 사람들이 다른 이들의 무례함을 인내하는 것을 불가피하게 한다. 바쁜 사회에서 개인들은 이기적이고 다른 이들에 대해 신경을 쓰지 않는 경향이 있다. 게다가, 사람들은 무례함에 대한 인내심을 키워 왔다. 이러한 이유로서, 나는 세상이 바쁘고 복잡해졌기 때문에 사람들이 다른 이들로부터 예의를 기대해서는 안 된다는 진술에 찬성한다.

Sample Essay 2 | DISAGREE   p.194

대도시 지역에는 수많은 사람들이 거주하고 있으며, 대부분의 사람들은 타인과 팔을 부딪치거나, 감정을 상하게 할 의도 없이 누군가를 툭 쳤던 경험을 몇 번쯤 가지고 있을 것이다. 일부는 사회가 바쁘고 복잡해졌기 때문에, 서로에게 예의를 기대해서는 안 된다고 주장한다. 하지만 나는 다음의 이유로 그 주장에 강력히 반대한다. 대인 관계는 오늘날 극도로 중요해지고 있으며 타인에 대한 무례함은 특정 종류의 업무를 지연시킬 수도 있다.

첫째, 다양한 분야의 많은 사람들을 아는 것은 오늘날 사회에서 가장 중요한 요소 중의 하나이다. 수년에 거쳐 우리의 생활 방식이 향상됨에 따라, 다른 이들과 어울릴 때 훌륭한 매너를 갖추는 것은 중요해졌다. 예를 들어, 연구에 따르면 90퍼센트의 직장인들이 부적절한 발언이나 태도를 보인 동료를 참을 수 없으며 그 사람과 함께 하는 단체 업무를 꺼린다는 결과가 나왔는데, 이는 예의 없는 사람들이 다른 이들과 친밀한 관계를 형성하는데 어려움을 겪게 될 것임을 보여 준다.

둘째, 사람들로 붐비는 상황에서 다른 사람들에게 예의를 갖추면 시간이 절약된다. 다른 이들에게 무례한 태도를 보이는 것은 시간을 낭비할 뿐만 아니라, 사람들 사이에서 불쾌감을 일으킨다. 예를 들어, 2011년 3월의 지진 이후 물을 얻기 위해 긴 줄을 섰던 일본인들의 행동은 타인에 대한 존중으로부터 온 것이었으며, 그러한 행동은 세계인들을 놀라게 했다. 사람들이 새치기를 시도했더라면 물을 얻는데 더 오랜 시간이 걸렸을 것이고 심지어 폭력을 야기할 수도 있었을 것임은 분명하다.

다른 사람에게 불쾌감을 일으킬 수 있는 불가피한 상황이 있을 수 있다는 점은 사실이다. 하지만, 예의는 다른 사람들과 어울릴 때 필수적이기 때문에 사람들은 이러한 상황을 피하려고 노력한다. 게다가, 다른 사람들을 존중하는 것은 사람들이 문제를 보다 효율적으로 해결하는데 도움이 될 것이다. 이러한 이유로서, 나는 세계가 바쁘고 복잡해졌기 때문에 다른 이들로부터 예의를 기대해서는 안 된다는 진술에 반대한다.

TOEFL MAP
ACTUAL TEST
New TOEFL Edition

Writing 1